To: Sase

From: Mary

Christmas 1993

365

DEVOTIONS

• • • • • • • Sixty-five • • • • • •

**A Scripture, Thought, and Prayer
for Every Day of the Year.**

DEVOTIONS

· · · · · · · · · · ·

JANUARY

Eileen H. Wilmoth, *Editor*
Volume 36
January, February, March
photo by H. Armstrong Roberts, cover photo by Dennis Frates
© 1992 The STANDARD PUBLISHING Co., 8121 Hamilton Avenue, Cincinnati, Ohio, 45231, a
division of STANDEX INTERNATIONAL Corp. Topics based on Home Daily Bible Readings,
International Sunday School lessons, © 1989 by the Lesson Committee. Printed in U.S.A.

PREPARED TO ANSWER

SCRIPTURE: Acts 2:29-37

VERSE FOR TODAY: Thy word have I hid in mine heart, that I might not sin against thee (Psalm 119:11).

HYMN FOR TODAY: "Thy Word Is Like a Garden, Lord"

During one of his pre-presidential political campaigns, Abraham Lincoln is reported to have heard that his opponent drew a crowd of 400 at a small-town rally. Turning in his well-worn Bible to 1 Samuel 22:2, Lincoln read his reply: "Every one that was in distress, and every one that was in debt, and every one that was discontented, gathered themselves unto him; and he became a captain over them: and there were with him about four hundred men."

Lincoln's answer was ready-made, provided in familiar, Spirit-inspired Scripture before the occasion arose. The Bible answers all kinds of questions for its readers before they are asked; and it solves problems before they arise.

On the Day of Pentecost Peter met the occasion by citing familiar facts concerning Jesus, reinforced by Scriptures probably learned in his boyhood. Peter certainly spoke by inspiration of the Holy Spirit—the Spirit combining inspired Scripture with inspired observation and empowered language. It is a combination available in lesser measure to each of us as we use the Spirit-inspired Word to answer—and frequently to prevent—life's problems before they occur.

PRAYER THOUGHTS: We praise You, dear God. May we make full use of Your Word, the sword of the Spirit, to realize Your triumphs in the name of Jesus, Your Son. Amen.

January 1-3. **Edwin V. Hayden** is the Editor of the Adult Bible Class. He travels extensively and is the author of numerous books and articles.

PLEADING, FOR GOD

SCRIPTURE: Acts 2:38-41

VERSE FOR TODAY: We are ambassadors for Christ, as though God did beseech you by us: we pray you in Christ's stead, be ye reconciled to God (2 Corinthians 5:20).

HYMN FOR TODAY: "Seeking the Lost"

He was a good man, but not a Christian. He helped his family in starting a new congregation in their community, but made no personal commitment. He listened patiently to a series of supply preachers who filled the pulpit before a minister could be secured, but steadfastly refused the gospel invitations. At long last, however, he confessed Jesus as Savior and Lord, being baptized into His name.

Why? Who and what convinced him? "It wasn't any one sermon or preacher," he said, "but as each man tried to give us a Biblical base for the new church, they all said essentially the same thing. That kind of cumulative persistence finally got to me."

Those ministers reflected a part of Peter's Spirit-inspired Pentecost preaching that is very important, but not spectacular: "With many other words he warned them; and he pleaded with them, 'Save yourselves from this corrupt generation'"(Acts 2:40, *New International Version*). The warning and pleading came after the inspired gospel message with its directive to baptism in the name of Jesus Christ, but before the harvest of 3,000 believers. Don't be ashamed to beseech for God!

PRAYER THOUGHTS: Give us, please, dear God of glory, a generous portion of Your seeking spirit. As You have been patient and persistent with us for our salvation, so may we be patient and persistent in dealing with beloved friends for their family relationship with You, now and forever. In Christ our Lord, amen.

THE FAMILY OF GOD

SCRIPTURE: Acts 2:42-47

VERSE FOR TODAY: As we have opportunity, let us do good to all people, especially to those who belong to the family of believers (Galatians 6:10, *New International Version*).

HYMN FOR TODAY: "The Family of God"

Among the deepest impressions of ten weeks spent among Christian missionaries in and around Harare, Zimbabwe, was the effect of furloughs on the missionaries' houses, furniture, automobiles, pets, and house plants! Almost nothing went unused during the months of a missionary's absence! Houses and "flats" became havens for home-hunters, or were left as guest lodging for visitors. If rental property was surrendered by a departing missionary, his furniture was used for the interim by another. The furloughing missionary's automobile—difficult or impossible to replace—was nevertheless given over to another's use.

A similar spirit was evident even when the owner was present. Material possessions were held very loosely, always available for the use of others in the family of Christ. Since the missionaries were strangers together in a foreign land, it was perhaps rather natural for them to do as did the earliest Christians, who lived as pilgrims and strangers in an unfriendly world. A more vital sense of family relationship in every congregation, recognizing their position "in the world but not of the world," would greatly empower the Great Commission in our own time.

PRAYER THOUGHTS: Thank You, our Heavenly Father, for Your other children, our brothers and sisters in the family of Christ. May we enjoy fully our relationship, using our material possessions wisely to Your glory and for the expression of our love to those who are also blood-bought and precious to You. Amen.

WORSHIP HIS MAJESTY

SCRIPTURE: Psalm 8

VERSE FOR TODAY: Give unto the Lord the glory due unto his name; worship the Lord in the beauty of holiness (Psalm 29:2).

HYMN FOR TODAY: "Majesty"

We live in a very casual age. Everyone seems to be on a first-name basis. Even the President of the United States does not get much respect. Do you remember when Jimmy was President? That was right before Ronnie. At least, up to the present, the media has not called President Bush, Georgie!

The problem of familiarity appears to have invaded our relationship with God. We dropped Thee and Thou from our prayer vocabulary some time ago. If we refer to God in public at all, we are likely to call Him "the man upstairs." Our attitude toward Him is about as respectful as if we considered Him some kind of cosmic Santa Claus. We still respect Him in anticipation of what He can give us, but we think of Him as though He were in the early stages of senility.

What ever happened to our concept of the majesty of the Almighty? When we talk about God today, we are likely to emphasize forgiveness and forget about judgment.

We need to emphasize the idea of coming into His presence with reverence and godly fear. After all, we do worship Him as Creator of the universe. "O Lord our Lord, how excellent is thy name in all the earth!" (Psalm 8:1).

PRAYER THOUGHTS: We come to You, O Lord, knowing that You are the Lord of all the earth. Like Isaiah of old, may we approach You as the one who is high and lifted up. We thank You for reaching down to us by becoming like us in Christ Jesus. Amen.

January 4-10. **Ross Dampier** is the Senior Minister with a church in Bristol, Tennessee.

THE FAITHFULNESS OF GOD

SCRIPTURE: Hebrews 10:19-25

VERSE FOR TODAY: Your faithfulness continues through all generations (Psalm 119:90, *New International Version*).

HYMN FOR TODAY: "Great Is Thy Faithfulness"

When the Bible tells us that we are to draw near to God in full assurance of faith, it simply means that God will keep His promises. It does not mean, however, that God is going to do everything for us. We must respond to that faithfulness upon His part by being faithful to Him.

When Hudson Taylor, founder of the China Inland Mission, was on his way to the Orient, his ship was becalmed. For days the wind did not blow. The captain, who was not a Christian, was so concerned that he asked Mr. Taylor to pray that a wind would be sent that would bring them to port. Mr. Taylor said that he would be glad to pray, but that there was a condition. The captain must first set the sails. The captain refused. "The men will think I am crazy if we set full sail in this calm sea." Hudson Taylor replied, "Then I will not ask God to send the wind. If we are going to pray, we must act as though we expected results." The captain finally agreed, and only then did the missionary begin to pray. It wasn't long before the prayer was answered and the ship was heading once more toward her destination. This is the full assurance of faith. It is believing that God will provide for our needs if we ask Him, and then acting as though we believed it.

PRAYER THOUGHTS: Lord, give us wings to our prayers that they may go up to You, but teach us to put feet on them, too. If we pray to get rid of the weeds, teach us to pray with a hoe in our hands. Only then can we pray in full assurance of faith. Amen.

THE LANGUAGE OF LOVE

SCRIPTURE: 1 Corinthians 13:1-7

VERSE FOR TODAY: We love him, because he first loved us (1 ⸱

HYMN FOR TODAY: "Love Divine, All Loves Excelling"

Love is far more than saying "I love you." It is demonstrated by everything that we do and say.

One day two missionaries were traveling through the back country far from their mission station. A small leak in a gasoline line went unnoticed until the tank was drained and they were stranded some distance from the nearest town. The older missionary remained with the vehicle and started to repair the leak while the younger man caught a ride with a passing native who would take him to a place where he could get more fuel. As they rode toward town, he began to talk with the driver about his older companion. "He speaks the language so poorly," he said. "It must be very difficult for people to understand what he is saying when he preaches." "Yes, it is," the native agreed. "We sometimes smile to ourselves, but we would never mention it to him. We would not want to hurt him because we love him very much. For more than twenty years he has worked among us. He has nursed us when we were sick. He has taught us a better way to grow our crops. Most of all, he has taught us about the love of God, and how we should love one another. We would not hurt him, because although he speaks our language very poorly with his mouth, by the way he lives he speaks the language of love."

PRAYER THOUGHTS: We thank You, Father in Heaven, for loving us enough to send Christ to die for us. Help us to show our love by what we do and say. In Jesus' name we pray, amen.

THE GIFT OF GOD

SCRIPTURE: 1 Corinthians 13:8-13

VERSE FOR TODAY: God commendeth his love toward us, in that, while we were yet sinners, Christ died for us (Romans 5:8).

HYMN FOR TODAY: "To God Be The Glory"

Robert Browning adds a beautiful character to the world of literature in a little girl whose name is Pippa. She works hard in a factory and has only one holiday a year, New Year's Day. She decides to spend the day by going to the four happiest houses in the town and singing for each of them.

She goes to the home of Sebold and Othima who are the richest people in the community. She walks at noon past the home of Jules who has just brought his bride to live there. In the evening she passes the tower where Luigi, the youngest patriot, lives. As darkness falls she comes to the church where the bishop represents to her the love of God.

As Pippa comes to each home, she does not guess the problems which lie within. Sebold and Othima are guilty of a crime, and her song makes them cry for mercy. Jules and his bride realize that their home is far from ideal, and they are reconciled. She rouses Luigi from secret cowardice, and her song keeps the bishop from permitting a serious injustice. In each case her song ministers to the lives of those whom she assumes are the rich and powerful.

That message of the love of God may just be the greatest gift we can give to people today. "God's in His Heaven, all's right with the world."

PRAYER THOUGHTS: Lord, we thank You for the challenge that You give to us to witness to the world. Make us realize that the success of our neighbors does not keep them from needing Your love. In Jesus' name, amen.

THE POWER OF THE RESURRECTION

SCRIPTURE: 1 Corinthians 15:20-28

VERSE FOR TODAY: It is a faithful saying: For if we be dead with him, we shall also live with him (2 Timothy 2:11).

HYMN FOR TODAY: "He Lives"

Jesus rose from the dead. This basic fact is the foundation upon which the church is built. It is the evidence which demonstrates beyond a doubt that Jesus is indeed the Christ, the Son of the living God. Taken by itself, however, the resurrection of Jesus is not complete. It is only when we realize that the risen Christ must live in us that the power of the resurrection is unleashed.

The minister was preparing his Easter sermon. His seven-year-old son came into the study eating what was left of a box of cookies. When he asked what his father was doing, the minister saw a chance to practice his sermon, so he began to summarize while the boy sat quietly eating cookies. When he had finished, the father asked if his son understood what the death and resurrection meant. The boy thought a moment and said, "Yes, it's sorta like this box of cookies." The father's heart sank. Surely the boy had missed the point. Then the son continued. "In a minute this box is going to be empty and I am going to be full."

The empty tomb is the means by which our empty lives can be filled with the risen Christ. Paul tells us, "As Christ was raised up from the dead by the glory of the Father, even so we also should walk in newness of life" (Romans 6:4).

PRAYER THOUGHTS: Heavenly Father, our lives are so empty, so powerless. Fill us with the power of Christ's resurrection. Make us new creatures through Him who died and rose again for our salvation. In Jesus' name, amen.

THE BLESSED HOPE

SCRIPTURE: 1 Peter 1:3-12

VERSE FOR TODAY: Looking for that blessed hope, and the glorious appearing of the great God and our Saviour Jesus Christ (Titus 2:13).

HYMN FOR TODAY: "We Shall Behold Him"

Whenever the word *hope* is used in the New Testament, it is usually connected with the second coming of Christ.

On October 30, 1938, many people in the United States believed that the end of the world was near. The Mercury Theater of the Air broadcast events described in H. G. Wells's *War of the Worlds* as though it were a live newscast. Orson Wells was the announcer, and he described how men from Mars were landing in New Jersey and preparing to advance on New York City. The militia who had attempted to stop them were wiped out with poison gas and death rays.

People were dashing about, telling their friends that the world was coming to an end. One man ran to the home of his neighbor, and as he hurried past he cried, "I have to go. The world is coming to an end, and I have an awful lot to do."

When Jesus comes back, will we be ready or will He find us with many tasks unfinished? Our Scripture for today tells us that if we are born again we will be ready for that glorious event. How will you fare on that great day? The blessed hope of His appearing should hold no terror for the Christian. Each day we live should find us ready to receive our Lord and to accept the eternal inheritance which His Word speaks about.

PRAYER THOUGHTS: Lord, make us ready for Your coming. Remind us that it will be when we least expect it. Keep us living daily for You so that we will be ready in that great day. In Jesus' name, amen.

A CALL TO HOLY LIVING

SCRIPTURE: 1 Peter 1:13-25

VERSE FOR TODAY: Follow peace with all men, and holiness, without which no man shall see the Lord (Hebrews 12:14).

HYMN FOR TODAY: "Living for Jesus"

The Christian is a person who is called upon to live a special kind of life. It is not good enough to be just average. We have to do our very best for Christ every day. We have to be holy; that is, whole or complete.

A farmer often remarked that he was a pretty good man. He would sometimes get mad and swear, but it didn't happen very often. Once in a while he admitted to cheating, but most of the time he was honest in his dealings. He gave generously to worthy causes. He never got drunk, and so he was of the opinion that God surely approved of him because he was above average.

One day he sent his hired man to build a fence around a field. He gave careful instruction—nothing fancy, just a good, average fence. When it was done, he went out to inspect it. Some places were strong, but others were woefully weak. There were even places where the wire was double and other places where there was no wire at all. Needless to say, the farmer was furious. "This kind of fence is of no use to me. The cattle will walk around the strong parts and get through the gaps." "Well," replied the hired man, "I figured that if you could average things out with the Lord, it would be all right to average it out with the cows."

It is not enough to just "average it out." The kind of life Christ requires demands complete and total obedience.

PRAYER THOUGHTS: Lord, help us to understand that what may be good enough for the world is not good enough for You. In Jesus' name, amen.

MAKING PERSECUTION PRODUCTIVE

SCRIPTURE: Acts 8:1-8

VERSE FOR TODAY: On that day a great persecution broke out against the church at Jerusalem, and all except the apostles were scattered throughout Judea and Samaria (Acts 8:1, *New International Version*).

HYMN FOR TODAY: "No One Ever Cared For Me Like Jesus"

A Florida couple took a lemon and turned it into lemonade. The husband—a champion swimmer, basketball player, and racer—was concerned that he had to use such heavy equipment for the sports. He and his wife were both handicapped; they knew something about wheelchairs and the special needs of people. As a result, they developed a chair with fifty percent less weight and a great deal more maneuverability. Said the man, "We looked at our problem in the light of its possibilities for helping others."

The early church faced persecution. Stephen was stoned. The believers were scattered. Suffering consequences for violating God's commands is not persecution. The loss of respect from society because of the inconsistency between words and lives is not persecution.

Persecution for the sake of principle is a reality. The Bible is a story of God's people in less than favorable circumstances. Faithfulness to God sent Joseph to prison and the apostle Paul on a life-long mission to hostile lands. To claim exemption because we're Christians is to misunderstand the method God uses to mold us in His image.

PRAYER THOUGHTS: O God, sometimes in life we are faced with crisis situations. Help us in these moments to remember Your promise that You will never forsake us. Through Christ we pray. Amen.

January 11-17. **E. Ray Jones** is the Senior Minister of a growing congregation in Clearwater, Florida.

UNLIKELY CONVERTS

SCRIPTURE: Acts 8:9-13

VERSE FOR TODAY: But when they believed Philip as he preached the good news of the kingdom of God and the name of Jesus Christ, they were baptized, both men and women (Acts 8:12, *New International Version*).

HYMN FOR TODAY: "I'm Redeemed"

A church leader asked for the prayers of his fellow elders in knowing how to deal with his new neighbors. "They are," he said, "the most immoral people I've ever encountered." One suggestion was to invite them to come to church. The leader laughed and said, "It's not likely that they'd be interested."

However, he made an effort to be a friend. When their first child was born he invited the family to church. They began attending, and a year later became Christians.

Simon the magician was an unlikely prospect for conversion. Jerome, a Christian leader of the fourth century, claimed to quote from Simon who said of himself, "I am the word of God; I am the almighty; I am the comforter; I am all there is of God." But when Philip came to Samaria with news about a powerful and loving God, some Samaritans—including Simon—believed that truth, rejoiced in the wonder of it, and were baptized. Simon did not fully understand the implications of becoming Christian and he had to be confronted about some personal attitudes. Christians must care enough to share the Word with love and mercy.

PRAYER THOUGHTS: O God, keep us sensitive to the fact that sometimes those who seem to be the most unlikely candidates for conversion are near the door of salvation. Help us to keep faith in the power of the gospel to touch the most hardened heart and bring about a new birth through Christ. Amen.

NEW LIFE, OLD PROBLEMS

SCRIPTURE: Acts 8:14-25

VERSE FOR TODAY: When Simon saw that the Spirit was given at the laying on of the apostles' hands, he offered them money (Acts 8:18, *New International Version*).

HYMN FOR TODAY: "Standing on the Solid Rock"

Temptation for the Christian can be compared to an irritating dog who is banished outside but stands waiting at the door to jump back inside the moment the door is opened. Simon reminds us of that truth. Simon became a Christian. Just as the Samaritans believed and were baptized, so Simon also believed and obeyed.

We must not assume that Simon, because of his sin, had lost his salvation. But he was in danger. Peter told Simon that he had no part in the ministry that the apostles were performing, because he had a crooked heart. Simon allowed himself to fall captive to sin. If he continued in it, it would ultimately result in the loss of his soul.

Though an individual may undergo a genuine conversion, he still must battle with temptation. Some patterns of conduct are changed only through great agony and over a period of time. Other temptations stay with people all their lives.

Be on guard against being overcome. To come into the environment of former sins is to be attracted and enslaved. Victory in the Christian life comes by allowing the Holy Spirit to strengthen and sustain us so that we don't fall victim to the lure of the past.

PRAYER THOUGHTS: O God, save us from that arrogance that assumes that once we have escaped the entanglement of sin we can never again be enslaved therein. Walk with us through the wilderness of life. Teach us that by depending upon Your strength we can withstand the evil intentions of the devil. We pray through Christ, amen.

POWER OF PERSONAL CONTACT

SCRIPTURE: Acts 8:26-40

VERSE FOR TODAY: He started out, and on his way he met an Ethiopian eunuch . . . This man had gone to Jerusalem to worship (Acts 8:27, *New International Version*).

HYMN FOR TODAY: "Into My Heart"

A national sports magazine tells the story of Lynn Jennings, two-time winner of the World Cross-Country Championship. At this writing, Miss Jennings is single, and her long hours of running have provided few opportunities for meeting eligible bachelors. However, she and her fiancé will soon march down the aisle. Miss Jennings did not meet him on the track or in her travels. He is the United Parcel Service driver who has been delivering Lynn's running shoes to her for the last five years. It was the personal contact that touched her life and won her heart.

We see the importance of the personal touch in the conversion of the Ethiopian official. God called Philip from Samaria where he was ministering to many, to a mission designed to meet the needs of one individual. Atheists have stated, "In the long hall of history the individual doesn't matter very much." But God says, "In the long haul of history nothing matters so much as the individual."

The Ethiopian official reminds us of the potential inherent in one person. There is reason to believe that the treasurer established the Coptic church in Africa. One never knows what spiritual powers are set in motion when one soul is brought into a saving relationship with Christ.

PRAYER THOUGHTS: Help us, our Father, that in our emphasis on improving mankind we will not neglect the needs of individual men and women. In the name of Jesus. Amen.

PETER'S REPORT

SCRIPTURE: Acts 11:1-8

VERSE FOR TODAY: So when Peter went up to Jerusalem, the circumcised believers criticized him . . . Peter began and explained everything to them precisely as it had happened: (Acts 11:2, 4, *New International Version*).

HYMN FOR TODAY: "So Send I You"

I grew up in an atmosphere of conflict. In our extended family some relative was always angry over something. However, when I became a Christian, I was not prepared to encounter conflict in the church. I expected the church to be a place of reconciliation. Instead I found conflict that was intense enough to sever church fellowships.

Conflict began very early in human history. Adam and Eve chose to disobey an explicit command of God. So, God himself had to engage in conflict with His creation.

It should not be surprising that conflict became a problem in the early church. A major conflict occurred over the issue of who was eligible for salvation.

Conflict in the world and in the church will not be completely resolved until the events described in Revelation 21 and 22 occur. However, concerned believers must pray about their responsibility in conflict. We must avoid conflict when possible, and act in a spiritual manner when conflict is inevitable. We must strive to work out our differences, and show love to one another.

PRAYER THOUGHTS: We recognize, our Father, that conflict is a part of the human condition. We pray that You will help us to understand the source of conflict as well as to find the strength to deal with conflict in a constructive, honest, upright, and Christian way. Through Christ, amen.

RECAPTURING THE MOMENT

SCRIPTURE: Acts 11:9-18

VERSE FOR TODAY: He will bring you a message through which you and all your household will be saved (Acts 11:14, *New International Version*).

HYMN FOR TODAY: "The Love of God"

One Saturday morning, I was sitting on the porch. Suddenly I became aware of what was going on around me. A squirrel was running up a tree trunk with its breakfast in its mouth. The lizards were dining on insects. Grapefruit hung heavily from the branches of the tree. The grass glistened with the morning dew. I realized that for weeks I had been sitting on that porch, but this was the first time I had appreciated what was going on.

It is a common failure that at certain points we all witness majestic moments, but, because we're in a hurry or have seen those things so often, we miss their importance.

Two thousand years of Christian history have dulled our senses to what took place in Ceasarea Phillipi. By revisiting the event, we can recapture some of the importance.

Cornelius was a man of moral virtues. Yet the centurion was told to send for Peter, who "will bring you a message through which you and all your household will be saved."

Here was a powerful, moral man who was willing to accept his imperfections and admit his need of forgiveness. Peter, a citizen of a captive nation, brought freedom to his captor. This is one of the watersheds of Biblical history.

PRAYER THOUGHTS: Open my eyes, Lord, that I may not miss life's great moments. Help me create those moments by taking advantage of the opportunities to share Your message of love and forgiveness. Enlarge my vision to include the whole world. In Christ, amen.

EFFECTIVE LEADERSHIP

SCRIPTURE: Acts 11:19-30

VERSE FOR TODAY: He was a good man, full of the Holy Spirit and faith, and a great number of people were brought to the Lord (Acts 11:24, *New International Version*).

HYMN FOR TODAY: "Jesus Calls Us"

The church in Antioch is a model for local congregations. It was the first local church to become officially involved in worldwide evangelism. It was the training ground for Christian leaders. It was led by Barnabas, one of the greatest and often least-appreciated leaders of the New Testament church. The quality of his leadership is defined by three characteristics.

1.) *Goodness.* He had personal character. Effective leadership flows from good character.

2.) *Indwelling of the Holy Spirit.* Effective leaders allow the Spirit of God to enter and take control of every aspect of life. The Holy Spirit will be in control of the thought life, financial priorities, recreational activities, work responsibilities, and family responsibilities. The fullness of the Spirit will flow out in the fruits of the Spirit.

3.) *Faithfulness.* Effective leaders are people of faith. Confident of the power of God, they're willing to risk. They'll launch endeavors that cause the faithless to fear. Men of faith begin churches, witness in homes, confront sin, and stand firm for moral virtues in the community. They are, in the words of Charles Spurgeon, "Before God like a lamb, before the world like a lion."

PRAYER THOUGHTS: O God, we pray for our leaders. May they express those qualities of effective leadership. And may we respond to their leadership with willing hearts. In Christ, amen.

EULOGY

SCRIPTURE: Romans 1:8-15

VERSE FOR TODAY: First, I thank my God through Jesus Christ for you all, because your faith is being proclaimed throughout the whole world (Romans 1:8, *New American Standard Bible*).

HYMN FOR TODAY: "I Would Be True"

In a little cemetery at Cane Ridge, Kentucky, one grave stands out from the rest. On its tombstone are the words: "Barton W. Stone . . . minister of the Gospel of Christ and distinguished reformer of the nineteenth century." Stone was a leader in the great 1801 Cane Ridge Revival—over 20,000 attended—that led to the first Christian churches of Kentucky.

When the apostle Paul wrote to the Romans, he, too, paid tribute to their faithful Christian service. Interestingly, the New Testament puts less emphasis on the *success* than on the *faithful performance* of Christian service. In the parable of the talents (Matthew 25:14-30), the slaves who had earned five and two talents, respectively, received the same commendation: "Well done, good and faithful slave; you were faithful with a few things, I will put you in charge of many things, enter into the joy of your master" (Matthew 25:21, *New American Standard Bible*).

How would you like your life to be remembered? Whether you are a famous Christian leader or an uncelebrated servant of Jesus, there surely could be no greater tribute than for God to say, "Well done, good and faithful Christian!"

PRAYER THOUGHTS: Our Heavenly Father, thank You for the example of dedicated Christians who have gone before us. Amen.

January 18-24. **Richard Koffarnus** is a college professor in Moberly, Missouri. He and his wife, Patti, have two children.

WHAT A FELLOWSHIP!

SCRIPTURE: 1 Corinthians 1:4-9

VERSE FOR TODAY: God is faithful, through whom you were called into fellowship with His Son, Jesus Christ our Lord (1 Corinthians 1:9, *New American Standard Bible*).

HYMN FOR TODAY: "Leaning on the Everlasting Arms"

Over a decade ago, while I was doing graduate studies, I received a call to teach at Central Christian College of the Bible in Moberly, Missouri. Later, I learned that my name had been suggested to Central by a good friend who was then preaching in nearby Columbia. Bill has since moved on to other fine ministries in other states, but I have found a home at Central.

I'm sure many partnerships have been made because of the efforts of friends-in-common, but none more important than the one described in 1 Corinthians 1:9. We usually think of Christ as the One who enables us to have fellowship with God. But it is equally true that God calls us into fellowship with Christ. How? By the preaching of the gospel (2 Thessalonians 2:14). Thus, 1 John 1:3 says, ". . . what we have seen and heard we proclaim to you also, that you also may have fellowship with us; and indeed our fellowship is with the Father, and with His Son Jesus Christ" (*New American Standard Bible*).

Why is this fellowship so important? Through it we receive an "eternal inheritance" (Hebrews 9:15). In other words, salvation means more than just spending eternity in Heaven. It means we've been called into a marvelous, eternal fellowship with God and His Son.

PRAYER THOUGHTS: We praise Your name, Heavenly Father, for calling us into eternal fellowship with Your Son and with Yourself. May we be faithful to proclaim Your call to others. In the name of Jesus. Amen.

BLEST BE THE TIE

SCRIPTURE: 1 Corinthians 1:10-17

VERSE FOR TODAY: Now I exhort you, brethren, by the name of our Lord Jesus Christ, that you all agree, and there be no divisions among you, but you be made complete in the same mind and in the same judgment (1 Corinthians 1:10, *New American Standard Bible*).

HYMN FOR TODAY: "Blest Be the Tie That Binds"

In 1772, John Fawcett was a young, talented preacher with the little Baptist church at Wainsgate, near Hebden Bridge, England. When the Carter Lane Baptist Chapel in London offered Fawcett £40 a year to minister there, it seemed a golden opportunity.

The church at Wainsgate could not match such a salary or position. All they had to offer was their love. They pleaded with Fawcett to stay, and stay he did. To commemorate his decision, Fawcett wrote the hymn, "Blest Be the Tie That Binds."

Some Christians seem eager to separate themselves from Christ's body. An unkind word or a difference of opinion and they are gone. Paul, however, exhorted the Corinthians not to allow such differences to divide the church. But how can we avoid divisions? Paul says, in Philippians 2:3, that a Christian must regard others as more important than himself. And how can we learn to do that? By imitating Christ, Who loved us so much that He gave up everything on our behalf (Philippians 2:5-8, 1 John 3:16).

You see, Christ is the "tie that binds" Christians together. The more Christlike we are, the more spiritual we become, and the stronger are our Christian bonds. Truly, "The fellowship of kindred minds is like to that above."

PRAYER THOUGHTS: Heavenly Father, help us to put the needs of others ahead of our desires, so that the kingdom might be stronger and Christians might be united in love. In the name of Jesus, amen.

FOOLISH PREACHING OR PREACHING FOOL?

SCRIPTURE: 1 Corinthians 1:18-25

VERSE FOR TODAY: For the word of the cross is to those who are perishing foolishness, but to us who are being saved it is the power of God (1 Corinthians 1:18, *New American Standard Bible*).

HYMN FOR TODAY: "Go Ye Into All The World"

We were walking into Busch Stadium to see the St. Louis Cardinals play when we heard him, a modern-day John the Baptist. Near the gates, surrounded by vendors hawking pennants and peanuts, he stood on a soapbox, Bible in hand. "Repent! The world is dying and so will you unless you come to Jesus today!"

Some fans paused to listen briefly. Others laughed and made sarcastic remarks. Most people just ignored him—or pretended to ignore him. I felt embarrassment for the man, exposing himself to such ridicule for an obvious exercise in futility (whoever heard of people being converted at a baseball game?).

Then I began to feel embarrassed *for myself.*

What did Paul say about preaching "in season and out"? And didn't he warn us that the world would think God's Word is nonsense, but that people would be saved by it anyway? I realized that I had been acting like a spectator, not a preacher. That Bible-thumping preacher was out there in the thick of the action, while I was content to sit back in the stands and criticize his performance. I was a foolish preacher, but he was a preaching fool!

PRAYER THOUGHTS: Father, let us not be bystanders in the work of preaching the gospel, but be willing to share Christ with anyone, anywhere, anytime. In His name we pray, amen.

I AM THE GREATEST!

SCRIPTURE: 1 Corinthians 1:26-31

VERSE FOR TODAY: . . . no man should boast before God (1 Corinthians 1:29, *New American Standard Bible*).

HYMN FOR TODAY: "I Surrender All"

On May 1, 1991, fans of major league baseball witnessed the setting of two impressive records. Fireballing Texas Ranger pitcher Nolan Ryan threw his seventh career no-hitter—three more than anyone else in major league history—beating Toronto, 3-0. Meanwhile, Oakland Athletics outfielder, Ricky Henderson, recorded his 939th career stolen base, surpassing Lou Brock's long-time record.

While Ryan reacted calmly to his accomplishment, the flamboyant Henderson grabbed a microphone and announced to the world, "Lou Brock was a great base-stealer, but now I am the greatest!" Not surprisingly, most sportswriters reporting the events much preferred Ryan's humility to Henderson's boasting.

The contrast between the two ball players brings to mind Paul's admonition, "no man should boast before God." There are those today, as in the first-century Roman empire, who believe that they deserve to go to Heaven because of their intellect, their sanctimonious life-styles, or their worldly accomplishments. But Paul reminds us that no mortal is smart enough, pure enough, or great enough to deserve eternal life. Salvation is a free gift from God and comes only through submission to Jesus Christ. So "let him who boasts, boast in the Lord" (1 Corinthians 1:31, *New American Standard Bible*).

PRAYER THOUGHTS: Thank You, Father, for granting eternal life. May I never forget that my salvation is a gift, purchased with the blood of my Savior, Jesus Christ. In His name, I pray. Amen.

WHAT DO YOU KNOW ABOUT JESUS?

SCRIPTURE: 1 Corinthians 2:1-5

VERSE FOR TODAY: For I determined to know nothing among you except Jesus Christ, and Him crucified (1 Corinthians 2:2, *New American Standard Bible*).

HYMN FOR TODAY: "I Know That My Redeemer Liveth"

Shortly before his death, in 1790, Benjamin Franklin answered a letter from Ezra Stiles, President of Yale. Stiles, a theologian and a scientist, asked Franklin about his religious beliefs. Franklin replied, "As to Jesus of Nazareth . . . I have some doubts as to his divinity; though it is a question I do not dogmatize upon, having never studied it, and think it needless to busy myself with it now, when I expect soon an opportunity of knowing the truth with less trouble."

A strange reply, coming from a man whose name is synonymous with scientific curiosity! This is the same Franklin who invented bifocals and experimented with lightning. How could he have so much interest in these endeavors and none in the greatest question of all?

Contrast Franklin's attitude with Paul's in 1 Corinthians 2:2. Paul was quite familiar with Greco-Roman literature and philosophy. But he also had his priorities straight. He came to preach Jesus Christ, not to discuss Homer and Plato, because only Christ can give eternal life.

There are still people today who have no time to learn eternal truths. They should heed the advice of *Poor Richard's Almanac*: "Never leave till tomorrow what you can do today."

PRAYER THOUGHTS: Our Heavenly Father, thank You for revealing to us the truth about Your Son, our Savior. Give us the courage to share that truth with those who have not yet believed it. In His name, I pray. Amen.

I HAVE A SECRET

SCRIPTURE: 1 Corinthians 2:6-16

VERSE FOR TODAY: We speak God's wisdom in a mystery, the hidden wisdom, which God predestined before the ages to our glory (1 Corinthians 2:7, *New American Standard Bible*).

HYMN FOR TODAY: "Thy Word Have I Hid in My Heart"

My daily junk mail recently brought a catalog advertising mail-order videos. Some were familiar Hollywood movies and others were of historical interest, but most were designed "to help the buyer get more out of life."

There was a recurring theme to these self-help videos. One claimed to unlock the health secrets of the Orient. Another offered to reveal the secrets of the unknown: UFOs and suchlike. Still another was to supply information to win a state lottery!

It seems that everyone wants to know a secret that will make him healthier, smarter, or more successful. That's nothing new. In the apostle Paul's day, many Greek and Roman cults attracted followers by making similar promises.

Christianity, however, offers people a different kind of mystery. The gospel is not a secret "ticket to success" which a man can discover by himself. It is a secret which God revealed through Jesus and the preaching of His apostles, to all people, to point the way to salvation.

Today the "secret" of salvation is a secret no more. It is available to anyone who will follow the teaching of the New Testament. Do you know the secret?

PRAYER THOUGHTS: Our Heavenly Father, thank You for revealing to man, through Christ, the secret of salvation. Help us to share that secret with others so they, too, can be saved. Amen.

January 25

AND THE WALL CAME TUMBLING DOWN

SCRIPTURE: Ephesians 2:11-22

VERSE FOR TODAY: For he himself is our peace, who has made the two one and has destroyed the barrier, the dividing wall of hostility (Ephesians 2:14, *New International Version***).**

HYMN FOR TODAY: "Dear Lord and Father of Mankind"

We Americans watched in thrill and amazement in 1989 when the infamous Berlin Wall came tumbling to the ground. The wall which for so many years had cruelly separated families and friends was abolished amidst shouts, tears, and the realization that a long-awaited peace had come.

This wall, however, was only a mere reflection of a greater wall torn down—a dividing wall of hostility between the Gentiles and Jews; and, most importantly, a dividing wall between God and us.

Because of Christ's death on the cross, we can now go boldly before the throne of God, knowing we can have peace with Him. Because of Christ's death, barriers between our brothers and sisters can—and *must*—be torn down. Too often Christians work harder at strengthening those walls instead of tearing them down to build bridges.

Is there a wall between you and someone else today? Go to God. Ask for help. Then pick up His hammer of love to tear down that wall of hostility and build a bridge of love.

PRAYER THOUGHTS: Christ Jesus, thank You for providing peace with our Heavenly Father. Please forgive us when we do not share that peace with others. Give to us the wisdom and compassion to tear down walls. May we be one in You. In Your name, amen.

January 25-31. **Pam Coffey** is a minister's wife and mother to twin boys. She lives in Arcadia, Indiana.

A MYSTERY REVEALED

SCRIPTURE: Ephesians 3:1-13

VERSE FOR TODAY: This mystery is that through the gospel the Gentiles are heirs together with Israel, members together of one body, and sharers together in the promise in Christ Jesus (Ephesians 3:6, *New International Version*).

HYMN FOR TODAY: "The Family of God"

The world loves a good mystery. The vast number of mystery novels, movies, and television shows are proof of that.

A good mystery will often include someone who has died. As the plot reaches its concluding climax, the reader finally discovers who did it and why.

Paul had a mystery which he excitedly revealed to the Christians in Ephesus—and to us today. Who died? Christ Jesus. Who did it? We *all* are responsible. Our sins put Him there—but He allowed it. Why? So that *everyone* together might be able to inherit the promises of God and approach His throne with freedom and confidence."

This was probably a shock to those who have ever felt that they were the "only ones." And it must have been a real thrill to those who have ever felt they will never be good enough to be included in God's special family.

Yes, the *whole world* is included, for God is "not wanting anyone to perish, but everyone to come to repentance" (2 Peter 3:9, *New International Version*).

Go share this exciting mystery with a friend—or an enemy—today.

PRAYER THOUGHTS: Dear Lord, thank You for making it possible for us to be adopted into Your family. Please help us to remember that this gift is for everyone. May we share it with love in Your name. Amen.

FILLED UP WITH LOVE

SCRIPTURE: Ephesians 3:14-21

VERSE FOR TODAY: I pray that you, being rooted and established in love, may have power, together with all the saints, to grasp how wide and long and high and deep is the love of Christ (Ephesians 3:17, 18, *New International Version*).

HYMN FOR TODAY: "O the Deep, Deep Love of Jesus"

Let's pretend. . . . The apostle Paul comes up to you at this moment and says, "(Your name), I want to pray for you right now that you may know the love of Christ."

What would your response be? "Great! Thanks, Paul. I really need that." Or, "Super, Paul, but (you glance at your watch), can you make it quick? I have an appointment in twenty minutes."

It is easy to take Christ's love for granted. We reach out for snatches of it as we dash from one activity to another. Paul wasn't praying for the Christians in Ephesus to just taste samples of the love of Christ. He wanted them to *know it* and be *filled with it* so that they, in turn, could be united in love and shower Christ's love on the rest of the world.

Don't just breathe a prayer and rush on your way today. Take time to consider how wide, how long, how high, and how deep the love of Christ is. Allow Him to strengthen you and fill you up with His love. And may that love overflow to your family and friends, co-workers and classmates, and to the members of the family of God.

PRAYER THOUGHTS: Lord, to You who are able to do immeasurably more than all we ask or imagine, according to Your power at work within us, to You be glory in the church and in Christ Jesus throughout all generations, forever and ever! Amen. (Adapted from Ephesians 3:20, 21.)

WATER BALLOONS AND FIERY DARTS

SCRIPTURE: Ephesians 4:1-6

VERSE FOR TODAY: Make every effort to keep the unity of the Spirit through the bond of peace (Ephesians 4:3, *New International Version*).

HYMN FOR TODAY: "We Are One In the Bond of Love"

One summer I attended a fun-filled week with fourth and fifth graders at a Christian camp. One special event stood out in my mind, and that was a game of water-balloon volleyball. Each member of a team was to grab an edge of a sheet, stretch it out and use it to toss a water balloon over the net to the other side. The other team had to catch the water balloon with its sheet and, in the same manner, toss it back.

I watched as bodies got drenched with water and little arguments erupted as certain members would declare his or her way to be the best. But slowly the campers learned that if they were going to get the job done, they would have to grab hold of the sheet and work together. By the end, I saw my team change from sixteen individual personalities to one working unit—and I was proud.

In our churches, we may not toss water balloons, but we do have to fight off Satan's fiery darts, and we *can't* do that when each person is pulling his or her own way. We have to grab hold of God's love and work together. We may be different, but we still can become *one*. Our Team Captain is watching. Let's make Him proud.

PRAYER THOUGHTS: Heavenly Father, please help us to keep our eyes on You and to grab hold of Your love and peace. Help us to follow our leader, Jesus Christ. May we be united in Your name. Amen.

WE NEED EACH OTHER

SCRIPTURE: Ephesians 4:7-16

VERSE FOR TODAY: So in Christ we who are many form one body, and each member belongs to all the others (Romans 12:5, *New International Version*).

HYMN FOR TODAY: "I Love Thy Kingdom, Lord"

Have you ever played the comparison game? Have you ever felt grossly inadequate? Have you ever retreated from Christian service because you were overwhelmed by those who seem to be able to do it all—and do it well? Have *you* ever been caught doing it all because no one else seemed capable or willing to help?

If you are saying "Yes" to any of the above, stop and reconsider. This comparison game is one of Satan's greatest tools to destroy the unity of the church.

The truth is, *we need each other*. We need the differences. We need to appreciate each other's gifts and acknowledge our own. We need to take what we are, hand it over to God, and say, "I realize I'm not perfect, but please use me, God." And we need to encourage others, telling them specifically what they do well, and praising God for what He can do, or is doing, through them.

What is your gift of service? Take time now and thank God for making you in a special way. Then write a note of thanks to someone who has a different gift and watch God strengthen your unity in Him.

PRAYER THOUGHTS: Dear God, thank You for making us different and giving us special gifts. May we use them for You, and may Your name be glorified. In the name of Jesus. Amen.

OLD CLOTHES—NEW LIVES

SCRIPTURE: Ephesians 4:17-24

VERSE FOR TODAY: Therefore, if anyone is in Christ, he is a new creation; the old has gone, the new has come! (2 Corinthians 5:17, *New International Version*).

HYMN FOR TODAY: "Living For Jesus"

I have a friend who laughingly warned me that if I stopped by her house one day, I may see her in her overalls. Continuing to chuckle, she described that they were old and worn, but were, "oh, so comfortable!"

My curiosity was aroused, so I watched for those overalls, and she was right. They were old and worn, but they did look comfortable (and I secretly wished for a pair myself).

We may laugh at our favorite old clothes, but when it comes to our favorite old lives, the laughing needs to stop. When we first become Christians we gladly shed our old selves for a new and sparkling identity; but after a time of wearing, we may find that our "new clothes" may not always feel as comfortable as those old ones. Those old habits and life-styles may beckon like old shoes and jeans crying, "Wear me . . . wear me." Harsh words and old attitudes may crop us subtly. Before long, we're wearing our old selves once again.

Let's take a look into God's heavenly mirror each day and ask, "What spiritual clothes am I wearing today?"

PRAYER THOUGHTS: Thank You, Heavenly Father, for making us new. Please forgive us for the times we go back to our old ways. Give us strength to follow You. Please clothe us in Your righteousness and may we reflect You to the world. In the name of Jesus, amen.

January 31

. . . AND LET IT BEGIN WITH ME

SCRIPTURE: Ephesians 4:25-32

VERSE FOR TODAY: Be kind and compassionate to one another, forgiving each other, just as in Christ God forgave you (Ephesians 4:32, *New International Version*).

HYMN FOR TODAY: "Let There Be Peace On Earth"

Today is Sunday. Do you have on your "new selves" as you prepare to meet God's people in worship? (Or, if you have already lived your day, look back and see how you did.)

Be prepared. Satan works hard to build barriers all week. He works especially hard on Sundays, for a spirit of unity for the Lord is a blow against him.

Paul was aware of the pitfalls around God's people, so he gave us some specifics in this passage. (Stop and read today's verses again.) He deals with anger and bitterness. He encourages talk that builds up rather than tears down. And he continues to remind us to be compassionate and forgiving toward others—just as God has been toward us.

Sometimes it's hard to show compassion, especially with fellow Christians. We seem to expect more of each other. But unity, forgiveness, compassion, and kindness must happen here. If we are ever going to reach the world with Christ's love, then we must begin with each other.

God gave us His peace; the price was His Son.

To Him be the glory as we become one.

PRAYER THOUGHTS: Heavenly Father, thank You for Your love and forgiveness. Please help us to unite as Your people so that the world may be won to You. In Jesus' name, amen.

DEVOTIONS

. . . .

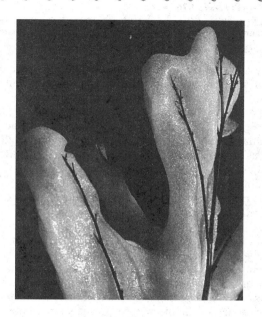

FEBRUARY

photo by Tom Stack

THE WAY OF THE CROSS

SCRIPTURE: Luke 23:26-34

VERSE FOR TODAY: "Jesus said, "Father, forgive them, for they do not know what they are doing" (Luke 23:34, *New International Version*).

HYMN FOR TODAY: "The Way of the Cross Leads Home"

They are all there—the participants and the bystanders, the Roman soldiers and the religious leaders, the mourning women and the criminals, the opportunists and the unwilling participants, the condemned and the condemning, the innocent and the guilty. The sadness of Luke's account of the journey from Pilate's judgment hall to the place of the skull almost leaves us breathless in stunned grief and horrified anticipation. It is almost as if all of creation stands still to observe this awful drama of death.

Jesus moves toward His death. A stranger is forced to carry the instrument of death. A great cry of mourning arises and follows the procession. Jesus speaks to the mourners, and those in the crowd are left to ponder what lies in store for themselves as well as what lies in store for Him.

When we come face-to-face with Jesus, we come face-to-face with ourselves. Our history is bound up in His, just as truly as those in Luke's narrative were bound up in His.

Think today of the meaning of Christ's crucifixion for you. In your imagination, stop for a moment at the foot of the cross. Hear again His words of forgiveness and give thanks.

PRAYER THOUGHTS: Dear God, help me never to forget the Christ of the cross and the price of Your love for me. In the name of Him who gave His life for me. Amen.

February 1-7. **Ward Patterson** is a college professor and author of numerous books and articles. He lives in Cincinnati, Ohio.

THE PEOPLE STOOD WATCHING

SCRIPTURE: Luke 23:35-43

VERSE FOR TODAY: The people stood watching, and the rulers even sneered at him. They said, "He saved others; let him save himself if he is the Christ of God, the Chosen One" (Luke 23:35, *New International Version*).

HYMN FOR TODAY: "Were You There?"

The people stood watching as Jesus was crucified. Some mocked. Some taunted. Some laughed. Some wept. One sought forgiveness.

A few years ago we had a "way of the cross" at a retreat I attended. At one of the stations the crucifixion was simulated. I remember our weeping eyes and choked throats as we stood in the moonlight and looked toward the cross. We thanked God for Jesus and asked for forgiveness of the sins that took Him there.

Another such time came in the German town of Oberammergau as I joined thousands of others in witnessing the Passion Play. I watched as the cross was raised and the villager portraying Jesus was suspended on the cross. There was a hush in the theater. We realized that it was this event that had brought us together from the far corners of the earth and united us in shared wonder.

These portrayals are attempts to help us imagine ourselves at the foot of the cross. Though we live long after the actual event, we, too, have a part in the drama of the cross. Jesus said, "If anyone would come after me, he must deny himself and take up his cross daily and follow me. For whoever wants to save his life will lose it, but whoever loses his life for me will save it" (Luke 9:23, *New International Version*).

PRAYER THOUGHTS: Our Father, we deserve death, but thank You for Jesus who took our sins upon himself. Amen.

THE DEATH OF THE RIGHTEOUS ONE

SCRIPTURE: Luke 23:44-56

VERSE FOR TODAY: And the curtain of the temple was torn in two. Jesus called out with a loud voice, "Father, into your hands I commit my spirit" (Luke 23:45, 46, *New International Version*).

HYMN FOR TODAY: "At the Cross"

The skies darkened. The temple veil tore. The Roman soldier praised God. The mockers and onlookers, in dismay, beat their chests and departed. Jesus' friends looked on from a distance. Jesus cried out, "Father, into your hands I commit my spirit." A prominent man put the body in his own tomb. Women prepared spices for the burial.

With these stark details, Luke records the death that shook the world. Matthew sketches these events in more dramatic detail. He notes that the temple veil was torn from top to bottom, that the earth shook and the rocks split, that tombs were opened and that the formerly dead were seen alive again in Jerusalem.

Jesus' death was unlike any other. It touched nature, it touched people alive and dead, and it touched the spiritual realm. The tearing of the temple curtain between the Holy Place and the Holy of Holies spoke of a new relationship between man and God made possible by the blood of Christ.

Has the death of Christ touched you? Think today on the impact and meaning of Christ's death for you.

PRAYER THOUGHTS: Father of mercy and love, You loved us so much that You gave Your righteous Son for our sins, so that we might be counted righteous before You. Thank You, Lord. Amen.

HE IS RISEN

SCRIPTURE: Luke 24:1-12

VERSE FOR TODAY: "He is not here; he has risen! Remember how he told you, while he was still with you in Galilee: 'The Son of Man must be delivered into the hands of sinful men, be crucified and on the third day be raised again'" (Luke 24:6, 7, *New International Version*).

HYMN FOR TODAY: "Christ Arose"

The humorist, Grady Nutt, used to say that the average preacher, standing before the empty tomb on the morning of the resurrection, would say, "Now, this illustrates three things...." Thus he poked fun at our way of turning dramatic, exciting, and world-changing events into dull precepts.

A few days ago we noted the breathlessness of Luke's account of the mournful journey from Pilate's judgment hall to Calvary. It was almost as if we could not breathe for the sorrow of it all. In his account of the resurrection, there is another kind of breathlessness, the breathlessness of head-long movement, joy and excitement, bewilderment and consternation. The stone of the tomb is rolled away, the body of Jesus is missing, the angels announce that Jesus has risen, the women rush to tell the disciples, Peter rushes to the tomb to see for himself.

The question of what became of the body of Jesus is one of utmost urgency today as well. The message of the resurrection is the heart of the gospel and the foundation of our understanding of who we are and what our eternal destiny will be.

PRAYER THOUGHTS: Father God, help us never to be complacent about the resurrection of Christ. Help us to have some of the same excitement as those early followers of Him who rushed to examine the empty tomb and who later rushed to tell the world of the meaning of that empty tomb. We seek Your blessing, in the name of Jesus. Amen.

WALKING WITH THE RISEN LORD

SCRIPTURE TEXT: Luke 24:13-27

VERSE FOR TODAY: "Did not the Christ have to suffer these things and then enter his glory?" (Luke 24:26, *New International Version*).

HYMN FUR TODAY: "Open My Eyes, That I May See"

Luke does not record many of the appearances of Christ after Christ's resurrection, but he does focus on one that Mark alludes to briefly.

It is interesting to note the kinds of people to whom Jesus appeared after His resurrection. None of them expected to see Him alive again. They were all amazed and bewildered by His appearances. Yet, they had one characteristic in common—they were seekers for truth.

If I had been arranging the appearances, I would have had Jesus appear to Pilate or King Herod or to the high priest or to a session of the Sanhedrin. But Jesus didn't do things that way. Instead, He stepped in beside those who were seeking to understand Him. He came alongside those who were willing to ask the big questions of life and who were receptive to what He had to say.

The bewilderment of the two on the road to Emmaus opened the door to a wonderful experience, though they did not truly understand it at first. Jesus began with the words of Moses and the prophets and explained to them what was said about himself. The things that they were experiencing were the culmination of God's plan, set in motion so many years before. How His teaching must have comforted them! All is well. God is in control. God is at work.

PRAYER THOUGHTS: Dear Father, thank You for coming alongside me in my moments of bewilderment. Thank You for the living presence of the risen Lord and His resurrection power in the life of the believer. Amen.

KNOWN IN THE BREAKING OF BREAD

SCRIPTURE: Luke 24:28-35

VERSE FOR TODAY: Then the two told what had happened on the way, and how Jesus was recognized by them when he broke the bread (Luke 24:35, *New International Version*).

HYMN FOR TODAY: "Break Thou the Bread of Life"

The miles must have gone quickly. All too soon Cleopas and his companion found themselves at their destination. They had been greatly comforted by the words of this stranger at their side who spoke with such assurance and confidence in the Word of God. There were so many more things they wanted to ask. They urged Him to stay with them.

The table was spread and they reclined on the floor beside it. The stranger reached for the bread that they had placed on the table. Slowly, He took that bread, prayed, and broke it.

Was it the way He prayed that first caused their eyes to open to who He was? Was it the depth of thanksgiving that His words conveyed? Or was it a characteristic way that He broke the bread and distributed it to each of them? Something struck a special chord of recognition. Something in that simple ceremony made them realize that they were in the presence of the One who had died on the cross but was alive from the dead. Suddenly, they knew Him! And just as suddenly He vanished from their sight.

Open eyes. Burning hearts. Rushing feet. Joyful news. Though very late in the day, they rushed back to Jerusalem to tell the disciples their personal experience of the resurrection. Would that we all were as excited as they about what we have come to know of the broken body and the empty tomb!

PRAYER THOUGHTS: Dear God, give us hearts that burn for Your truth and lips that tell what You have made known to us. Fill our hearts with the excitement of His resurrection. In the name of Jesus. Amen.

HE OPENED THEIR MINDS

SCRIPTURE: Luke 24:36-49

VERSE FOR TODAY: He told them, "This is what is written: The Christ will suffer and rise from the dead on the third day, and repentance and forgiveness of sins will be preached in his name to all nations, beginning at Jerusalem (Luke 24:46, 47, *New International Version*).

HYMN FOR TODAY: "Our God Reigns"

The two travelers, having returned to Jerusalem, were eager to recount their experience on the Emmaus road. But before they could speak, the disciples greeted them with their own news, "It is true! The Lord has risen and has appeared to Simon." How eagerly they all must have compared their experiences.

Then, suddenly, Jesus stood in their midst. He showed them His hands and feet and ate fish in their presence. Then He taught them that everything they were experiencing was the fulfillment of Scripture: "The Christ will suffer and rise from the dead on the third day, and repentance and forgiveness of sins will be preached in his name to all nations, beginning at Jerusalem" (Luke 24:46).

The pierced hands and feet of Jesus were His identifying marks. They were marks of His love and His victory over death.

The apostles were eye witnesses of this unique event in history. Millions of people have lived and died, but only one has conquered death. Paul and the other apostles focused their lives around this reality. He wrote to the Philippians, "I want to know Christ and the power of his resurrection and the fellowship of sharing in his sufferings, becoming like him in his death, and so, somehow, to attain to the resurrection from the dead" (Philippians 3:10, 11, *New International Version*). This should be our prayer as well.

PRAYER THOUGHTS: God of life, we thank You that there is hope for us in the resurrection of Jesus Christ. Amen.

IN JESUS ONLY

SCRIPTURE: Galatians 3:21-29

VERSE FOR TODAY: So the law was put in charge to lead us to Christ that we might be justified by faith (Galatians 3:24, *New International Version***).**

HYMN FOR TODAY: "I Know Whom I Have Believed"

There was a popular TV series years ago where the detective made famous the words, "Just the facts, ma'am, just the facts." The facts are these: we all are sinners and we cannot save ourselves from sin. It is not the degree of our sin that condemns us, but the fact of sin. Before God we stand as sinners—not great sinners or little sinners, but sinners. How do we know that? The law has told us that we are sinners. "The soul that sinneth, it shall die . . ." (Ezekiel 18:20). Sinners are people who have missed the mark. The law exposes our crime and our helplessness. The prophet Isaiah tells us that our righteousness is nothing but filthy rags before God (Isaiah 64:6). We have nothing to offer God. Good works are not enough —being a law-abiding citizen will not do. The purpose of the law is to show us our guilt, not to save us.

Is it all hopeless? Are the cynics right when they call out that all is despair and without reason? Paul writes that the law was our teacher to bring us to Christ. Only the mercy of God can restore our relationship to God that has been broken by sin. It is in Christ, not the law, that we are made whole!

PRAYER THOUGHTS: Father, there are times when my earth-bound thoughts hold fast to what I can see and touch. Nonetheless, I KNOW that You alone are the source of my salvation. Thank You, Father, for this inestimable gift! I believe! Help me in my unbelief. In the name of Jesus, amen.

February 8-14. **Willard Walls** is a campus minister and college professor living in Muncie, Indiana.

YOU CAN BE A SOMEBODY!

SCRIPTURE: Romans 9:1-5

VERSE FOR TODAY: Consequently, you are no longer foreigners and aliens, but fellow citizens with God's people and members of God's household, built on the foundation of the apostles and prophets, with Christ Jesus himself as the chief cornerstone (Ephesians 2:19, 20, *New International Version*).

HYMN FOR TODAY: "Moment by Moment"

Today's verse is a wonderful reminder of the truth confirmed in yesterday's devotion. We are no longer alienated and disenfranchised from God's fellowship. Why not? Are we not sinners? God's mercy and our faith in Jesus Christ has changed our relationship. We are God's children.

For twenty years I have been associated with a ministry that nurtures and directs the university student through difficult times. One of the most exacting demands on the student's personal development is his self-identity. For some it is a laborious struggle to break loose from the expectations and pressures of others. It is a wonderful experience to know who you are and what God wants of your life.

As Christians we are God's adopted. We know who we are; we know our family. Do you know that God has no grandchildren, but only children? That's right. You cannot be adopted into the family of God through the faith of someone else. No matter how godly your parents or grandparents are, their faith cannot bring you into God's family. It begins with your faith in a Person with a promise.

PRAYER THOUGHTS: Father, for Your merciful love and compassion I offer my gratitude. Your Word has comforted me in my loneliness and isolation. It has reminded me that I belong to You. To Your name be glory. Amen.

LIVING WATER

SCRIPTURE: Romans 9:6-18

VERSE FOR TODAY: I rejoice at Thy word [promise], as one who finds great spoil (Psalm 119:162, *New American Standard Bible*).

HYMN FOR TODAY: "Wonderful Words of Life"

Promises are important. We put our trust in people who can keep their promises. Broken promises are tragedies that scar. Do we dare put our trust in another's promise? Are we to risk another hurt?

Into these kinds of questioning lives Jesus brings a promised gift. It does not depend, writes Paul, on man's desire or his effort, but totally on God's mercy.

Jesus revealed that promise to the Samaritan woman at Jacob's well: "If you knew the gift of God, and who it is who says to you, 'Give Me a drink,' you would have asked Him, and He would have given you living water" (John 4:10, *New American Standard Bible*). Sin has affected us all to the harm and hurt of ourselves and others. But there is more. . . sin has brought death.

It is here that the promise of God comes into employment. The remedy for death is Jesus' promise of living water. On the feast of Tabernacles, as the priests poured water around the altar of sacrifice, Jesus cried out to the crowd, "If any man thirst, let him come unto me, and drink" (John 7:37). Let us go to Jesus who has the promise and the power to take away death with living water and to satisfy our thirst for salvation.

PRAYER THOUGHTS: O God, may my "love . . . abound more and more in knowledge and depth of insight . . . filled with the fruit of righteousness that comes through Jesus Christ—to the glory and praise of God" (Philippians 1:9, 11, *New International Version*). In Jesus' name, amen.

LOOKING IN THE RIGHT PLACE

SCRIPTURE: Romans 9:19-29

VERSE FOR TODAY: I love the Lord, because He hears my voice and my supplications (Psalm 116:1, *New American Standard Bible*).

HYMN FOR TODAY: "Thank You, Jesus"

A colleague, who constantly misplaces his car keys, bought a key ring that makes a sound when he claps his hands. He defended the necessity for the new contrivance by saying that he always looked for the keys in the wrong place!

Today's text illustrates how the Israelites, God's chosen people, were looking for God's gift in the wrong place. They were pursuing God's grace and mercy through works and not by faith. Jesus became the "stumbling stone" and not a stepping-stone into the kingdom.

The present generation's behavior is not unlike Israel's. In the emptiness of life, people seek fulfillment in all the wrong places. When you look for meaning in drugs, wealth, prodigious careers, fame, and promiscuous relationships, you are looking in the wrong places. When you seek God's approval by being legalistic, narrow, and religiously correct, you are looking in the wrong places.

"The one who trusts in him will never be put to shame" (Romans 9:33, *New International Version*). A Syrophoenician woman learned this truth when she approached Jesus with the request that He cast out the demon from her little daughter. Her trust in the mercy of God healed her daughter (Mark 7:24-30). Your trust in a merciful God, who loves you and wants the very best for you, is the only way to wholeness and meaning.

PRAYER THOUGHTS: Father, it is my goal to bear the fruit of the Spirit during my waking hours to Your honor. In the Savior's name, amen.

OUR FAITH

SCRIPTURE: Romans 9:30-33

VERSE FOR TODAY: "See, I lay in Zion a stone that causes men to stumble and a rock that makes them fall, and the one who trusts in him will never be put to shame" (Romans 9:33, *New International Version*).

HYMN FOR TODAY: "You Shall be Holy"

Pascal, the Christian mathematician of the seventeenth century, said that there are by-streams of happiness, affection for others, doing good, but the real source of happiness is a life that is right.

Righteousness comes only from God. Verses 30 and 31 of the text contain both a wonderful statement and a terrifying statement. The wonderful news is that the Gentiles attained righteousness because of their faith. On the other hand, the Jews tried to produce righteousness through the Mosaic law. When we accept the salvation of Jesus, He treats us as though we are righteousness. His blood covers our sins. This is a robe of righteous received by faith.

The planet Uranus, discovered in 1781, was regarded as the outermost of the planets. The study of Uranus by the astronomers revealed certain deviations and perturbations that could not be accounted for by any of the known laws and theories. It was proposed that these perturbations were caused from the action of another planet. After midnight on the morning of September 14, 1846, a student astronomer discovered the planet named Neptune. The astronomers' faith in the laws of the universe had led them to the discovery. The eye of faith saw it long before it was seen through the telescope.

PRAYER THOUGHTS: O God, I have been robed in righteousness by Your Son and my sins forgiven. Praise be to God. Amen.

February 13

CALLING ON THE NAME OF JESUS

SCRIPTURE: Romans 10:1-13

VERSE FOR TODAY: For it is with your heart that you believe and are justified, and it is with your mouth that you confess and are saved (Romans 10:10, *New International Version*).

HYMN FOR TODAY: "Reach Out to Jesus"

Augustine said that by trampling our sins and vices under our feet, we frame a ladder by which we rise on our dead selves to higher things. Once we make that decision, Jesus places our foot on the first rung. That is love and grace. To the woman at the well, Jesus said, "Go call your husband." To another He may say, "Go call your wife, your child, your mother and father." Or He may say, "Bring your checkbook or record of that wrongful business transaction."

A young student once asked the discoverer of chloroform, Sir James Simpson, what he considered his greatest discovery. Simpson replied, "The greatest discovery I ever made was when I discovered that I was a great sinner and that Jesus Christ is my Savior." We are sinners with a heart to believe and a mouth to confess that Jesus is Lord. For "everyone who calls on the name of the Lord will be saved" (Romans 10:13, *New International Version*).

The opportunity to climb the ladder that Augustine described must be made available to the whole world, for God desires that *all* people be saved. As Christians we are to be envoys of good news to those who have not heard. Are you a member of God's envoy to an unbelieving world?

PRAYER THOUGHTS: Father, may my conversation lead another to You. Through my walk and conversation, Lord, I desire that the gospel be preached with power and conviction. In Jesus' name, amen.

GOD'S ENVOYS

SCRIPTURE: Romans 10:14-21

VERSE FOR TODAY: Consequently, faith comes from hearing the message, and the message is heard through the word of Christ (Romans 10:17, *New International Version***).**

HYMN FOR TODAY: "I Believe You, Jesus"

Paul uses the Old Testament (cf Joel 2:32) to demonstrate that salvation is by faith. To "call upon the name of the Lord" means to believe in the Lord Jesus Christ. Both Jew and Gentile need to do this. He quotes Isaiah 52:7 which says, "How lovely on the mountains are the feet of him who brings good news, who announces peace and brings good news of happiness, who announces salvation and says to Zion, 'Your God reigns!'" (*New American Standard Bible*). God calls beautiful the feet of those who bear glad tidings.

A visitation team called on an elderly man who was known for his obstinate and resistant behavior when anyone spoke with him about Christ. The elders were barraged with shouting and cursing when the man answered the door. When they returned to the church office, they wrote on the card, "Don't call on this man again." The next day the minister read the message and made out a new card. The new card was given to another team! Within an hour the visitation team arrived at the church building with the elderly man. He had confessed the Lord and wanted to be baptized! What the elders had not seen was clearly discerned by the second team—the man was under conviction, and he was wrestling with the good news. How beautiful are the feet that bring the Word of God.

PRAYER THOUGHTS: Father, I praise You in thanksgiving for making me an heir of salvation. In Jesus' name, amen.

WHAT IF?

SCRIPTURE: Philippians 2:1-11

VERSE FOR TODAY: Your attitude should be the same as that of Christ Jesus (Philippians 2:5, *New International Version*).

HYMN FOR TODAY: "In My Life Lord, Be Glorified"

Have you ever played the group game, "What If?" Half of the group writes down situations, and the other half writes results, without knowing what the others are doing. The two responses are read and are often quite humorous. One example might be "Ted was three hours late to work," followed by, "so the ice cream melted all over the floor."

So much for the game. Now let's consider my life if I were to make some changes.

What if I decided to exalt Christ in my life? What if my motivations for serving were purely out of love for Christ? What if I had a servant attitude? What if I had used my money and possessions for the growth of the kingdom of God? What if I quit using people? What if I understood and accepted myself as God did?

I would respect each individual because they are made in God's image. I would love each person I came in contact with—regardless of how unloving or obnoxious they might be—by the strength given by the Holy Spirit. I would become like Christ, even in the midst of conflicts. I would honor God even above myself, my family, my friends, and my country.

PRAYER THOUGHTS: Lord Jesus, I want You to be King in my life today. I desire to praise and honor You through my life. I trust in You, and I ask You to increase my faith. I need Your strength to be obedient to You and to serve others. Amen.

February 15-21. **Judy Johnson** is an administrative assistant living in Cincinnati, Ohio. She volunteers with the Bethany House for homeless women and children.

WHAT ARE YOU WEARING?

SCRIPTURE: Romans 13:8-14

VERSE FOR TODAY: Rather, clothe yourselves with the Lord Jesus Christ, and do not think about how to gratify the desires of the sinful nature (Romans 13:14, *New International Version*).

HYMN FOR TODAY: "My Desire"

During my first visit to New York City, there was a garbage strike, and people were literally throwing garbage onto the streets. At dusk I was leaving Times Square area as others were arriving for evening entertainment. In those days the ladies wore long gowns, furs, and a lot of jewelry. Totally engrossed in their own happenings, little did they realize what they were walking on! In their own minds they looked, smelled, and acted very properly, and only an outsider could observe what actually was happening to them.

That reminds me of life around me. Sometimes we are so involved in making sure we are right, in protecting ourselves from others' anger and hostility, and in appearing to be so righteous, that we are not aware of reality. We want our spiritual and emotional appearance to be proper. Our desire to always appear proper may cause us to be a stumbling block to others.

However, Jesus has instructed us to clothe ourselves with humility so that we can serve others. Our emotions and actions need to be genuinely humble because of our relationship with Christ, our Savior.

PRAYER THOUGHTS: Heavenly Father, too many times I am concerned about me. I confess to You my sins of jealousy, pride, and dissension. I ask that You mold me into a person who loves You and who can then love others. In the name of Jesus. Amen.

February 17

GARBAGE IN, GARBAGE OUT

SCRIPTURE: Romans 14:1-12

VERSE FOR TODAY: Who are you to judge someone else's servant? To his own master he stands or falls. And he will stand, for the Lord is able to make him stand (Romans 14:4, *New International Version*).

HYMN FOR TODAY: "Search Me, O God"

Those who work with computers are familiar with GIGO—"Garbage In, Garbage Out." A computer really does not think; it requires a human mind to program it. If it receives wrong information, the computer uses wrong information.

Our minds work very much like that. We are being programmed every minute. Experiences, books, magazines, what we observe around us, commercials, movies, etc., are all inputting information into our subconscious minds. Then we live out our lives through our own filters.

To become like Christ we must renew our minds by His Word and by the power of the Holy Spirit. We must enter new information that will be used to live out our lives. What has become so ingrained in us must now be examined and evaluated to see if it is Christ-honoring.

Once our minds are renewed, we begin to act differently. Our relationships take on new dimensions. If we cannot survive contact with sinners and their activities without sinning, our faith is weak, and we should avoid the temptation. If our faith is strong, we can pursue being a light in a dark world. Neither of us is to be judged by the other.

PRAYER THOUGHTS: Heavenly Father, I ask You to renew my mind today. Help me to understand areas in my life where I am weak. Help me to have Your thoughts toward others and not to be judging. I need Your presence in my life at this moment. Amen.

WHOSE RULES?

SCRIPTURE: Romans 14:13-23

VERSE FOR TODAY: Therefore let us stop passing judgment on one another. Instead, make up your mind not to put any stumbling block or obstacle in your brother's way (Romans 14:13, *New International Version*).

HYMN FOR TODAY: "Bind Us Together"

One summer day I was at a community pool with two children, and they both wanted to race me across to the other side. The younger one, who was just beginning to swim, set her rules: "I'll start in the middle, and you give me a head start." The older one, who was more experienced, said, "Give me just a little start, and we can't breathe." The end goals were the same—to be the first one across the swimming pool—but the rules were different.

We Christians are striving to become Christlike, and Christ has given us freedom to live by grace in His Spirit. Satan has made us feel nervous about that freedom, and we have set up our own rules on how to achieve Christlikeness.

Sometimes our rules are a real hindrance to others who are racing. The "strong" Christian may flaunt his freedom in Christ and thereby offend others, while the weaker brother may set up many petty rules, trying to fence others in. The result is the same: dissension.

To grow in our faith we must be aware of Satan's attacks on us. We need to live by grace and not by our own rules.

PRAYER THOUGHTS: Heavenly Father, I praise You for Your lovingkindness to me. I confess my weakness of listening to Satan too many times and then setting up my own rules of conduct instead of living by grace through Your Spirit. Help me to love my brother as You love us both. In the name of Christ. Amen.

INTERDEPENDENCE

SCRIPTURE: Romans 15:1-6

VERSE FOR TODAY: Each of us should please his neighbor for his good, to build him up (Romans 15:2, *New International Version*).

HYMN FOR TODAY: "Make Me A Blessing"

At work one day a phone line went dead, so I promptly called the phone company for service. The next day they checked the equipment and told me the trouble was the building's security system. Their service people arrived and said to contact the phone-system service. They told me the problem was the answering machine. By the end of the week, I was frustrated with the way each piece of equipment was tied with the other. I was ready for the simple life!

Relationships are not simple, either. They are often very difficult. When they go awry, we are tempted to isolate and protect ourselves from others. It would be easier just to be independent of others, but that is not God's plan.

Recently we have heard a lot about co-dependents, people who let another person's behavior affect them and are, in turn, obsessed with controlling that person's behavior. That results in much pain, anger, and frustration. That, too, is not God's plan.

On the other hand, there are people who are dependent upon others, in an unhealthy way, to provide for their emotional strength. That, too, is not God's plan.

God wants us to be interdependent upon each other. We live for the good of others as we are led by God. We are not people-pleasers, but God-pleasers.

PRAYER THOUGHTS: Lord, Your love is so perfect. I need You to help me love and serve others out of a true love for You. Help me find my strength in You. In the name of Jesus. Amen.

BRINGING PRAISE TO GOD

SCRIPTURE: Romans 15:7-13

VERSE FOR TODAY: May the God who gives endurance and encouragement give you a spirit of unity among yourselves as you follow Christ Jesus, so that with one heart and mouth you may glorify the God and Father of our Lord Jesus Christ. Accept one another, then, just as Christ accepted you, in order to bring praise to God (Romans 15:5-7, *New International Version*).

HYMN FOR TODAY: "I Love You With the Love of the Lord"

Just when I think I've got it licked, it rears its ugly head again. I find it difficult to accept others. I think I accept them, and then all of a sudden I'm irritated by someone's mannerisms, speech, ways of thinking, dress, weaknesses, etc. I want them to change so that I will be more comfortable.

I'm glad that God doesn't treat me that way. Yes, He desires changes in my life for my sake as well as for the kingdom, but He accepts me for me today. In Him, I am able to accept and love my brothers and sisters in Christ.

Scripture teaches that I should accept others as Christ accepts me. Why? It brings praise to God. It shows that I have relied upon God's strength to love and accept a brother. The praise goes to God because I could not do it myself. God's mercy toward me is so great that I am filled and overflowing with gratitude. This enables me to express that love and mercy toward others.

PRAYER THOUGHTS: Heavenly Father, I am overwhelmed because of Your mercy toward me. I thank You for the gift of salvation through Jesus Christ. I thank You that Your love can be channeled through me toward those around me. Give me strength to love and accept them as You do. In the name of my Savior, Jesus Christ. Amen.

GLORY TO GOD

SCRIPTURE: Romans 15:14-21

VERSE FOR TODAY: Therefore in Christ Jesus I have found reason for boasting in things pertaining to God (Romans 15:17, *New American Standard Bible***).**

HYMN FOR TODAY: "To God Be the Glory"

Have you ever been stirred by some special music in a church service and then people began clapping? Sometimes it is a spontaneous outburst of clapping, and other times it is only a ripple of noise.

In some circles clapping in church is a real issue of spirituality. To some, the practice is viewed as giving praise to the musician. To others, it is viewed as giving praise to the God of the musician for what He has done through the life and the message that the musician brings.

So, who is to get the glory? For Paul the issue was settled. All glory went to God for what had been done.

When we understand God, we know that He works through us and others to accomplish what is to be done. We have no power to bring about great results alone. Only through prayer and the working of the Holy Spirit can God's work be accomplished here on earth.

So, the real glory goes to God for what He has done. Let's applaud God and give Him the glory!

PRAYER THOUGHTS: God, we praise You for the great things You have done. You have created the world, You have changed lives, You have brought about healing to a broken world. We cannot do this, and we recognize Your greatness. Through Christ we pray, amen.

THE GIFT OF ENCOURAGEMENT

SCRIPTURE: 2 Timothy 1:3-14

VERSE FOR TODAY: Therefore encourage one another, and build up one another, just as you also are doing (1 Thessalonians 5:11, *New American Standard Bible*).

HYMN FOR TODAY: "Reach Out to Jesus"

A friend and I were commiserating about our lack of finances—she for her business and I for our struggling ministry. We shared our mutual doubts of being able to continue. Then she smiled and said, "But I can't quit. I keep thinking of what God has waiting for us just around the corner." Her comment reminded me of a song I used to hear frequently on the radio: "Don't Give Up On the Brink of a Miracle."

A few days later, a visiting missionary spoke of God's provision—even from unexpected sources—when we are walking in His will.

When two of our friends faced a crisis that would bring about changes in their life-style, they were wrapped in the loving arms of a Bible school class—not just for a while, but for months.

Paul's "pep-talk" to Timothy in today's Scripture reminded him of his heritage of faith, his own gifts, a shared experience, and a reminder of the power of God. Encouragement comes in many forms: a note, a phone call, a sermon, helpful suggestions, a ministering act, a hug, or a prayer.

Who have you encouraged today?

PRAYER THOUGHTS: Father, help us to trust You and to remind others of Your loving care. Amen.

February 22-28. **June Lang** is an editor with *Alive* magazine for senior adults. She and her husband live in Cincinnati, Ohio.

February 23

WHAT'S YOUR EXCUSE?

SCRIPTURE: 2 Timothy 2:1-13

VERSE FOR TODAY: Suffer hardship with me, as a good soldier of Christ Jesus (2 Timothy 2:3, *New American Standard Bible*).

HYMN FOR TODAY: "In the Service of the King"

The temperature was in the 90s. Our city had issued a heat alert. Our church kitchen, which is not air-conditioned, was like a sauna. One of the ladies had draped a small towel across her shoulder with which she frequently mopped her brow as she prepared treats for snack time. The children were restless and noisier than usual as they gathered around the tables we had set for them. I thought of a number of places I would rather have been.

One of the workers wondered aloud why we continued to have VBS in such circumstances. "It's not <u>our</u> VBS," the head of the kitchen crew reminded her. "It's <u>God's</u> VBS. He loves those little critters and so do I! That's why I'm working in this kitchen right now." Her simple statement put things in proper perspective.

It isn't always convenient to be busy doing the work of the kingdom. I can think of a lot of excuses for not taking on a project, not attending a planning meeting, or not making a call.

Then I wonder: what child might not hear of the love of Jesus if I don't teach? What soul might be lost if I fail to share the gospel? What heart might not be comforted if I do not share my gift of music? What lonely person might surrender to despair if I am too busy to visit or offer encouragement? What person might become homeless if I did not share my material goods?

PRAYER THOUGHTS: Heavenly Father, forgive my selfish actions when I fail to seize the opportunities You give me to serve. In Jesus' name, amen.

APPROVED UNTO GOD

SCRIPTURE: 2 Timothy 2:14-19

VERSE FOR TODAY: Be diligent to present yourself approved to God as a workman who does not need to be ashamed, handling accurately the word of truth (2 Timothy 2:15, *New American Standard Bible*).

HYMN FOR TODAY: "More About Jesus"

A visitor from another congregation was discussing with me the growing number of church leaders who are deserting their wives and families and leaving behind them a wide path of destruction in the church. She lamented that her former minister had excused his behavior with, "God wants us to be happy." I told her that I knew an elder who had left a wife and four children because he wasn't "happy."

"How can someone so well-versed in Scripture act like that?" I asked. "Paul explicitly instructs Christian men to love their wives with an 'agape' love" (Ephesians 5:25).

"They either ignore the Scripture or twist it to mean what they want," she replied. Then she added, "I guess we need to be careful that we don't do that ourselves."

She's right, I thought. It's easy to be disappointed or downright angry with others who do not "rightly divide the word of truth," especially when they do so much harm to the church. But what about my own life? Are there admonitions I conveniently ignore or try to explain away? I need to pray daily that I will stay true to God's Word and not fall into temptation— that I might be a worker approved unto God.

PRAYER THOUGHTS: Loving and forgiving Father, help me to be careful to stay close to Your Word. Give me understanding and strength to obey. Help me to remember to pray for the leaders of my church that they might not fall into temptation. In the name of Jesus. Amen.

WINSOME CHRISTIANS

SCRIPTURE: 2 Timothy 2:20-26

VERSE FOR TODAY: Now flee from youthful lusts, and pursue righteousness, faith, love and peace, with those who call on the Lord from a pure heart (2 Timothy 2:22, *New American Standard Bible*).

HYMN FOR TODAY: "Living for Jesus"

When I was a teenager, my parents occasionally shared with me what they thought were compliments. "Mrs. So-and-so told me, 'June is such a sweet (or good) girl,'" my mother would tell me. I did not feel complimented. I felt put-upon.

Why do they say these things? I would ask myself. *Don't they know that I get angry, that I have thoughts and desires that aren't Christian? I wish they wouldn't say those things. It puts too much responsibility on me. If I do something wrong, I'll feel like I'm letting them down.* I did love the Lord and tried to live to please Him, but I didn't want the added responsibility of not being a stumbling block. Could it be that my parents had an ulterior motive in sharing those compliments with me?

Perhaps we Christians should remind one another of our responsibility of being winsome. Paul encourages us in today's Scripture to avoid such youthful traits as impatience and argumentativeness, and to concentrate on patience, love, and gentleness—even in presenting the truth of the gospel. Our purpose is not to alienate but to draw others to Christ. We have a responsibility to teach by word and example.

PRAYER THOUGHTS: Lord, whether I like it or not, I know that people are influenced by my behavior. May I never be guilty of keeping someone from following You. Help me to walk by Your Word. Amen.

BACK TO BASICS

SCRIPTURE: 2 Timothy 3:1-9

VERSE FOR TODAY: For since in the wisdom of God the world through its wisdom did not come to know God, God was well-pleased through the foolishness of the message preached to save those who believe (1 Corinthians 1:21, *New American Standard Bible***).**

HYMN FOR TODAY: "Rescue the Perishing"

Today's Scripture is a frightening description of present-day America. There was a time in this country when so-called moral expectations were pretty much in line with Biblical principals. Not so today. Christian motivation and behavior is as foreign and incomprehensible to society as it was to the Greeks and Romans to whom Paul preached.

How have we Christians allowed this to happen? Complacency? Over-tolerance? Timidity? Neglect? An "Ignore it and it will go away" syndrome? Refusal to be involved in politics? A "live and let live" philosophy?

I vividly remember a sermon preached years ago by Earl Hargrove, Chancellor of Lincoln Christian College. With reference to Exodus 1:8, Earl asked the question, "How had it come about that 'a new king arose over Egypt, who did not know Joseph'? Was it the neglect of the Israelites?"

Have we Christians neglected to remind our country that it was founded on God-fearing principles? Should we say, "Tsk, tsk," and throw up our hands in despair, or should we take action? Can Christian principles be restored to our government? If so, what part should you play to bring this about? Where will you begin?

PRAYER THOUGHTS: Dear Heavenly Father, forgive our negligence in doing our part to keep this a Christian nation. Help me to do my part to restore Christian guidelines to our government. Amen.

AN OVERLOOKED ROLE

SCRIPTURE: Titus 2:1-8

VERSE FOR TODAY: In speech, conduct, love, faith and purity, show yourself an example of those who believe (1 Timothy 4:12, *New American Standard Bible*).

HYMN FOR TODAY: "Make Me a Channel of Blessing"

In his book, *The Measure of a Woman,* Gene Getz emphasizes the important role of the older women in training the younger women to be Christian wives and mothers. We were using this book in conjunction with a Bible study for women, and I asked the question, "Has anybody in this group experienced the teaching guidance of an older woman in the church?" Without hesitation, three of the women named the same lady. "I'm not sure I'd have made it as a new Christian without the encouragement of Mrs. DeMaris," one of them declared. Without fanfare, this godly woman had made herself available to these young mothers. Her advice, ability to listen, gentle correction when needed, her role model, and her prayers played a vital role in their Christian nurture.

To my knowledge, not many churches concentrate on this aspect of teaching, but perhaps it need not be a structural area of Christian education. The responsibility is not strictly that of women. I have seen young men, whom my father had spent time nurturing, become responsible leaders in the church. I know a couple who have a ministry of teaching young families.

If you are an older adult, consider the possibility of taking a younger person under your wing. If you are young, seek out the advice of an older, experienced Christian.

PRAYER THOUGHTS: Lord, I thank You for the godly men and women who helped me to grow. May I be a nurturer also. In Jesus' name. Amen.

PASS IT ON!

SCRIPTURE: Titus 2:9-15

VERSE FOR TODAY: In all things show yourself to be an example of good deeds, with purity in doctrine, dignified (Titus 2:7, *New American Standard Bible*).

HYMN FOR TODAY: "My Tribute"

Some time ago I read of an incident in which a "Good Samaritan" came to the rescue of a stranded motorist. When the grateful motorist asked what he owed, his benefactor simply smiled and waved the proffered money aside. "Just do the same for someone else when you have the opportunity," he admonished as he drove away. The motorist replied that he had always tried to follow that example.

No doubt you have often wondered how you could possibly repay a kindness shown you by a caring friend, a neighbor, or even a stranger. When you come to the conclusion that you can't, you usually feel motivated to be more helpful to others.

Today's suggested hymn asks the question of how we can say thanks for the things the Lord has done for us. No amount of money can pay for our salvation. It seems the best we can do is to bring the knowledge of salvation to those we meet along the way of life. Paul's instructions to Titus are that we should be an example of good deeds, zealous in our efforts for the Lord. Of course, our deeds and evangelistic efforts are not going to pay for our salvation. They are simply our way of expressing gratitude for the gift of salvation God has given us.

Pass it on!

PRAYER THOUGHTS: Lord, I am so thankful for the priceless gift You have given me. Help me not to be guilty of taking Your gift for granted. May I always be reminded to pass it on. In Jesus' name, amen.

Psalm 150

Praise the Lord!
Praise God in His sanctuary;
Praise Him in His mighty expanse.
Praise Him for His mighty deeds;
Praise Him according to His excellent greatness.

Praise Him with trumpet sound;
Praise Him with harp and lyre.
Praise Him with timbrel and dancing;
Praise Him with stringed instruments and pipe.
Praise Him with loud cymbals;
Praise Him with resounding cymbals.
Let everything that has breath praise the Lord.
Praise the Lord!

My Prayer Notes

My Prayer Notes

DEVOTIONS

MARCH

photo by Luoma Photos

March 1

CHRIST, THE OMEGA POINT

SCRIPTURE: John 1:1-5

VERSE FOR TODAY: In the beginning was the Word, and the Word was with God, and the Word was God (John 1:1).

HYMN FOR TODAY: "His Name Is Wonderful"

Have you ever played "Scrabble" and wished for the all-time high point word? You know. The one that includes all those obscure consonants like "Q", "Y", or "Z"! Poets and philosophers down through history have sought for words or a word that would explain our existence.

The apostle John told us of The WORD! This Word was with God and was God. Furthermore, the apostle went on to say in this chapter and 1 John 1, that this Word has walked among us as a man. Jesus backed up John when He said, "I am the way, the truth, and the life" (John 14:6).

If we really grasp the significance of these statements, we will understand that the Lord Jesus Christ is the sum of all things spiritual. He is all in all.

Talk about a "high point word!" Many people talk about the importance of tradition, method, morals, gifts, etc., but of all things we can possibly pursue, the most important of all is God's Son, the Word, who came to be among us. Find Him and You have found the essence of LIFE!

PRAYER THOUGHTS: Heavenly Father, thank You for the simplicity that is the Lord Jesus Christ. Amen.

March 1-7. **Angus MacDonald** is a minister and writer who lives in Gainesville, Virginia. He and his wife, Susan, have three children, Joshua, Martha, and Zachary.

THE GIFT GIVEN TWICE

SCRIPTURE: John 1:6-13

VERSE FOR TODAY: He came unto his own, and his own received him not (John 1:11).

HYMN FOR TODAY: "O Sacred Head Now Wounded"

It is easy to advertise a "winner." But when you have a product people are not sure of, like Wilbur and Orville's airplane, then you have a job. John the Baptist was to advertise one who would be rejected by His own people. I asked my son to share how he would feel if he were John. He answered with a story:

One Christmas, a boy made a sculpture for his father. It was to him the most beautiful of all his sculptures. It was an eagle that seemed real enough to break its pose and fly. After applying the final touches, He wrapped it, and placed it under the tree, marked "To Dad." He could hardly sleep that Christmas eve.

In the morning his dad unwrapped beautiful gifts of great expense. Finally, he came to his son's gift. A faint smile crossed his father's face, and he said dully, "an eagle." The boy realized his father did not value his creative masterpiece as much as he did, and this was confirmed later when the boy found it in the trash, buried among the wrappings.

Years later, the child became a famous artist, and the same eagle, valued as one of his early works, was sold for thousands of dollars. The boy then presented the money to his father who now understood the value of the rejected gift.

Not everyone we witness to now will understand the value of our Lord, but one day they will.

PRAYER THOUGHTS: Our Heavenly Father, thank You for witnesses like John the Baptist who have brought attention to the greatest gift of all. Help us to do the same. In the name of Jesus. Amen.

REAL COMMUNICATION

SCRIPTURE: John 1:14-18

VERSE FOR TODAY: No man hath seen God at any time; the only begotten Son, which is in the bosom of the Father, he hath declared him (John 1:18).

HYMN FOR TODAY: "There's Something about that Name"

Two men meet in a hallway. One yells, "How are ya?"; the other responds, "How are ya?" Both are quite satisfied with this incredibly incomplete conversation.

Most of our conversation is on a superficial level and we like it that way. We reserve real questions about a person's state for a few we really love. "How are you?" over the dinner table would never be satisfied with a "How are you?" back.

Our passage tells us that the Lord Jesus Christ is "the Word." Not only is this profound, it is also a truth simple and sweet. God wants to communicate how much He means when He says, "I love you!" He shows us in His only begotten Son who "was made flesh, and dwelt among us" (John 1:14).

By coming as an infant in a manger to a poor couple, Jesus demonstrates His love to us. By taking on human nature, He shows us He does not look down on our humanity. By suffering natural limitations and temptations, He shows us He can identify with our pain and failures.

The law through Moses pointed man to the impossible, exposing his fallibility. Grace in Jesus Christ shows God's unconditional love descending to all mankind.

PRAYER THOUGHTS: Dear Heavenly Father, help us to realize Your genuine love for us. Help us to see in the life of our Lord Jesus Christ that You do not despise our company but desire to be with us. Amen.

"HALT, WHO GOES THERE?"

SCRIPTURE: John 1:19-28

VERSE FOR TODAY: He said, I am the voice of one crying in the wilderness, Make straight the way of the Lord (John 1:23).

HYMN FOR TODAY: "No One Ever Cared for Me Like Jesus"

During the Vietnam era, soldiers were taught strenuous rules regarding guard duty. The punishment on the front line for falling asleep was drastic. The Pharisees of Jesus' day thought of themselves as guardians of Israel. Their "Halt, who goes there?" to John the Baptist was an insistence that he identify himself. He never told them his name, from what we see in Scripture. He only told of his mission. But to John, his mission *was* his identity.

Much is made of "identity" today. To find one's identity, we are told, one must assert himself boldly and think only on those things that are positive about himself. John the Baptist found his full identity in the task of being a voice, preparing the way for the Messiah.

John's identity was like that of a picture frame, with the Lord Jesus Christ as the center. Modern men are like picture frames without pictures. The focus is on the frame instead of the more important content within.

All men have one purpose according to Scripture: to glorify God. As we allow the Lord Jesus Christ to be the center and focus of our lives, our identity is clear, and we are at peace.

PRAYER THOUGHTS: Thank You, Heavenly Father, for the identity that You have given us. We are temples of Your Holy Spirit, and Christ within is our hope of glory. Forgive us for stooping to lesser identities. Our task defines us, and that is to glorify You! Amen.

March 5

HE'S THERE AMONG YOU

SCRIPTURE: John 1:29-34

VERSE FOR TODAY: This is he of whom I said, After me cometh a man which is preferred before me: for he was before me (John 1:30).

HYMN FOR TODAY: "Be Thou My Vision"

If Jesus was in a crowd, could you identify Him? Most people think they would. They'd look, perhaps, for a holy glow or a winsome look, or even a pale, almost ghostly face.

Scripture consistently plays down the physical looks of our Lord. A Messianic chapter in Isaiah indicates that He had "no form nor comeliness . . . that we should desire him" (Isaiah 53:2). Interestingly, John the Baptist himself didn't recognize Him at first. Perhaps it was because Jesus was a cousin of John the Baptist.

In Nazareth the same thing occurred. People didn't have faith in Jesus because He was only a hometown boy. They knew his sisters as well as His parents. To them He was just the carpenter's kid.

Suppose our Lord walked into our town today. Would we recognize Him? Probably not. We can be assured of this because we regularly miss His presence in our lives right now, today. In Matthew 7 we read of a group of men who are castigated because they did ministry in the name of Jesus Christ but never came to know Him. He says to them, "Depart from me. I never knew you!" Can we identify Jesus? Can we identify Him now, in our lives? Do we know Him?

PRAYER THOUGHTS: Dear Lord, forgive us for losing You in the crowded days of our lives. Thank You that You never lose our identity. You will never lose us in the crowd. Our Savior, let us not fail to identify You and know You, that we may teach others to know You too. Amen.

EVANGELISM ON TIME

SCRIPTURE: John 1:35-42

VERSE FOR TODAY: He first findeth his own brother Simon, and saith unto him, We have found the Messiah, which is, being interpreted, the Christ (John 1:41).

HYMN FOR TODAY: "So Send I You"

A perfume seller came to the door of a missionary's home and said, "Would you like Eternity?" The missionary responded, "I already have eternity." The young saleswoman asked, "Is someone else working my sales area?" "No," said the missionary. "I mean eternity in the presence of God." The person at the door, once perplexed, was now uncomfortable.

Evangelism requires great tact, but most of all, timing. Jesus was never in a hurry but was always on time. Many, reading the account of the call of the disciples are convinced that Jesus just walked right up and said "follow me."

As you look at this passage, note that the first two disciples the Lord approached were disciples of John the Baptist. This relationship link is followed intensely through family lines, neighborhood, and village, until virtually every one of the disciples is chosen. Judas may be the only disciple without a link to the family or neighborhood of these first men.

Add to this relationship link the approach of the Lord. Rather than starting with "Follow me!", He begins with "Come and see." He invites them *into His life.* Evaluate your approach to evangelism. Is it with strangers and at arms' length? The example of our Lord is to start at home and work out.

PRAYER THOUGHTS: Dear Jesus, we thank You that You said "Come and see" to those first disciples. Open our hearts and then open our homes to our family first and then to those around us. Amen.

"COME AND SEE!"

SCRIPTURE: John 1:43-51

VERSE FOR TODAY: And Nathanael said unto him, Can there any good thing come out of Nazareth? Philip saith unto him, Come and see (John 1:46).

HYMN FOR TODAY: "Tell Me the Story of Jesus"

"Come and see" are wonderful words. They are perhaps the rarest of all in evangelism. Why is this so? None of us like others to see us at less than our best, so we don't invite them to "Come and see." In the military, Inspector Generals show up routinely on military bases. Before their arrival, feverish activity prepares the buildings, implements, and men and uniforms to better-than-normal conditions. In reality, an unannounced visit would have found the men as they were and would have provided a more accurate inspection.

When we are "doing evangelism," we like to make sure our clothes are pressed and our smiles are unwilted. Ours is not a "Come and see" evangelism. That approach would place before the scrutiny of the world our vulnerable areas. If people come and see, we are fearful they may detect our weaknesses.

But *who* are we presenting? Christ or ourselves? Andrew knew when he said "Come and see" that it had nothing to do with him. It was Jesus who was to be seen. What a great breakthrough it would be if we understood that our vulnerability and weakness allows the Lord to shine through! Then we would be less hesitant to say "Come and see!"

PRAYER THOUGHTS: O Lord, how often we have felt that evangelism depended on our putting up a front of perfection. You are our Perfection. Help us, dear Lord Jesus Christ, to allow You to live through us, even in our humanness as we tell others to "Come and see." Amen.

BORN TO LAST

SCRIPTURE: John 3:1-8

VERSE FOR TODAY: For you have been born again, not of perishable seed, but of imperishable, through the living and enduring word of God (1 Peter 1:23, *New International Version*).

HYMN FOR TODAY: "Where the Spirit of the Lord Is"

While my old friend Vincent poured me a cup of his own choice tea in his favorite tea house, he shared some of the wisdom of Chinese maxims. The waiter listened intently. Then on the back of our menu for the day the waiter penned the following Chinese maxim:

"As the pine is to the flower, so good is to evil;

The pine, unlike the flower, is cooly aloof; But on the day the frost falls, Only the pine and not the flower is seen."

In the same way the Spirit-breathed life keeps on blessing others after troubles wither up human willpower.

Sometimes I forget that truth. Excited by pride and my senses, I'm sure I can succeed on my own. I carelessly promise to do more than I possibly can. Money runs short. Legal procedures run long. Equipment breaks down. People get sick. In short, human strength fails.

Vincent is always aware of human weakness because disease has robbed him of over three-fourths of his ability to breathe. The life he now lives reminds me that the Spirit-breathed inner life supplies strength for wisdom, love, joy, and peace beyond normal limits, as will eternal life.

PRAYER THOUGHTS: Heavenly Father, thank You for offering us birth into spiritual life. In Jesus' name. Amen.

March 8-14. **Gary Anderson** ministers in Emmett, Idaho. For many years, he ministered with the Chinese in Hong Kong. He and his wife, Joyce, have three children, Sandra, Steven, and David.

LIFT UP CHRIST WITHOUT DELAY

SCRIPTURE: John 3:9-15

VERSE FOR TODAY: That everyone who believes in him may have eternal life (John 3:15, *New International Version*).

HYMN FOR TODAY: "If I Be Lifted Up"

My good friend Joe asked me to speak at his wedding. Since I didn't really know the church or minister, my family and I arrived early. Not seeing Joe, we sat near his friends and family and visited with them.

As the church filled, I kept watching for Joe but didn't see him. Finally, ten minutes after the wedding was supposed to start, Joe rushed past me. I overheard him explain to the minister that the wedding couldn't start because someone hadn't yet arrived. When Joe walked by again only two feet away, I tried to get his attention, but he looked straight through me. My daughter Sandi said, "He's so nervous; he doesn't see you." So I hurried to catch him. He soon confirmed my fears. He was delaying the wedding because he thought I wasn't there. My presence had failed to catch his attention.

In the same way, our friends and neighbors are delayed from enjoying life forever in Christ. They miss out, even when they know that their lives are lacking, because we fail to lift up Christ so that His presence, as the answer to their needs, catches their attention.

PRAYER THOUGHTS: Good Father, thank You for sending Christ so that we can live in Him forever. Keep our hearts attentive to Him even in the bustle of our lives. Help us to bravely lift up Christ so that our friends might also be drawn to eternal life in Him. Amen.

THE ONE AND ONLY

SCRIPTURE: John 3:16-21

VERSE FOR TODAY: "For God so loved the world that he gave his one and only Son, that whoever believes in him shall not perish but have eternal life" (John 3:16, *New International Version*).

HYMN FOR TODAY: "All Hail the Power of Jesus Name"

"How can Christ be both God and man?" you may ask. "How can He be both the Son of God and God? How can God be one and yet have this Son who is also God?"

It's difficult to grasp who Christ is. But that's because Christ is one of a kind. We have nothing familiar with which to compare Him. And nothing to compare can be found.

If you like, climb the cliffs of Mount Everest in air almost too thin to breathe. Plumb the blackest depths of Carlsbad's Lechuguilla Cave. Sound the murkiest underwater recesses of the Pacific Ocean's Izu Trench. Question the countless gurus of Calcutta's pagan shrines. Even travel at light speed to Andromeda's Galaxy NGC-205. Perhaps you will find life forms who sin and need salvation like us, but you won't find anyone to compare with Christ.

Christ was God's rarest, priceless treasure, His very best—His one and only Son. Yet God gave Christ to the world anyway. So we see just how much God's care for us is truly beyond compare. We can rest assured that such care is enough to meet our deepest needs.

PRAYER THOUGHTS: Dear Lord God, we praise You because You are greater than even the greatest human understanding. Thank You for showing us that Your love in Christ is beyond compare. Each day we find Your comfort in the midst of our trials. We also find strength to fulfill our duty. May You be glorified. Amen.

LET CHRIST SHINE

SCRIPTURE: John 3:22-30

VERSE FOR TODAY: I have been crucified with Christ and I no longer live, but Christ lives in me. The life I live in the body, I live by faith in the Son of God, who loved me and gave himself for me (Galatians 2:20, *New International Version*).

HYMN FOR TODAY: "Let the Beauty of Jesus"

I was watching a concert on television filmed in black and white nearly forty years before. The poor quality of filming and sound recording were distracting. And the obviously aged conductor had such poor eyesight that he was conducting entirely from memory.

Yet I was fascinated. People would go away from his concerts feeling as if they had never known music so well as when he conducted it. The TV station considered his concert worth airing on prime time. The conductor was Arturo Toscanini.

What distinguished Toscanini as a great conductor? One factor seems to have been that, like John the Baptist to Jesus, Toscanini was intensely devoted to the service of the great master composers. His purpose was not so much to present something new and innovative of his own, as to truly understand how the composer would have wanted his music to sound and then wholeheartedly produce just that sound in the greatest detail.

May we, too, seek to conduct our lives so that Christ's great masterpiece of saving grace (rather than our personal innovations) shines forth in the greatest detail.

PRAYER THOUGHTS: Divine Lord, we praise You for taking human history and composing in it the greatest masterpiece of love and grace. Guide us to fulfill our parts well so that the beauty of Christ might shine forth in all its glory. Amen.

ABOVE MERE WEALTH AND CREDENTIALS

SCRIPTURE: John 3:31-36

VERSE FOR TODAY: Such a high priest meets our need—one who is holy, blameless, pure, set apart from sinners, exalted above the heavens (Hebrews 7:26, *New International Version*).

HYMN FOR TODAY: "Jesus, Name Above All Names"

Few countries had navies larger than Aristotle Onassis' fleet. Yet all that money couldn't stop the rare muscle failure (myasthenia gravis) that killed him in 1975.

Over ten years later, a lady in New York City got sicker and sicker. New York has some of the world's finest doctors, but many doctors examined her before one saw that she had this rare muscle failure. Yet she was considered too old for the surgery that could have stopped it for good.

A couple of years later, this rare muscle failure put my mother in a Boise, Idaho, intensive care unit, unable to move. What could Dad and we expect? Surgery seemed out of the question since Mom was older than the other lady. Boise didn't have world-class doctors. We weren't rich, but we had Christ, who is over all. We prayed to God in His name. The doctor performed surgery.

Mom recently phoned. She'd been gardening and attending church activities. As I write, she is flying alone to Wisconsin to visit family. We learned that Christ and what He can do is indeed above all that youthful vitality, wealth, and human credentials can do.

PRAYER THOUGHTS: Heavenly Father, we praise You for caring enough to show us that Christ is worth trusting. Thank You for the comfort of knowing that His ministry of saving love is unaffected by lack of money or fame. Help us also to do our part in this ministry. Amen.

CHRIST PRAYS FOR OUR PROTECTION

SCRIPTURE: John 17:1-11

VERSE FOR TODAY: Holy Father, protect them by the power of your name—the name you gave me—so that they may be one as we are one (John 17:11, *New International Version*).

HYMN FOR TODAY: "I Have Found a Hiding Place"

In 1978, Vietcong soldiers were so cruel that many Vietnamese saw no way to live except to flee their homeland by sea. Many were shot without mercy when caught. If they escaped these dangers, they found the South China Sea no less cruel. As winter approached, the ship Huey Fong under Captain Shu rescued over 3,000 such folk, including 1,352 children from certain death at sea.

Yet their troubles were not over. Two days before Christmas, Hong Kong blocked their entry just about forty miles from where I lived. While the world watched, other countries refused them passage. They ran out of drinking water. Only biscuits were left to eat. Disease was spreading. Bad weather was looming.

Finally, on January 17, 1979, 600 family heads on board united in signing a letter to Captain Shu, pledging to shoulder all criminal charges if he would run the blockade while they knelt on deck pleading to God for him and for their own salvation from destitution. Captain Shu not only obliged, but insisted on bearing the blame himself.

God heard their pleas. Even now, Christ intercedes to protect His own, bearing the blame himself—that we might be one.

PRAYER THOUGHTS: O God who hears the cries of Your destitute children, teach us to hear, and with one voice to plead for and minister to, souls in darkness, the starving, the orphaned, the oppressed, and the crippled. Amen.

OUR LOVE IS GOD'S

SCRIPTURE: 1 John 4:7-12

VERSE FOR TODAY: Dear friends, let us love one another, for love comes from God (1 John 4:7, *New International Version*).

HYMN FOR TODAY: "I Love You With the Love of the Lord"

"Among the most persuasive words you can say to an audience are an honest recounting of how God has affected you." That's what I told six ordinary Chinese men in "Effective Preaching" class. "So," I continued, "would you each please come forward and persuasively speak to us of God's truth?"

Y. T. Chan began. "I'm going to talk," he said, "about God's love. Had it not been for faithful Christian friends and their patient teaching, I wouldn't know God's love." Although his theme was God's love, his message interestingly was Christian love.

I recalled that he'd been an illegal alien, a spirit medium in martial arts and probably on drugs. Faith moved him to turn himself in to immigration authorities for imprisonment and extradition. I also recalled that Christians even appealed to the highest authorities for his pardon.

When he finished, S. K. Chan stood up. "Had it not been," he said, "for Christian love when my elbow was crushed. . . ." And another story—of God's love—began to unfold.

More persuasive than any words were loving actions that manifested the loving presence of God.

PRAYER THOUGHTS: O God of love, teach us Your thoughts that we might understand true love. Let our hearts dwell on Your loveliness till we think that which is lovely. Fill us with Christ's Spirit that our every move might be a move of love. Amen.

THIS CLAIM DEMANDS A RESPONSE

SCRIPTURE: John 8:48-59

VERSE FOR TODAY: "I tell you the truth," Jesus answered, "before Abraham was born, I am!" (John 8:58, *New International Version*).

HYMN FOR TODAY: "I Love to Tell the Story"

"I can jump out of the upstairs window of my house," the stocky boy announced suddenly to my other first-graders. His black eyes flashed, daring someone to challenge his statement. The other children listened with mixed reactions. A few seemed to accept his claims, but others shook their heads in disbelief. One boy responded jeeringly, "And I can fly, too!" A ripple of giggles followed.

Quickly trying to defuse the rising emotions I calmly said, "Let's all turn to page 100 in our workbooks." In a matter of seconds everyone's attention was focused on the reading lesson at hand. The boy's foolish claim needed no response.

But the claim which Jesus made to the Jewish leaders could not easily be ignored. He clearly said that He existed before Abraham was born. His statement undeniably proclaimed His divinity. It was a claim which not only demanded a response back then but continues to call for one today. Jesus said that He is God. The Jewish leaders responded by seeking to stone Him for blasphemy. Blinded by their own sin, they did not see the truth. But what about us today? His claim still demands a response.

PRAYER THOUGHTS: Loving Father, thank You for reminding us today that the claims of Jesus demand a response. Help us to accept the challenge of discovering who You really are. And use us to tell others that You are exactly who You said You are. We give You praise. In His name, amen.

March 15-21. **Sharon Beth Brani Loy** is a teacher and free lance writer living in Normal, Illinois.

NOW I CAN SEE

SCRIPTURE: John 9:1-7

VERSE FOR TODAY: This is the message we have heard from him and declare to you: God is light; in him there is no darkness at all (1 John 1:5, *New International Version*).

HYMN FOR TODAY: "Turn Your Eyes Upon Jesus"

It was a Sunday morning I'll never forget. Having recently moved to Illinois, my spirit was unsettled and lonely as I sat on the pew in church. I, a bride of just twenty days, greatly missed my family and friends in Virginia. But suddenly my attention was drawn to the female soloist. She, a blind lady, was singing "Satisfied With Jesus" with deep feeling. I watched as her fingers moved across the braille. There was no doubt that Jesus was her Light. God was strengthening her faith and using her in a mighty way. My heart that day was encouraged to let Him fill all my needs with himself.

It's easy to allow ourselves to question, "Why did this happen to me?" or "What did I do wrong?" Regardless of the reasons for our suffering, Jesus has the power to help us deal with it. In this fallen world, innocent people sometimes suffer. But as we ask Him to give us strength through the trial and a deeper perspective on what is happening, our faith grows and God is glorified. His light brightens all the dark places of our life when we turn to Him in faith.

PRAYER THOUGHTS: O Lord, we thank You today that You are still giving sight to the blind and shedding light in dark places. Help us, in whatever our circumstances, to see them with Your eyes. Draw us closer to You and may all we do and say glorify God. In Jesus' name, amen.

THE BEGINNING OF FAITH

SCRIPTURE: John 9:8-12

VERSE FOR TODAY: And Jesus answering saith unto them, Have faith in God (Mark 11:22).

HYMN FOR TODAY: "Have Faith in God"

I'm sure that one could have sensed electricity in the air as the people pressed around the blind man who had just been healed. With mud still covering his eyes, he had found his way to the Pool of Siloam. There he had scrubbed away every trace of mud. When he opened his eyes, eyes which had never seen before, he could see everything clearly. With excitement he raced back. People who had known him for years shook their heads in surprise and skepticism. They wanted to know what had happened.

The man's response at this point was very limited. Although he did not understand everything, he knew that the man called Jesus had healed him. Faith grows from a tiny seed. At the beginning we may not even know what is happening in our lives. But if we respond to God with believing hearts, that little seed of faith will grow. We must not let the questions of skeptics discourage and confuse us. Instead, we need to hold on to the reality of His touch in our lives. We need only to trust and obey Him. That belief will become strong and vibrant as we grow in Him.

PRAYER THOUGHTS: Heavenly Father, at times my faith seems so small. But it's so exciting to see that You will cause it to grow the more I know You. Help me to be patient with new Christians and to encourage them in their faith. In Jesus' name, amen.

WHO DO YOU SAY HE IS?

SCRIPTURE: John 9:13-23

VERSE FOR TODAY: And I say unto you, Ask, and it shall be given you; seek, and ye shall find; knock, and it shall be opened unto you (Luke 11:9).

HYMN FOR TODAY: "Ask Ye What Great Thing I Know"

Oh, how I looked forward to the days that Mary came to clean my house. She not only made everything shiny, but we had long talks about Jesus. At first Mary was hesitant to say very much about her faith. But gradually she began to share. Although she had attended Sunday school and church as a child, it wasn't until she was an adult that she really came to know the Lord in a personal way.

"How did it happen?" I asked one day.

"Well, my life was all messed up," she explained. "My marriage was breaking up, and I, with two small children, was at the end of myself. I remembered back to what I had heard about Jesus as a child. And I knew that I had to decide for myself if He really was who He said He was.

"I turned to Him and discovered that He is everything He claimed to be. I know that He is my Lord and Savior."

Like the blind man, Mary had shown consistent, growing belief in Jesus. The hearts of the Pharisees were blinded by skepticism and jealousy. But while questioning and debating about Jesus, people were being healed and lives were being changed. So it is today.

PRAYER THOUGHTS: Thank You, Father, for the wonderful way You continue to make Yourself known to us when we seek You. We praise You that You are our Lord and our Savior. In Jesus' name, amen.

JUST TELL WHAT YOU KNOW

SCRIPTURE: John 9:24-34

VERSE FOR TODAY: Then spake Jesus again unto them, saying, I am the light of the world: he that followeth me shall not walk in darkness, but shall have the light of life (John 8:12).

HYMN FOR TODAY: "Heavenly Sunlight"

As I sat with my friend in the restaurant one evening, my hands began to tremble. "How do you explain it?" she asked with growing sharpness in her voice. I didn't know what to say. I didn't know how to answer her. I simply froze in panic.

"Jesus, help me," I whispered silently.

I had prayed for months for an opportunity to share what God had done in my life with my friend. So while we were eating I had slowly begun to tell her about the miraculous change in my life. But her response was to bombard me with difficult questions.

I took a deep breath.

"You have asked many questions tonight. I do not know all the answers. But I do know this. Jesus has changed me. I am not the same person as I was. He has set me free. And He wants to do the same for you." My friend was very quiet, and I could tell that she was under deep conviction. How grateful I was for the opportunity to share Christ with her. Like the man who had been blind, I didn't need to know all the answers in order to tell others about Jesus.

PRAYER THOUGHTS: Loving Father, sometimes I am afraid to tell others about You. Help me to boldly share what You have done for me, and then to trust You to use my words so others may believe in You, too. In Jesus' name, amen.

A GLORIOUS DISCOVERY

SCRIPTURE: John 9:35-41

VERSE FOR TODAY: And they said, Believe on the Lord Jesus Christ, and thou shalt be saved, and thy house (Acts 16:31).

HYMN FOR TODAY: "I Know Whom I Have Believed"

"How can I stop doing such bad things?" I asked my mother one night as she tucked me in bed. Even at a young age, I was aware that I was a sinner and that I needed a Savior. My mother gently held me in her arms and showed me Acts 16:31-33. At that moment I believed in the Lord Jesus Christ. As the years have passed, I have grown to know Him better. Today I can look back and see how He has tenderly guided me to a greater faith. And I anticipate a future of continuing to grow in spiritual strength. Yes, life has become a glorious adventure!

The man who had been blind gained not only physical sight but also spiritual sight. First, he recognized Jesus as Master, then prophet, and then Lord. The longer he experienced his new life, the more confident he grew in the One who had healed him. How true it is that the longer we walk with God the better we understand who He is.

Let's encourage those struggling with doubts and questions to embrace Him. He so wonderfully takes each seeking person and leads them into greater discoveries.

PRAYER THOUGHTS: Dear Lord, thank You for reminding us that the walk of faith is a glorious adventure. Each day draw us closer to You and open our eyes to more discoveries of who You really are. Thank You for transforming all our fears into faith. In Jesus' name, amen.

HE GOES BEFORE US

SCRIPTURE: John 10:1-9

VERSE FOR TODAY: I am the good shepherd: the good shepherd giveth his life for the sheep (John 10:11).

HYMN FOR TODAY: "Savior, Like A Shepherd Lead Us"

"O Lord, I'm so afraid," I cried out to Him one night. Thoughts of my soon-approaching wedding and then the leaving of job and family and friends filled me with increasing dread. And although I knew that God had miraculously brought about this dramatic change in my life, I still wrestled with many fears and apprehensions about the future. With tears streaming down my face, I reached for my Bible and began to turn the familiar pages. My eyes suddenly rested on these verses. Somehow, as I read again that Jesus is our Good Shepherd, my emotions began to quiet and a sense of peace enfolded me. Just being reminded that He cares for me just as the shepherd cares for his flock comforted my trembling heart. Realizing that Jesus always goes before His sheep and that He was already preparing the way began to transform my fears of the future into faith.

Oh, there were other times when sickening fears would threaten to overwhelm me, but just remembering that Jesus, my Shepherd, always leads His sheep continued to fill me with fresh courage so that I could take one more step.

PRAYER THOUGHTS: Heavenly Father, thank You for so tenderly caring for each one of us. Thank You that as the Good Shepherd You always go before us and You are preparing the way. We give You praise. In Jesus' name, amen.

WALK IN THE LIGHT

SCRIPTURE: John 11:1-11

VERSE FOR TODAY: Jesus answered, "Are there not twelve hours in the day? If anyone walks in the day, he does not stumble, because he sees the light of this world" (John 11:9, *New King James Version*).

HYMN FOR TODAY: "Walk in the Light"

My grandson, Stevie, loves to play with flashlights! A flashlight is better than any toy to him. The flashing light holds a certain fascination for him. When he presses a button, the light goes on; presses again, it goes off. For an adult, a flashlight holds a greater purpose—without a light we can stumble and fall in the darkness. With the light, we can walk without fear. A flashlight is more than a toy to us. It is a necessity. So is God's Word.

We can compare this to walking in the sunshine of God's knowledge and will for our life or stumbling around, hurting ourselves (and others) in a dark life of sin. We need to read the Word daily so we know what God's will is for us. We need to know how God thinks and His Word will tell us. Psalm 119: 105 says, "Your words are a flashlight to light the path ahead of me, and keep me from stumbling" (The Living Bible).

Though Jesus' disciples reminded Him that the Jews wanted to kill Him, Jesus knew He could go to Judea because He walked in the daylight, in the knowledge of God's will.

PRAYER THOUGHTS: Lord, help me to take time every day to read Your Word so that I may walk in the daylight, knowing Your will for my life, and not stumble. In Jesus' name, amen.

March 22-28. **Kathleen Thompson** is a homemaker and free lance writer who lives in Westlake, Ohio.

GREAT FAITH

SCRIPTURE: John 11:12-23

VERSE FOR TODAY: Then Martha said to Jesus, "Lord, if You had been here, my brother would not have died" (John 11:21, *New King James Version*).

HYMN FOR TODAY: "I Know Whom I Have Believed"

So often Martha is belittled because she was always busy. It did appear that she was often busy to the extent that she neglected spiritual matters. In Luke 10:38-42, Jesus tells her what really matters when she complains to Him about Mary sitting at His feet while Martha worked.

But these Scripture verses show that Martha had great faith. She believed that if Jesus had been there, He would not have let her brother die. She knew she could call on Him to answer her prayer. She loved her brother and knew that Jesus did too.

Someone once said that God answers prayer in one of four ways: yes, no, maybe, and—you have to be kidding!

Jesus had a greater purpose in mind than a healing. Jesus said to her, "Your brother will rise again." And he did. Martha prayed and God answered—but in His way.

So often we ask God for something only to be given something else instead. We may think God didn't answer our prayer. But if we thank Him anyway and wait, we will see that He had a greater purpose in mind in His answer to our prayer. We can trust Him to answer in the best way possible.

PRAYER THOUGHTS: Lord, we thank You that You take our shallow prayers and turn them into miracles of Your love and concern for our lives. Amen.

POWER OVER LIFE AND DEATH

SCRIPTURE: John 11:24-29

VERSE FOR TODAY: Jesus said to her, "I am the resurrection and the life. He who believes in Me, though he may die, he shall live" (John 11:25, *New King James Version*).

HYMN FOR TODAY: "I Will Sing of My Redeemer"

So often these words are read at a funeral service to give comfort to the friends and relatives who are mourning the death of a loved one. Often, too, a death brings us more serious thoughts of our own coming death, and these words can hold comfort in that way, also. These words, however, were meant to hold more than comfort. They were meant to reveal that Jesus has power over life and death, as He soon proved in raising Lazarus from the dead.

Death came into the world in the Garden of Eden when Adam and Eve sinned—physical death of the body and spiritual death of the soul. Spiritual death came when God sent them out of His garden, and their physical death came later. We can be saved by Christ's entrance into our lives—a choice of the will to put our lives into His hands.

Though we do not understand now how God can raise us to life, we can believe it and put our faith in Him, because Jesus said it and proved what He said.

What is the key to this faith? It is found in the next verse as Jesus continues and says, "He who believes in Me, though he may die, he shall live. . . ."

PRAYER THOUGHTS: Jesus, I thank You that You paid the penalty for sins. I am set free! I put my faith in You, for You are the resurrection and the life. Amen.

March 25

THE FACES OF GRIEF

SCRIPTURE: John 11:30-37

VERSE FOR TODAY: "Therefore, when Jesus saw her weeping, and the Jews who came with her weeping, He groaned in the spirit and was troubled (John 11:33, *New King James Version*).

HYMN FOR TODAY: "Be Still, My Soul"

It was Mary's turn to make her statement of faith. She fell down at Jesus' feet and said, "Lord, if You had been here, my brother would not have died," (John 11:32, *New International Version*). Sound familiar? Martha had said these same words.

Mary's grief was as deep as Martha's, but she expressed it differently. Martha hurried about, always keeping busy while Mary sat quietly, silently waiting.

I have been at funerals and heard one person say about another: "They're not even crying. Don't they care?" The people in question may have cried their eyes out the night before. Or they may do their crying when the funeral is all over and the realization comes that they will never see their loved one again in this life.

We are all human beings—the same, yet created individually by God. Each of us expresses emotions differently, and we should be cautious of judging another. We can't see all that is going on inside a person.

Jesus, though, understood both Martha and Mary. He wept because they wept. He loved them and He loved their brother, Lazarus. Their grief was His grief. Yet Lazarus would not be dead for long. Jesus would soon turn their grief into joy.

PRAYER THOUGHTS: Lord, You understood Martha and You understood Mary even though they were so different. I thank You that You understand me. May I never judge others by outward appearance but entrust them into Your loving hands. Amen.

ANSWERED PRAYER

SCRIPTURE: John 11:38-44

VERSE FOR TODAY: Jesus said to her, "Did I not say to you that if you would believe you would see the glory of God?" (John 11:40, *New King James Version*).

HYMN FOR TODAY: "Now Thank We All Our God"

One of the hostesses for our Bible study group had just moved into her own apartment. She had just about everything she needed, but the chairs we sat on around her dining room table for Bible study were folding chairs—not comfortable for one of the ladies who had a back problem. We decided to pray for chairs. Not two weeks later, we were sitting on regular dining room chairs! A friend of hers had called her very shortly after we had prayer and asked her if she needed any dining room chairs! She had bought new ones and didn't want to throw the old ones away because they were still good. We were all amazed! But we shouldn't have been.

Have you ever said a prayer and then been surprised when it was answered? Sometimes we pray hoping God will answer, but we don't really expect Him to answer.

Mary and Martha were a little like this. They thought the time for answered prayer for their dear brother Lazarus was over. But Jesus knew better. He told them Lazarus would rise from the dead, yet they were surprised when he did!

We tend to put limitations on God. We need to remember that we have a great God, and He can do anything!

PRAYER THOUGHTS: Lord, we thank You for the privilege of prayer. Help us to have great faith to believe that You will answer our prayers. You are a great God and can do anything! Amen.

BEARER OF TALES

SCRIPTURE: John 11:45-53

VERSE FOR TODAY: But some of them went away to the Pharisees and told them the things Jesus did (John 11:46, *New King James Version*).

HYMN FOR TODAY: "O God, the Rock of Ages"

Jesus raised Lazarus from the dead. Many saw and became believers, but some did not. The Son of God showed His deity clearly, yet some people still refused to believe.

The people who were suspicious and didn't understand Jesus went to the chief priests and the Pharisees and told them what had happened. Caiaphas, the high priest and leader of the Sadducees, spoke a prophecy about Jesus. Caiaphas was not a believer, yet God used him. He heard the facts, but he did not want to pay the cost of believing. He was a selfish, prideful man, and he played a direct part in Jesus' death because of it.

Don't let yourself be the bearer of tales. You may think you know all the facts, but you can only see one side of the story—your side. Tell only what Jesus has done for you.

Proverbs 10:19 says, "In the multitude of words sin is not lacking, But he who restrains his lips is wise" (*New King James Version*). Many times Jesus himself told people not to tell anybody what He had done for them.

From that day on, they plotted to put Jesus to death. Seemingly innocent words taken from a true story were used to the advantage of evil men, and Jesus had to retire from the public eye.

PRAYER THOUGHTS: Dear Heavenly Father, we ask that You help us to think a while and pray before we speak. Help us to honor You in all we say and not tell tales that can harm others. We can only do this through Jesus Christ our Lord. Amen.

PLOT OF DEATH

SCRIPTURE: John 11:54-57

VERSE FOR TODAY: Therefore Jesus no longer walked openly among the Jews, but went from there into the country near the wilderness, to a city called Ephraim, and there remained with His disciples" (John 11:54, *New King James Version*).

HYMN FOR TODAY: "Jesus Paid It All"

This last miracle ended the public ministry of Jesus, for plans had been laid for His death by His enemies. He withdrew to Ephraim with His disciples.

It was the time of the Passover. People wondered if Jesus would come. Anyone seeing Him was to report to the chief priests and Pharisees, for they wanted to arrest Jesus. They thought that the killing of Jesus would be their triumph, but it was all part of God's plan.

It was the plan of salvation—not only for Israel, but for all of God's children. All people everywhere would be drawn to Jesus. Jesus said, "And I, if I am lifted up from the earth, will draw all peoples to Myself" (John 12:32 New King James Version). Salvation is God's gift to us. But it did not come without a cost. The cost was the sacrificial death of God's only Son for our sins, that we might have eternal life with God forever.

Have you experienced becoming one of God's children? Praise God if you have and tell others! If you haven't, you can do it now by accepting what Jesus did for you on the cross. Give your heart to the Lord and receive forgiveness for all your sins and the free gift of salvation!

PRAYER THOUGHTS: Dear God, we thank You for sending Your only Son to die on the cross for our sins. We accept Jesus as our Lord and Savior. We praise You and thank You for loving us. In Jesus' name, amen.

PRAISE FOR PRODIGALITY

SCRIPTURE: John 12:1-8

VERSE FOR TODAY: "Wherever this gospel is preached throughout the world, what she has done will also be told, in memory of her" (Matthew 26:13, *New International Version*).

HYMN FOR TODAY: "Take My Life and Let It Be"

When Mary of Bethany raided her most treasured possessions to find that big alabaster box of pure, costly perfume, and took it to where Jesus reclined at the table with Lazarus, then broke it open, pouring the whole sixteen ounces over the Master's head and feet, the practical men present protested, saying, "To what purpose is this waste?" (Matthew 26:8). They had just witnessed a classic example of *prodigality*, which is, by dictionary definition, "extravagance in expenditure; excessive liberality; waste." Could not the money it represented have been put to better use?

Jesus didn't think it could! Not long after that, Nicodemus would use a hundred pounds of spices in preparing the Lord's body for burial, but Mary had already performed that work of love; love does not count the cost. It is like the prodigality of God, who would "throw open the floodgates of heaven and pour out so much blessing that you will not have room enough for it" (Malachi 3:10, *New International Version*). It approaches the lavish love of God, who gave His Son to save ungrateful sinners. And what is prudent or practical about that? But it is marvelously worth remembering.

PRAYER THOUGHTS: O, boundlessly loving Father, help us to see and understand Your grace. May we learn to follow in Your way. We pray in His name, who gave himself for us. Amen.

WHAT A KING!

SCRIPTURE: John 12:12-19

VERSE FOR TODAY: Rejoice greatly, O daughter of Zion; shout, O daughter of Jerusalem: behold, thy King cometh unto thee: he is just, and having salvation; lowly, and riding upon an ass, and upon a colt the foal of an ass (Zechariah 9:9).

HYMN FOR TODAY: "All Hail the Power of Jesus' Name"

"After the Good Prince Charming came to the throne there was no more suffering in all the land. Peace, prosperity, and happiness followed ever after."

Such is the material of fairy stories. It was even the expectation of the Israelites when they came to the prophet Samuel demanding a king "like all the nations." Samuel warned them that their kingdom would be heavy with forced labor and taxes, but they still had stars in their eyes. Their king would "judge us, and go out before us, and fight out battles" (1 Samuel 8:20).

Samuel was right, of course, in his dire predictions. And the people were right in their words, although not in their expectations. Zechariah described the later King whom God would send to them, righteous in judgment and compassionate in His reign. Isaiah described the manner of the King's going before His people to fight their battles against Satan and sin. He would lead them in the way of life eternal. He would endure the cost of victory for all who would accept His rule.

And there is the sticking point—accepting His rule and following as He leads. The eager crowds at Jerusalem celebrated that rule, but relatively few among them followed this one-of-a-kind King to victory. Will we?

PRAYER THOUGHTS: May we open the gates of heart and life, our Heavenly Father, to the King of glory whom You sent to save us. Amen.

A MATTER OF DEATH AND LIFE

SCRIPTURE: John 12:20-36

VERSE FOR TODAY: He that loveth his life shall lose it; and he that hateth his life in this world shall keep it unto life eternal (John 12:25).

HYMN FOR TODAY: "Hallelujah, What a Savior!"

The siren-scream of a speeding ambulance proclaims an emergency. Normal traffic rules are ignored. This is a question of life and death, with death pushed away for a time while life is gripped with slipping fingers. Death may be defeated now, but it stands yet in the shadows awaiting a final victory over the body of its prey. Our material experience is always a matter of life and death—in that order.

In Christ, the opposite is true! His gospel is a matter of death and life! He won life by way of death! From the beginning of Jesus' ministry, He anticipated the destruction of His bodily temple, and its restoration afterward (John 2:19-21). Jesus began early to teach His apostles about His coming death and resurrection, but they didn't hear what He said about rising again (Matthew 16:13-23; Luke 18:31-34). Only after His resurrection did they finally understand.

The believer's experience in Christ is also a matter of death and life. It begins with a willing death to sin, with burial in Christian baptism, and rising to walk in newness of life (Romans 6:1-11). It continues with a constant surrender of what is material and temporary for the sake of what is eternal with God. Then indeed life has the last word!

PRAYER THOUGHTS: Thank You, our Father God for Jesus' conquest over death and the grave! May we always give this matter of death and life with Him our highest priority. Amen.

DEVOTIONS

APRIL

April 1

NOT *MY* FEET, LORD!

SCRIPTURE: John 13:1-11

VERSE FOR TODAY: For by the grace given me I say to every one of you: Do not think of yourself more highly than you ought (Romans 12:3, *New International Version*).

HYMN FOR TODAY: "Not I, But Christ"

A Christian man stopped by a fellow church member's home for a visit. When he knocked on the door, a loud voice boomed from inside: "Come in; it's open!" The visitor found his friend reclining on the couch with a television remote in one hand and a cola in the other. The man remained focused on his television show as his guest tried unsuccessfully to converse. Before long, the visitor rose to his feet, and headed toward the door. "Is there anything I can get for you before I leave?" he asked.

"No," replied the host. "I'm just fine. See you Sunday."

The disciples had not intended to be rude to one another, and certainly not to Jesus. They simply became preoccupied with more pressing problems. If Jesus was going away, who would be their leader? If a kingdom was to be established, who would hold positions of high authority? When Peter recognized his blunder, he tried to refuse Jesus' hospitality. Only then could he reconcile his selfish behavior.

Today, show kindness toward others with an attitude of sincere humility. Free others to serve you by developing an atmosphere of mutual concern in all relationships. Only then will you escape the hazards of selfishness and experience the joys of Christian servitude.

PRAYER THOUGHTS: Dear God, give me the courage to let others serve me. Show me the needs of others that I might serve. Amen.

April 1-4. **Larry Jones** is Associate Minister with the First Christian Church in Clearwater, Florida. He and his wife, Jane, have two children, Nathan and Laura.

SERVING THE MASTER

SCRIPTURE: John 13:12-17

VERSE FOR TODAY: Now it is required that those who have been given a trust must prove faithful (1 Corinthians 4:2, *New International Version*).

HYMN FOR TODAY: "All For Jesus! All For Jesus!"

In a small Florida town a son sued his mother. The son had been awarded sixty thousand dollars for injuries sustained in an automobile accident. When he reached the age of eighteen, he requested what remained of the settlement after the payment of hospital bills. The money, amounting to around twenty-five thousand dollars, was gone, and the boy's mother, who had been given guardianship of the funds, could not explain its disappearance.

The Bible uses the word "steward" to describe God's servant. This term implies responsibility to one's superior for the use of given resources. When Jesus washed His disciples' feet, He commanded them to follow His example. He was the final authority in their ministry, and as they served they needed to recognize their accountability to Him.

We must be obedient to Christ in our service to others and as we let others serve us. Our decision to help others should not be determined by personal preference and our willingness to let others help us should not be discouraged by a false sense of independence. Today, let the mind of Christ rule your steps, and put on a servant's heart to meet the needs of your world.

PRAYER THOUGHTS: God, help me remember my responsibility to Your Son as I carefully consider the resources You have given me. Give me the courage to accept the service of others as they use the gifts You have given them. Amen.

DECEIVING OURSELVES

SCRIPTURE: John 13:18-30

VERSE FOR TODAY: The pride of your heart has deceived you (Obadiah 3, *New International Version*).

HYMN FOR TODAY: "Purer In Heart, O God"

A man recently caught in an extramarital affair was shocked at his own behavior. "I kept telling myself I had everything under control," he said. "Even in the most secret parts of my heart I was convinced I was doing nothing wrong."

In an adulterous affair, two words come to play: *rationalization* and *denial*. As the relationship escalates, both partners find reasons to justify their actions. Together, they deny any impropriety and staunchly defend themselves before any accusers. Only after the affair is fully known will their minds allow them to see the truth.

Like Judas, the modern Christian can create reasons for sin, or successfully deny his motives. This pattern will surely lead to spiritual disaster and possible public embarrassment.

Today, your greatest protection from this kind of tragedy is an honest relationship with Christ. Through the Holy Spirit and His Father's Word, He can show you the weaknesses of human reasoning. As you study His holy nature, you can no longer deny the reality of your sins. Fortunately, when we open our hearts in repentance, God is "faithful and just and will forgive us our sins and purify us from all unrighteousness" (1 John 1:9, New International Version)."

PRAYER THOUGHTS: Father, thank You for the freedom to approach You with a cleansed heart. Help me to be honest with myself and to keep my eyes closely focused on Your Son Jesus. Amen.

NOT OF THIS WORLD

SCRIPTURE: John 15:18-27

VERSE FOR TODAY: "No one can serve two masters. Either he will hate the one and love the other, or he will be devoted to the one and despise the other" (Matthew 6:24, *New International Version*).

HYMN FOR TODAY: "There Is Joy In Serving Jesus"

In the 1940 movie *Knute Rockne: All American,* Pat O'Brien plays the legendary Notre Dame football star. In a particular scene, a businessman offers coach Rockne ten thousand dollars to endorse a new liniment to be called Rockne Rub. Knute promptly tosses the offer in a nearby wastebasket. Such opportunistic acts threatened to trivialize the sport he loved.

The non-Christian world has trouble understanding Biblical values in an age of materialism. This fact demonstrates itself when the media gives national attention to Christian scandal. The more numerous contributions of the church go largely unnoticed because those who dislike the church find greater security in its weaknesses than its strengths.

Jesus sent His first disciples into a hostile world. They needed to remember the world's behavior had little to do with them personally, but with the One who had sent them.

As you uphold Christlike values, remember your role as a servant of your Master, Jesus Christ. You are a reflection of your Savior, and the response of others is a reflection of their inner soul. When you realize people are not rejecting you personally, you will be better prepared to witness effectively with a sincere spirit of love and compassion.

PRAYER THOUGHTS: Dear Lord, help me deal with the world's reaction to Your Son. Give me the patience and security to witness in a caring way. Amen.

KINDNESS OVERCOMES INJUSTICE

SCRIPTURE: John 19:1-6

VERSE FOR TODAY: Love your enemies and pray for those who persecute you (Matthew 5:44, *New International Version*).

VERSE TODAY: "Help Somebody Today"

Historians often commend the Roman empire for its vast and monumental system of justice. But the trial of Jesus was a mockery of the Roman system of justice. After Pilate had pronounced Jesus to be innocent, he yielded to pressure and condemned Him to death. Is this a sample of our world's justice? Unfortunately, it too often seems to be the case.

There is much that is unjust in our world today. We can find victims of injustice in every community. Innocent children often suffer from the sin of their parents. Too often they are the painful victims of broken homes. Perhaps it is too much to expect this world to be a just place. But in the face of injustice, there are two things that we who follow Christ can do. First, we can vow that we will never be party to any injustice ourselves. And, we can help to counteract the impact of injustice in society by extending kindness and compassion whenever we have an opportunity. This is what Jesus did, and it is what thousands who have walked in His steps have done. The world still sees Jesus in the lives of men and women who today reflect His love. YOU can be such a person today.

PRAYER THOUGHTS: Heavenly Father, help me to be sensitive to those about me who are hurting and then to reflect Your healing love. May I be one who does not yield to evil but overcomes evil with good. I ask in Jesus' name, amen.

April 5-11. **Henry E. Webb** is a minister and retired college professor. He and his wife, Emerald, reside in Johnson City, Tennessee, where they continue in service to Christ and His church.

THE CRUCIFIED KING

SCRIPTURE: John 19:17-21

VERSE FOR TODAY: But he was wounded for our transgressions, he was bruised for our iniquities: the chastisement of our peace was upon him; and with his stripes we are healed (Isaiah 53:5).

HYMN FOR TODAY: "There Is a Fountain"

Pontius Pilate ordered an inscription placed over the head of the Lord as He hung on the cross. It read: Jesus of Nazareth, King of the Jews. The inscription was intended to be a mockery. One doesn't expect to find a king hanging on a cross. Kings are usually self-serving. They live in ease and splendor, expecting others to serve them.

But Jesus was a different kind of king. He came, not to be served, but to serve. An essential part of that service was to give His life "a ransom for many" (Matthew 20:28). King Jesus was also "the Lamb of God, which taketh away the sin of the world" (John 1:29), and this could only be done through sacrifice. It is a profound mystery to human thinking how the concepts of King and sacrificial Lamb can be joined in one person; yet Jesus is both.

John's great vision in Revelation is based on this wonderful fact. Thousands of angelic voices blended in singing praise to the Lamb who was slain and who made it possible for men of "every tribe and language and people and nation" (Revelation 5:9, *New International Version*) to know God and share the promise of everlasting life. This is what our Savior does for us.

PRAYER THOUGHTS: Almighty Heavenly Father, it is not possible to understand the mystery of divine love that is shown to us in the suffering and death of Your Son when He purchased our salvation with His blood. But we can believe it, and we forever thank You for Him and His love. Amen.

SECRET FOR A VICTORIOUS LIFE

SCRIPTURE: John 19:22-27

VERSE FOR TODAY: Be faithful, even to the point of death, and I will give you the crown of life (Revelation 2:10, *New International Version*).

HYMN FOR TODAY: "I Would Be True"

"It is finished." With those words, Jesus marked the completion of His life's work. The great mission to save mankind was successfully completed when the great sacrifice for the sins of all humanity was made.

There is a purpose for every life. We may undertake a great many tasks in the course of a lifetime, but there should be an over-arching purpose for every individual. To fulfill this purpose makes life a success. Jesus knew what His life was to accomplish. He never wavered from His aim, though tempted to do so (Matthew 16:21-23). Paul, also, had the great satisfaction of fulfilling his purpose in life (2 Timothy 4:7).

It is worthwhile to spend time thinking about life's major purpose. Life is too precious to drift through it aimlessly. A secular songwriter raised the question: "What's it all about?" Too many modern people don't have an answer to this fundamental question. Jesus addressed it when He urged us to "seek . . . first the kingdom of God" (Matthew 6:33). Priorities are so important! If our priorities are right, other things will fall into place, and life will take on new meaning, become useful, and then be filled with satisfaction when "it is finished."

PRAYER THOUGHTS: Father of mercy and wisdom, help me to sort out my priorities and keep them in proper order. The world about me has many alluring distractions. Keep me on the path that leads to victory in this life and to the crown of surpassing worth in the next. In the name of my Savior, Jesus Christ, I pray. Amen.

WITH US IN DEATH

SCRIPTURE: John 19:28-37

VERSE FOR TODAY: Yea, though I walk through the valley of the shadow of death, I will fear no evil: for thou art with me; thy rod and thy staff they comfort me (Psalm 23:4).

HYMN FOR TODAY: "Does Jesus Care?"

At Christmas, we celebrate the fact that the Son of God became man, taking on human nature as a baby and growing to adulthood in the normal, human manner. He was called Emmanuel—GOD with us. We are told that His humanity was real, that He knew hunger, thirst, and weariness. He was no stranger to rejection, disappointment, and sorrow. But the extent of His humanity is nowhere so evident as when He went through the actual experience that humans fear—death. In identifying with us, He even shared suffering and death as we do.

Yet, it wasn't just the human nature of Jesus that died. A seminary professor once spoke of "the mystery of Christ's death." I objected: "What's so mysterious about death? It happens every day." I will never forget his reply: "Can GOD die?" I had made the mistake of thinking that only the human in Jesus tasted death, but Jesus was also the Son of GOD. He was not nicely divided into human and divine parcels; He was *one* person. When He died on Calvary, GOD also shared in the experience of death. It *is* a mystery, but it is also a fact: God knows from experience what it is like to die. And He will go with us "through the valley of the shadow of death." With this faith we can face the future without fear.

PRAYER THOUGHTS: Dear Father, we know that none of us will escape the experience known to us as "death." We are thankful that Jesus' death and resurrection proves that there is life after death! Amen.

A MEMORIAL TO JESUS

SCRIPTURE: John 20:1-10

VERSE FOR TODAY: He is not here; he has risen! Remember how he told you, while he was still with you in Galilee (Luke 24:6, *New International Version*).

HYMN FOR TODAY: "He Arose"

For centuries it has been customary for mankind to enshrine heroes and martyrs in magnificent tombs. Every national capital displays the crypts of those who have made their mark on history. But there is no crypt that holds the body of the Lord of life—only an empty spot somewhere in or near the city of Jerusalem, a place which held the body of Jesus for a scant three days. This is because it was impossible for death to hold the Lord of life (Acts 2:24). He broke the stranglehold of death and showed us that God created us to live. Furthermore, God intends to give Christ's followers this gift of life.

However, let us not overlook *the* memorial to Jesus' life and work. It is not a tomb—it is a table. On it one finds food and drink. How appropriate! In contrast to the opulence of many memorials, this one is very simple, as befits the life of Jesus. Furthermore, the memorial is life-giving—food and drink. This, too, is appropriate as a memorial to the Giver of life. And this remembrance can be observed, not just in Jerusalem, but in any spot on this earth. And every time believers meet about His table, they "proclaim the Lord's death until he comes" (1 Corinthians 11:26, *New International Version*).

PRAYER THOUGHTS: Father in Heaven, we rejoice that the tomb of our Lord is empty. We thank You for the hope of life that this gives to us who believe, that as we have shared in the likeness of His death we may also share in the likeness of His resurrection. Amen.

"I HAVE SEEN THE LORD!"

SCRIPTURE: John 20:11-18

VERSE FOR TODAY: We did not follow cleverly invented stories when we told you about the power and coming of our Lord Jesus Christ, but we were eyewitnesses of his majesty (2 Peter 1:16, *New International Version*).

HYMN FOR TODAY: "Open My Eyes"

"I have seen the Lord!" It was Mary Magdalene who first heralded the best news that mankind has ever heard. Mary was not speculating about a theory; rather, she was reporting on a fact—something she had seen with her own eyes. The Lord, whom she had seen die on a cross, stood alive before her and spoke to her. And her testimony was quickly confirmed by others to whom the Lord appeared on the day of resurrection.

Mary's eyes were tear-dimmed when Jesus first appeared to her, and she didn't recognize Him. It's still the case with us that our vision can become blurred and we don't see all that we ought to see, spiritually. Jesus tells us that the pure in heart shall see God. Perhaps the impurity in our hearts blinds us to spiritual realities we need to see. At any rate, Mary recognized Jesus when He spoke to her. His word was unmistakable. And so it is with us; He speaks to *us today* through His Word. And His Word generates faith and gives us hope for our days. This is because our faith rests in a living Savior who promises His presence with us "to the very end of the age" (Matthew 28:20, *New International Version*). Jesus lives!

PRAYER THOUGHTS: Thank You for the privilege of living in this day, which You have given me. Open my eyes that I might see the presence of the Lord in all of my surroundings and my relationships this day. I pray in the name of Jesus, amen.

THE RESURRECTION—A FACT

SCRIPTURE: John 20:19-30

VERSE FOR TODAY: God has raised this Jesus to life, and we are all witnesses of the fact (Acts 2:32, *New International Version*).

HYMN FOR TODAY: "How Firm a Foundation"

The resurrection of Jesus from the dead was no well-kept secret. He appeared to ten of His disciples on the very day of the resurrection. Missing was Thomas, the one apostle who would not accept the testimony of the others who saw the risen Christ. A week later, Thomas would confront the living Lord. He could no longer question the fact that Jesus was alive again. He had seen Him.

Facts are established in human thinking in several ways. One is to experience some event through our own eyes, ears, or touch. But such first-hand experience is denied us for all the facts of past history. For us, historic facts are established by credible witnesses. And credibility is strengthened by greater numbers of witnesses who give testimony to an event.

The resurrection of Jesus is the best attested fact in ancient history (1 Corinthians 15:3-8). And the credibility of the apostolic witnesses is established by the fact that they were willing to give their lives for their faith.

We are many centuries removed from this greatest event in human history; yet is as relevant to our situation today as it was centuries ago. Our faith is in a risen Savior who is able to promise life to us.

PRAYER THOUGHTS: Father in Heaven, how grateful we are that our faith in the living Christ is based on a firm, factual foundation. Grant that others may see the risen, living Christ in me today. In the name of the risen Christ Jesus I pray. Amen.

THE SON OF GOD WITH POWER

SCRIPTURE: John 21:1-8

VERSE FOR TODAY: Finally, be strong in the Lord and in his mighty power (Ephesians 6:10, *New International Version*).

HYMN FOR TODAY: "All Hail the Power of Jesus' Name"

Have you ever tried to look for someone in a crowded room? Sometimes it can be very difficult, especially if the person you're looking for doesn't have anything that makes him or her stand out from everyone else. But if you know the person well, there can be many clues to help you: hair color, voice, height, even a way of walking.

In the Scripture today, Jesus' apostles recognized Him not by any physical characteristics that they saw or by the sound of His voice. It was His power that made obvious who He was. That's what set Him apart from the crowd. It was also something with which the disciples were very familiar. They had seen that same power demonstrated hundreds of times.

We should be just as familiar with the power of Christ. We can do more than read about it in Scripture. We can experience it in our own lives. His power helps us to go beyond our own abilities, to overcome temptation, to spread the glorious message of salvation. Have you drawn on His power enough to recognize Him by it?

PRAYER THOUGHTS: Dear God, please help us to draw upon the power You have demonstrated in Christ. Help us to use that power to live triumphantly in the situations in which You place us each day. Amen.

April 12-18. **Paul Friskney** is an active Christian and Assistant Professor of English in Cincinnati, Ohio, where he lives with his wife, Ann, and their young daughter, Hannah.

ON A DAILY BASIS

SCRIPTURE: John 21:9-14

VERSE FOR TODAY: Therefore we do not lose heart. Though outwardly we are wasting away, yet inwardly we are being renewed day by day (2 Corinthians 4:16, *New International Version*).

HYMN FOR TODAY: "Moment by Moment"

In the old Shirley Temple movie, *The Little Princess,* the main character's father has been injured in war and gone through a severe illness. Even after he is physically healed, his mind remains confused and unable to connect with reality. Only the sound of his daughter's voice can bring him out of it.

In today's Scripture, the disciples are in a similar condition. They have gone through intense fear, exhaustion, panic, and confusion. They weren't sure where to turn next. They seemed to be just wandering around without any sense of direction. Jesus uses a very ordinary experience to bring them back to reality: eating breakfast.

One of the greatest joys in the Christian life is knowing that Jesus is nearby no matter what is happening in our lives. He's there in the moments of great testing and of great victory. But He's also with us when we're doing something as ordinary as eating breakfast. When we realize the completeness of His care for us, it frees us from worrying about everyday matters so that we can concentrate on the important work He has given us to do. We can now have joy in living.

PRAYER THOUGHTS: Dear Father, we want to thank You for the way You are always nearby so that we can lean on You and share all our experiences. Please help us to draw closer and closer to You so that we might feel both Your comfort and Your challenge. Amen.

WORDS (AND WORKS) OF LOVE

SCRIPTURE: John 21:15-19

VERSE FOR TODAY: Dear children, let us not love with words or tongue but with actions and in truth (1 John 3:18, *New International Version*).

HYMN FOR TODAY: "Make Me a Blessing"

When I was a small boy, my mother used to sing songs or recite poems that were meant to give me insights into life without me realizing it. One that I remember in particular was about three children named John, Nell, and Fan. Each child in turn told their mother, "I love you." But in two out of three cases, the child's actions contradicted the words. Only Fan realized that love is true only when it's demonstrated in actions and not just spoken in words.

Jesus is anxious to teach Peter the same lesson. Peter had been saying all along that he loved Jesus, but his actions hadn't quite lived up to his words. Jesus wanted him to see the need to bring the two in line. The truth is simple. If we love Jesus, we will live according to His pattern. We won't accept what others say we should do, and we won't go by what we want. Instead, we will be concerned with Jesus' will and the lives He wants us to touch. That's the only expression of love that means anything: one that's backed by the way we live each day.

PRAYER THOUGHTS: Dear Heavenly Father, we hear people all around us talking about love, but it's a much more shallow understanding of love than You want us to have. May our words and works be a blessing to those around us. Help us to look at Your example of love and use that for our pattern. In the name of Jesus. Amen.

WHAT ABOUT HIM?

SCRIPTURE: John 21:20-25

VERSE FOR TODAY: Make it your ambition to lead a quiet life, to mind your own business and to work with your hands, just as we told you (1 Thessalonians 4:11, *New International Version*).

HYMN FOR TODAY: "Search Me, O God"

The novel, *A Tree Grows in Brooklyn,* offers glimpses into many different personalities. One of the minor characters is the insurance man who comes to the apartment each month to collect the payment from the family. He is filled with gossip about all the families whom he visits. The mother of the family dislikes his gossiping and does everything possible to be sure that he doesn't have anything to tell about her family. Nevertheless, she can't help asking about what he knows about the other families in the building.

That's a very common human characteristic. Peter demonstrates it very clearly in today's Scripture. But Jesus moves him away quickly from his curiosity about others. Jesus points out that rather than worrying about what would happen to others, Peter should be concerned with following Jesus. It's a difficult lesson to learn, but a very important one. As long as we spend our time in everybody else's business, we won't have any time to take care of our own. God's given us a lot to do for Him. Let's get to work.

PRAYER THOUGHTS: Dear God, please forgive us when we are side-tracked by what others are doing or saying. Help us to concentrate on the work You have given us to do so that we can be Your faithful servants. In the name of Jesus. Amen.

WHILE I AM WAITING

SCRIPTURE: Acts 1:1-5

VERSE FOR TODAY: We do not want you to become lazy, but to imitate those who through faith and patience inherit what has been promised (Hebrews 6:12, *New International Version*).

HYMN FOR TODAY: "Have Thine Own Way"

In college, I had two roommates named John. Although they had the same name, they couldn't have been more different. One had a hard time getting anything accomplished. He was so relaxed that nothing really seemed to be important to him. The other John was always busy trying to fulfill some plan that he had made. At times, his desire to push ahead kept him from seeing warning signs or hearing or heeding words of instruction.

Somewhere between these two examples comes the true meaning of the patience God wants us to have. He expects us to wait patiently, not because we are too lazy to act on our own, but because we are committed to following His time schedule. The apostles had to learn this lesson, too. Many of them had suffered from the desire to move faster than Jesus. They had also known the feeling of wanting to hide from all responsibility. Jesus told them they needed to wait until they received power from Heaven. It was the only power that would get them through the lives ahead of them. The same thing is true for us.

PRAYER THOUGHTS: Dear Heavenly Father, so many times we are tempted to try to control things on our own or to let our circumstances control us. Help us to wait patiently for Your instruction and to follow Your time schedule. Help us to have confidence in You. In the name of Your son, we pray. Amen.

WORKMEN AHEAD

SCRIPTURE: Acts 1:6-11

VERSE FOR TODAY: For we are God's fellow workers; you are God's field, God's building (1 Corinthians 3:9, *New International Version*).

HYMN FOR TODAY: "To the Work"

Have you heard the old story about the man who was driving down a highway when he saw a sign that read, *Watch for Falling Rocks*? He immediately pulled over to the side of the highway and stopped his car. Then he got out, sat on the hood of the car, and stared at the hillside. He had gotten the words of the message, but he hadn't understood their meaning.

The apostles seem to have had a similar experience. Jesus gave them clear instructions for the future, but they were so caught up in all that they had seen and heard that they forgot to do anything. The angel needed to remind them that they had important things to do before Jesus returned.

Before we are too hard on them, though, we must realize that we sometimes fall victim to the same thing. If we're not careful, we can become so engrossed in the trappings of Christianity and in the questions that arise in our minds that we do the equivalent of standing around and staring. That's when we need to get back to the basics: Jesus will return, and we have work to do before His return.

PRAYER THOUGHTS: Dear God, the only way that we can become like You is to concentrate on the things that are important to You. Help us to do that and not be distracted, even by the good things of life. Give us wisdom to follow Your leading. In the name of Jesus, we pray. Amen.

TRANSFER OF POWER

SCRIPTURE: Acts 1:12-16, 21-26

VERSE FOR TODAY: From him the whole body, joined and held together by every supporting ligament, grows and builds itself up in love, as each part does its work (Ephesians 4:16, *New International Version*).

HYMN FOR TODAY: "Teach Me Thy Will, O Lord"

Since I grew up as a preacher's son, our congregation was my extended family. I remember one couple in particular who were my substitute grandparents during part of my early childhood. However, as years passed and that couple felt that they had less power in the church, they became bitter. Rather than accepting a role that would have benefitted the church, they backed away from their responsibilities and chose to criticize from the outside. Their decision brought pain for everyone involved, including them.

Today's Scripture holds an important contrast to the spirit represented by that couple. When we look at Matthias and Barsabbas, we see hearts of service. That attitude insures that their service will continue no matter what the outcome of the choice. Of course, Matthias stepped into his role as an apostle along with the eleven. He didn't withdraw because he wasn't "in control." Instead, he allowed God to direct his area of service. As a result, everyone was blessed.

PRAYER THOUGHTS: Dear Lord, help us not to be controlled by feelings of competition or bitterness. Help us to take joy in the abilities of others and to allow You to show us our own places of service. May we be understanding of other people's feelings. Give us wisdom to reach out to bring the whole body of Christ together in love, both young and old, to let the world know that You give love. Amen.

April 19

THE IMPORTANT LEFTOVERS

SCRIPTURE: John 6:1-14

VERSE FOR TODAY: When they had all had enough to eat, he said to his disciples, "Gather the pieces that are left over. Let nothing be wasted" (John 6:12, *New International Version*).

HYMN FOR TODAY: "Gentle Shepherd"

Jesus wanted to stress economy after the miraculous feeding of the five thousand..."that nothing be lost." Some of us can remember World War II and how our government urged us to salvage food scraps and metal scraps. Yes, many of us are wasteful! An old maxim is needed today: "Waste not, want not." A minister friend once described his wife's wastefulness of food in this fashion: "She throws more out the back door than I'm able to bring in through the front door."

Our Scripture today should remind us to reflect on some of life's fragments which are of great importance. We should gather the fragments of lessons learned from His Word. Have we yet learned that our adversities are His opportunities? Do we remember that Jesus never fails us if we obey and trust Him? Why haven't we filled all fragments of time with prayer?

When the disciples gathered the leftovers, there were twelve baskets full! What a lesson! We, too, must gather up our mis-spent moments, our sluggish enthusiasm, our neglected duties. Gather all opportunities and use them for His glory.

PRAYER THOUGHTS: Gracious Father, make us glad that we are alive and able to live in Your love and care. May we put our hearts and minds into all privileges and tasks. May we find happiness not in seeking it, but in bringing it to others. Help us to covet the things that most deeply concern our peace. We ask in His name, amen.

April 19-25. **Gladys Smith** is a speaker, lecturer, writer, and dramatist. She lives in Newnan, Georgia, with her husband, Evangelist J. B. Smith.

THEY WEATHERED THE STORM

SCRIPTURE: John 6:15-21

VERSE FOR TODAY: He maketh the storm a calm, so that the waves thereof are still (Psalm 107:29).

HYMN FOR TODAY: "'Til the Storm Passes By"

Jesus knew the people's hearts as He fed the five thousand with the little boy's lunch. They viewed Him as a hero and wanted to make Him their king. That group of people mistook the mission of Jesus, for He didn't come to feed men's bodies, but to save their souls.

Weary at the end of that busy day, Jesus directed the disciples to get into a boat and proceed to the opposite side of the sea. They obeyed, but a quick storm came and the disciples knew they were in trouble. Perhaps they felt their lives would end in a watery grave.

We are often tossed on stormy seas of trouble, adversity, financial problems, or sickness, but we are taught He intercedes for us with "groanings which cannot be uttered" (Romans 8:26).

Soon the disciples saw Jesus walking on the water toward them and heard Him say, "It is I; be not afraid." When Jesus came aboard, they realized they had weathered the storm.

Take Jesus aboard in your life, and one day you'll be at home on the other shore.

PRAYER THOUGHTS: Heavenly Father, may we lay aside all feelings of pride and self-sufficiency. May His statutes be our delight. May the Holy Spirit bind us together in a fellowship of saints who have one Lord, one faith, one love. In His name, amen.

DOING OUR BEST FOR HIM

SCRIPTURE: John 6:22-29

VERSE FOR TODAY: That all men should honour the Son, even as they honour the Father. He that honoureth not the Son honoureth not the Father which hath sent him (John 5:23).

HYMN FOR TODAY: "Open My Eyes, That I May See"

A businessman who had wide contacts and important connections made a vacation trip to Europe. During his travels, he was stricken with an illness that delayed his return for three months. His physicians ordered him to take a rest cure in the Swiss mountains.

While recuperating, he grew very anxious about his business affairs at home. Even though his associates assured him that all was going well, he would often imagine there were grave problems and that he was losing a great deal.

When he arrived home, however, he discovered that younger officials of his business had taken their responsibilities very seriously. They not only carried on admirably in his absence, but had brought increases in the volume of business and had improved, on the whole, the relationships with the clients. What a difference to be surrounded by loving concern and competence on the part of his employees and staff, and to realize his cherished business had been in excellent hands.

We need, likewise, to be saved from self-preoccupation, which is often a subtle form of pride. Let us trust in God who gives us the strong anchor of hope.

PRAYER THOUGHTS: Dear Father, we thank You for the Lord Jesus, the captain of our salvation who gave His life that we might be redeemed. Help us to serve each other in love for His sake. We thank You that we've been considered worthy, called into His fellowship. For Jesus' sake, amen.

"I AM THE BREAD OF LIFE"

SCRIPTURE: John 6:30-40

VERSE FOR TODAY: Jesus declared, "I am the bread of life. He who comes to me will never go hungry, and he who believes in me will never be thirsty" (John 6:35, *New International Version*).

HYMN FOR TODAY: "Let Us Break Bread Together"

The Bible has a great deal to say about bread. Jesus, you remember, accepted a boy's lunch and multiplied it to feed five thousand people. At the Lord's last supper with His disciples before He was crucified, we read, "He took bread, and gave thanks, and brake it, and gave unto them, saying, This is my body which is given for you" (Luke 22:19). So ordinary bread was sanctified as it became the symbol of His body, broken on the cross for our sakes. There is no spiritual life in bread baked in this world's ovens. This Divine Bread whom God gave, Jesus Christ himself, provides for every need of our souls.

Many years ago, one of my Bible School teachers taught an acrostic on the word bread:

> B . . . Bread must be *b*roken.
> R . . . Bread must be *r*eceived.
> E . . . Bread must be *e*aten.
> A . . . Bread must be *a*ssimilated.
> D . . . Bread must be *d*istributed.

Even the greatest saints walk through dry places, so there is a dire need for Living Water and Bread from Heaven.

PRAYER THOUGHTS: Dear God and Father, teach us the joy of feeding daily upon the manna of Your Word. Save us from food that is deceptive. As we grow in years, increase our spiritual hunger and appetite. In Jesus' name, amen.

April 23

CHRIST'S PULLING POWER

SCRIPTURE: John 6:41-50

VERSE FOR TODAY: For God so loved the world, that he gave his only begotten Son, that whosoever believeth in him should not perish, but have everlasting life (John 3:16).

HYMN FOR TODAY: "Jesus is All the World to Me"

All of us who are truly Christ's can give genuine testimony that we are "new creatures" in Him. "Old things" have passed away and "all things are become new" (2 Corinthians 5:17). We have a new spiritual life with a Christward pulling power. Everything now has a new meaning, and the new center of our lives is Jesus.

Our old ways of viewing things, old ways of judging people, old ideas for fun and pleasure, old hates, loves, habits, misunderstandings, prejudices, and old standards of values have passed away. "One thing I know, that, whereas I was blind, now I see" (John 9:25).

The outward evidence of this inward miracle is the way we live. A minister once asked a man, "Have you been converted?"

"Strangely enough," said the man, "I was converted in my sleep."

Then the minister commented, "That's certainly unusual, but we'd better see how you behave when you are awake."

Jesus, the source of life, gives us a new outlook on life. Everything will tingle with new significance. John Wesley said, "Our people die well." Yes, "in Christ" we even die well. "Behold, all things are become new!"

PRAYER THOUGHTS: Dear Heavenly Father, may this day be filled with power that shall bring us near to You and make us more like You. May we always live in the Spirit of Christ, the source of our lives. In His name, amen.

WE HEAR HIS VOICE!

SCRIPTURE: John 6:51-65

VERSE FOR TODAY: The Spirit gives life; the flesh counts for nothing. The words I have spoken to you are spirit and they are life (John 6:63, New International Version).

HYMN FOR TODAY: "Come, Thou Fount of Every Blessing"

"How do you know that your mother is upstairs?" a man inquired of his nieces and nephews.

One boy answered immediately, "I saw her go upstairs!"

"Do you mean you saw her start to go upstairs?" asked the uncle.

"I know she's up there, because I went to the foot of the stairs to call to her and she answered," remarked a little girl.

"You are right," said the uncle. "The disciples said they saw their Master ascend into Heaven, and they know He is living. I know that He is living because He answers my prayers."

I am so comforted each morning as I face a new day that I shall not live it by myself. His Holy Spirit was given to me as a gift when I was baptized into Christ. When I place myself in His hands, then His gentleness and wisdom will flow through me. This is the true rally spirit . . . God and me.

> "Take our soul and bodies' powers.
> Take our memory, mind and will.
> All our goods and all our hours.
> All we know and all we feel.
> All we think, or speak, or do.
> Take our hearts but make them new."
>
> —author unknown

PRAYER THOUGHTS: Dear God, our Father, help us in childlike humility and trust to take our Lord's words and receive His teaching. Help our unbelief, strengthen our grasp of the unseen, and bring us into living union with You. Thank You in the great name of Jesus. Amen.

April 25

HE IS LORD

SCRIPTURE: John 6:66-71

VERSE FOR TODAY: Then Simon Peter answered him, Lord, to whom shall we go? thou hast the words of eternal life (John 6:68).

HYMN FOR TODAY: "He Is Lord"

Jesus was a fearless leader and never misled His followers. They learned to expect from Him strong and assertive leadership. His was a well-defined message of truth, proclaimed aggressively, yet winsomely and reasonably—prompting them to love Him.

At this moment only a handful of disciples acknowledged Him as leader, but He saw beyond that moment. Owen Wister once said, "When a man lives among his fellowmen as a brother, they will acknowledge him, if he deserves it, as their superior." Because Jesus so lived, He was recognized by these disciples as Lord and Master. Jesus was not satisfied to utter grand truths . . . He lived them!

A missionary came home from India just at the time when the gospel hymn, "Hold the Fort," was popular. Everywhere he preached he heard that song. The more he heard the song, the more he disliked it. He finally protested the message of the hymn when he cried indignantly, "Hold the Fort? That is the devil's business. Our business as Christians is to follow the example of Christ and storm the fort." He is Lord and He came to storm the fort . . . just as God sent Him to do.

PRAYER THOUGHTS: We thank You, our Heavenly Father, for the gift of Your Son and the blessings He has brought to us. Teach us to follow His footsteps in the generosity of His deeds, His love, and His grace. We beseech You to hear our prayers and pardon our sins. In the name of Christ, amen.

SOMETHING WE CAN COUNT ON

SCRIPTURE: Isaiah 40:3-8

VERSE FOR TODAY: The grass withereth, the flower fadeth: but the word of our God shall stand for ever (Isaiah 40:8).

HYMN FOR TODAY: "Wonderful Words of Life"

"Daddy?"

"Yes, what is it?"

"You said I'd be your little girl forever. I want to be big someday."

Daddy put his book down and took his little girl in his lap. "When you graduate from college, get married, and have children of your own, you'll be a lady to everyone else, but you will always be Daddy's little girl. You will always be a part of my heart. I will always love you. Some things never change."

"Thank you, Daddy. You are in my heart too."

In a changing world, how comforting it is that there are some things we can count on. Above all, we can depend on God to keep His Word. He is a loving Father whose children are never too old to love.

Isaiah looked down through the ages and saw a man whose task it was to remind people of this wonderful love and wonderful Word. It was the voice of one that would prepare us all for the coming of the Lord. God's Word is true; a way for redemption was made.

Thank You, God.

PRAYER THOUGHTS: Thank You, God, for the beauty and strength in Your Word. Thank You for being so dependable and always keeping Your promises to me. Help me this day to cherish those words and hide them in my heart that I might always live by them. Amen.

April 26—May 2. **Essie Johnson** is a freelance writer, editor, and playwright. She is employed by the Gethsemane Christian Academy in Lafayette, Louisiana.

A SPECIAL GIFT

SCRIPTURE: Luke 1:57-66

VERSE FOR TODAY: What manner of child shall this be! And the hand of the Lord was with him (Luke 1:66).

HYMN FOR TODAY: "Where He Leads Me"

A business associate recently apologized for a late-night return call. His daughter, he explained, had experienced a difficult labor, but now his beautiful daughter and granddaughter were resting comfortably. Births have a way of scheduling themselves so everything and everyone else must simply adjust!

Zechariah and Elizabeth were an exception in some ways. They had wanted a child for a long time but never expected the blessing God had prepared for them. John's birth was unlike any other child's. Zechariah at first doubted, but then came to realize how special his son would be. His name was not selected by friends or relatives or even his parents. It was as God commanded: John. They raised him in the fear of the Lord, knowing that their child would impact history.

The destiny of our children may not be as John's, but when raised in the fear of the Lord they can become giants in the faith. They can make a difference in their households, communities, and country. Who knows what God has planned for the children in your family, church, and neighborhood if they are taught the ways of God? A child is a gift, a trust, and a demonstration of what God can do.

PRAYER THOUGHTS: Thank You for the gift of children, for the hope they bring into the world. Help us to guide them in the straight path. Help us to show them the way to You. Most of all, help us to live so that they might see You in us. Amen.

FOLLOW THE LIGHT

SCRIPTURE: Luke 1:67-80

VERSE FOR TODAY: To give light to them that sit in darkness and in the shadow of death, to guide our feet into the way of peace (Luke 1:79).

HYMN FOR TODAY: "Jesus, the Light of the World"

In the small southern town where I lived for many years, we would sometimes sit outside during the power outages. These would be fairly common on warm summer nights. There would be total darkness except for a few flashlights and candles in the windows. The flashlights of those walking from one house to another were easy to see. Theirs were the only lights, and because of the situation they seemed brighter than ever. Light in darkness is reassuring and comforting. We knew we were not alone when we saw the flashlights approaching.

While walking with a flashlight, we didn't have to worry about stumbling, falling, or walking into someone else. We could clearly see the path ahead.

And so it was with John. He was sent to share light with those who sat in darkness. Theirs was not a temporary state that could be corrected by the city in a few hours, but rather a way of life that could only be changed by the individual. John walked the lonely road with a light in his hand, offering it to all who listened to his voice. Have you accepted the Light?

PRAYER THOUGHTS: Thank You, God, for the gift of light into a world of darkness. Help me this day to let Your light shine through me, so that another might come to know and serve You. Help me to live a life full of love and compassion that comes only from the Light of the world. In His name, I pray. Amen.

WHISTLE-BLOWER FOR GOD

SCRIPTURE: Mark 6:14-20

VERSE FOR TODAY: The voice of one crying in the wilderness, Prepare ye the way of the Lord, make his paths straight (Matthew 3:3).

HYMN FOR TODAY: "Stand Up, Stand Up for Jesus"

Every little boy or girl wants to have friends. Every teenager knows how important it is to be a part of the crowd—to "fit in."

Adults know, too, the pressure to "go it alone" especially when powerful people are involved. Whistle-blowers risk losing their jobs and being mistreated for doing what they feel is morally right.

Herod knew that John was a just man, and he respected him, yet he didn't want to displease his wife and daughter. So he had John killed even when he knew it was wrong. He didn't have the strength to stand up for what was right.

John, no doubt, might have enjoyed having the favor of friends. There may have been times of loneliness, perhaps even sadness, but he knew what he had to do. He was meant for another life. He was a whistle-blower for God. He knew the risk, but he would not take sides with sin. Making the right decision—going against the grain—is difficult, but John had to do what was right and call sin "by it's right name." In the end it cost him his life, but in the end his life was safe with his Creator.

What price are we willing to pay for service to the Master? Are we willing to be whistle-blowers for God?

PRAYER THOUGHTS: Jesus, sometimes it's hard to be different, to stand up for You. Sometimes I just want to fit in, not stand out. Help me to stand up and represent You in all I do and say today. Amen.

SEEK GODLY COUNSEL

SCRIPTURE: Mark 6:21-29

VERSE FOR TODAY: Train up a child in the way he should go: and when he is old, he will not depart from it (Proverbs 22:6).

HYMN FOR TODAY: "Let Him In"

During the celebration of her daughter Caroline's wedding, one reporter casually made a comment to Jackie Onassis, former first lady. The reporter was surprised to discover what any mother could have told him. One of the most famous women in the world counted among her greatest achievements raising her children to be happy, loving, well-adjusted adults.

It is the burden of every godly mother's heart to raise her children in the fear and nurture of God. All through life the child will seek the support of the parents—the advice of those older and wiser.

Salome was offered an opportunity to have anything she wanted when her dancing pleased Herod. She sought her mother's advice. The answer resulted in John's unmerited death. Salome went down in history as a daughter whose mother's poor counsel caused the death of a spiritual giant. Perhaps Herodias thought the death of John would end her troubles. Perhaps she thought if she silenced the man of God, the voice of God would cease. Instead, she only involved her daughter in a more grievous sin than the first.

Parents must seek to be models and examples of holiness, that their children might follow in their paths.

PRAYER THOUGHTS: Heavenly Father, I am not wise enough to counsel Your people or even my own household. Grant me wisdom to offer wise counsel—Your counsel—to those who seek my advice and direction. In the name of Jesus, amen.

My Prayer Notes

DEVOTIONS

Spring Flowers

MAY

photo by H. Armstrong Roberts

A CHARGE TO KEEP

SCRIPTURE: Luke 3:15-20

VERSE FOR TODAY: I have fought a good fight, I have finished my course, I have kept the faith (2 Timothy 4:7).

HYMN FOR TODAY: "Keep On The Firing Line"

A promising career now a thing of the past. "Why," I ask, "Did you leave a great job?" *Why,* I wondered, *not wait until an early retirement rolled around with its security?*

"I tried to get away from God, but I had to do this ministry," the minister replied. It is a humble ministry counseling and teaching adults, teaching children, providing help, resources, and encouragement to those in need. The small mission office is nothing like his former executive suite, but this was the charge God gave him.

John's ministry, too, was a burden that had to be fulfilled. Humble, he would take no credit. Instead he told people of the one to come whose baptism would be one of fire. He counted himself unworthy even to untie his Lord's sandals. John was compelled by the love of God to share a revolutionary message. He sought no glory in this life, but he achieved the goals God set for him with dignity and power.

To each, God has given a task. What of you and I? Are we fulfilling the ministry set before us no matter what the cost? Will we be remembered as great successes by the world's standards or as humble servants of God by Biblical standards?

PRAYER THOUGHTS: Thank You, Lord Jesus, for allowing me to share in Your work in this world. Show me the things You would have me to do. Show me how to do them. Please help me to keep the charge You have given to me. Amen.

THE ADVANCE TEAM

SCRIPTURE: Matthew 11:7-15

VERSE FOR TODAY: For this is he, of whom it is written, Behold, I send my messenger before thy face, which shall prepare thy way before thee (Matthew 11:10).

HYMN FOR TODAY: "The Lily of the Valley"

The secret service makes a sweep of the area. The slightest irregularity comes under close examination. The President of the United States will be in town. The advance team must make sure that everything is in readiness. There are sites to secure, interviews to be arranged—the list goes on. When the President, who is considered to be the most important person in the country, comes for a visit, nothing can be left to chance.

John knew the world was to receive the most precious visitor it would ever know. It was a brief visit, to be sure—just a few years—but the world would never forget Him, and John would never forget the part he was to play in this great event. It was a task he never deserted, even when in his jail cell. "Go," he told his disciples. "Find out if this is the one." They did, and John knew his efforts were not in vain. The Promised One was here. What greater honor could any man receive than to be referred to by the Son of God as "more than a prophet" (Matthew 11:9). And so it was. He had performed the task God set before him. He prepared the way for the Son of God.

PRAYER THOUGHTS: I am so thankful to know that You are coming again for Your people. Help me to be ready, and help me to prepare the way for Your return by sharing Your gospel with others. Amen.

May 3

WHO SAID SO?

SCRIPTURE: Matthew 10:1-6

VERSE FOR TODAY: The prophecy came not in old time by the will of man: but holy men of God spake as they were moved by the Holy Ghost (2 Peter 1:21).

HYMN FOR TODAY: "Come, Thou Almighty King"

"Who said?" "No, I won't!"

Rebellion against authority is widespread in our society. Even the Bible is dismissed as "invalid." Christians accept God as the supreme, absolute authority, but we rely on God's Word as our only source. From Genesis to Revelation we realize God has been at work through the creation, history, and spiritual growth of His people.

Our Verse for Today was penned by the apostle Peter. Jesus promised His apostles that He would send the Holy Spirit to be His presence with them and to guide them into all truth (John 16:12-15). Jesus himself had received authority from the Father (John 5:27; Matthew 17:5; Matthew 28:18).

We have come full circle on the question of authority. Authority belongs to God (read Job 38-41 and Isaiah 41:21—46:12 for sheer wonder of and exultation in our God's magnificence). He gave all authority to Jesus, who conveyed it through the Holy Spirit to the apostles and His written Word. Thus we may preach, teach, speak, and write as long as our words are Scripturally sound, realizing that we shall be held accountable (Romans 14:12).

PRAYER THOUGHTS: We thank You, Father, that we have the backing of the Creator. Help us to know Thy Word. Amen.

May 3-9. **Jacqueline Westers** is a Christian writer and former editor of adult literature at Standard Publishing. She makes her home in Cincinnati, Ohio.

FOLLOWING INSTRUCTIONS

SCRIPTURE: Matthew 10:7-15

VERSE FOR TODAY: Examine yourselves, whether ye be in the faith; prove your own selves. Know ye not . . . that Jesus Christ is in you? (2 Corinthians 13:5).

HYMN FOR TODAY: "Standing on the Promises"

Many household items we buy carry the tag, "Some assembly required." So the first thing we look for in a package is the instruction sheet. Recently I bought a small lamp and found no instructions in the box. The shade was a mere brass skeleton of two circles separated by thin brass wires. Eight curved glass panels had to be attached, top and bottom. Using the picture on the box, a little common sense, and a screwdriver, I put the lamp together—and so far it hasn't fallen apart.

Jesus gave His apostles specific instructions when He sent them out. Today we have the Bible as our guidebook; but when we need help and guidance the most, we have difficulty finding appropriate verses. David wrote, "Thy word is a lamp unto my feet, and a light unto my path" (Psalm 119:105). But if we are stumbling in the dark, we cannot see clearly to read anything. God's Word should already be shining in our hearts, to light our way. As we read and ponder Scripture passages, we shall be fortified when temptation, suffering, and trials come. Read Deuteronomy 6:6-18; Psalm 1 and 119; 2 Timothy 3:16, 17; and 2 Peter 3:14-18.

PRAYER THOUGHTS: We thank You, Father, for Thy Word, which gives us not only instruction and comfort, but reproof and challenge, so that we may develop stability and reassurance in our daily lives. In the name of Jesus Christ, our Savior and Lord. Amen.

PRESS ON—AND ON

SCRIPTURE: Matthew 10:16-23

VERSE FOR TODAY: Fear none of those things which thou shalt suffer . . . be thou faithful unto death, and I will give thee a crown of life (Revelation 2:10).

HYMN FOR TODAY: "The Way of the Cross Leads Home"

Our college class spent a skip day climbing Mount LeConte in the Smokies. The path at the base spiraled upward and around the mountain, ever narrowing toward the height. Each of us carried his own lunch and other paraphernalia. As we climbed upward, the path became steeper, rougher, and harder on the legs and back. Our burdens also seemed heavier; but no one wanted to give up. We struggled on until suddenly the path widened and disappeared. We had reached the top, and our groans changed to shouts of joy.

The Christian life is much like that. We begin it with enthusiasm and energy, but sooner or later the way becomes wearing, our burdens heavy. There is no real trial or temptation on a joyful hike in the Smokies; however, along the Christian life Satan is there to put every kind of obstacle in the way—anything to make us turn aside. But Jesus is also there, and He is stronger than Satan. He assures us that we will not be burdened beyond our capability. He strengthens us for carrying the cross we have taken up for Him, and He walks beside us.

Just imagine what the view at the height will be like!

PRAYER THOUGHTS: We thank You, Father, for the promise that Jesus will be with us always. In times of strength or in times of weakness, help us, Lord, to rely on You, knowing that Yours are the everlasting arms. In the name of Jesus, our Savior. Amen.

LIKE TEACHER, LIKE STUDENT

SCRIPTURE: Matthew 10:24-28

VERSE FOR TODAY: Now are we the sons of God, and it doth not yet appear what we shall be: but we know that, when he shall appear, we shall be like him (1 John 3:2).

HYMN FOR TODAY: "O Master, Let Me Walk With Thee"

Our first-grade teacher passed the whole class into the second grade. But it was found that we were not adequately prepared for second-grade work. The whole class had to repeat the first grade. Whether it was incompetence or negligence, somehow I never cared about being like that teacher.

In college, one of my professors so impressed me with the importance of his courses that I couldn't think of attending a class unprepared. I felt that to do so would somehow disappoint him. I'm sure that he couldn't care that much about his students' daily assignments, but it was good motivation on my part. I had chosen to follow a good example.

All the fine attributes, good examples, fairness, and caring help that I observed in most of my teachers abound in the best of all teachers—Jesus Christ. I want to learn from Him, for His teachings are the truth; I want to obey Him, for His commandments are not grievous, but for my benefit; I want to follow Him, for He is the right way to walk; I want to live for Him, for He is the life. He is my example.

Who wouldn't want to be like Jesus?

PRAYER THOUGHTS: As we strive to be more like Jesus, dear Lord, help us to remember that others observe our comings and goings, our behavior and attitudes. May we be worthy examples for Your sake. Amen.

DETAILS, DETAILS

SCRIPTURE: Matthew 10:29-33

VERSE FOR TODAY: In thy book all my members were written, which in continuance were fashioned, when as yet there was none of them (Psalm 139:16).

HYMN FOR TODAY: "Moment by Moment"

When I burned my finger the other day, I didn't notify my brain, "A finger is being burned. Immediately send out the necessary units of white corpuscles to isolate the area. Alert the immune system to begin the healing process and restore the skin to its former state." No; all I did was apply a little soothing ointment and a bandage. Can you imagine how complicated and time-consuming it would be to blink our eyes and pump each heartbeat manually; to monitor the respiratory, circulatory, and nervous systems; to convey our food through the digestive system; and coordinate everything to function as smoothly as our bodies do now, automatically? But no, our God of details has taken care of all that. With David I am amazed that the God who controls the universe and the whole world of nature has provided me with the required number of little white cells to heal me automatically when I am careless enough to burn my finger. Why has He done this? Yes, He loves us; but another reason may be that God wants us to use our time and energy for more important matters—like serving Him, for instance.

What do you think?

PRAYER THOUGHTS: Thank You, Father, for the many things we receive every day that we take for granted. When we are preoccupied with major decisions, help us not to overlook the little things that also matter. In the name of Jesus. Amen.

NECESSARY CUTS

SCRIPTURE: Matthew 10:33-42

VERSE FOR TODAY: The word of God is quick, and powerful, and sharper than any two-edged sword, piercing even to the dividing asunder of soul and spirit (Hebrews 4:12).

HYMN FOR TODAY: "I Gave My Life for Thee"

After my mother was baptized into Christ, she learned that she was no longer welcome in her sister's home. One day Mother went to visit her, only to see the door shut in her face. She and my aunt never saw each other again. Mother came to America later, but not only the Atlantic Ocean kept the sisters far apart.

While the Word does divide families and friends, it also cuts into individual lives. If one is a new creature in Christ, old life-styles, habits, prejudices, and attitudes may have to be removed, and that may take a longtime. If the new creature had been addicted to alcohol, drugs, or other abuse, it may require a very slow and painful process to eliminate.

It comes down to a matter of allegiance. Following Christ means that we are now servants of righteousness, no longer to be dominated by unrighteousness (Romans 6). Jesus himself had to choose. He could have called down legions of angels to rescue Him from the cross and its agony. But you and I were too important to Him, and there was no other way to save us. The question is, how important to us is He?

PRAYER THOUGHTS: How can we adequately express our gratitude or praise You enough, dear Father, for all You have done for our salvation? May our lives reflect our appreciation by living sacrificially as You did. In the name of Your Son, and our Savior, Jesus. Amen.

WHAT IS THE GOOD NEWS?

SCRIPTURE: Matthew 11:1-6

VERSE FOR TODAY: This is the Lord; we have waited for him, we will be glad and rejoice in his salvation (Isaiah 25:9).

HYMN FOR TODAY: "O Zion, Haste"

"Behold, I bring you good tidings of great joy, which shall be to all people. For unto you is born this day . . . a Saviour" (Luke 2:10, 11). So said the angel to the shepherds when Jesus Christ was born.

Every religion has a founder, prophet, or deity. But no other religion offers to all people all over the world a Savior who frees man from sin and guilt, who died and rose again. What is the good news? The good news is that Jesus himself is the good news. He is at once high priest and sin-offering, the price and the prize. He is good news to the lame who stumble along their way; He makes the blind see the truth that makes them free; He gathers in the outcasts of society. Jesus is good news to the rich and poor, the strong and weak, the intellectual and the backward.

Jesus is God's gift to the world (John 3:16), but He invites individuals to himself (Matthew 11:28-30). He came to earth not only for everyone, but for every one, for people long ago, and for you and me now. He is our own good news.

No, John, we don't look for any other.

PRAYER THOUGHTS: Thank You, dear Father, for the good news in Christ Jesus, the only good news worth publishing all over the world. Help us to review our commitment to bringing Christ to those who do not know Him. We pray in His name. Amen.

WATER, WATER EVERYWHERE!

SCRIPTURE: John 4:1-14

VERSE FOR TODAY: "But whoever drinks the water I give him will never thirst. Indeed, the water I give him will become in him a spring of water welling up to eternal life" (John 4:14, *New International Version*).

HYMN FOR TODAY: "Springs of Living Water"

A group of Arabs were touring the United States. Their tour took them to such famous sights as Washington D. C., New York City, Mount Rushmore, Pike's Peak, and Niagara Falls. The Arabs, being from countries where water is more valuable than oil, were amazed at the great volume of water that poured over the falls. One of the Arab men asked the young American tour guide how the falls were turned off at night. The brash young man boastfully said, "We have so much water here that we leave the falls on all night long just to impress you tourists." The Arab guest was visibly distressed at the apparent waste of such a valuable resource. He abruptly said to the tour guide, "We men of the desert have learned to appreciate the value of water more than you wasteful Americans."

Jesus gives the Christian "a spring of water welling up to eternal life." Do you view His gift of water like the arrogant tour guide, as something to be taken for granted? Or do you gratefully appreciate salvation, like the man of the desert prizes water?

PRAYER THOUGHTS: Father, help me to be thankful for salvation. Help me always to remember the sacrifice that Jesus made for me on the cross. Help me to be grateful for the gift of grace. In the name of Jesus, amen.

May 10-16. **James Moore** ministers to the Calvary Christian Church in Stockbridge, Georgia. He and his wife, Becky, have two children, Catherine and Daniel.

"AND WHERE IS YOUR CHURCH?"

SCRIPTURE: John 4:15-24

VERSE FOR TODAY: Yet a time is coming and has now come when the true worshipers will worship the Father in spirit and truth, for they are the kind of worshipers the Father seeks (John 4:23, *New International Version*).

HYMN FOR TODAY: "O Worship the King"

"And where is your church located?" she asked me. I was at a loss to answer. You see, the church where I minister is in the middle of a major building/relocation program. We sold our old building and had to move out before the new building was completed. We don't have a church building! So I said to her, "We are located in at least 200-300 places all over the Atlanta area each day!" Actually we meet on Sunday in rented rooms at a local community college. But each day the Christians that call themselves Calvary Christian Church are located in their homes, at their jobs, on sports fields, at stores, and malls. . . . My church is wherever the members go!

In Jesus' day, the Jews worshiped in the temple in Jerusalem, the Samaritans in their place of worship on Mount Gerizim. These two sites for worship symbolized their conflict! But Jesus wants His people to worship "in spirit and in truth" (John 4:23). I have learned that worship is not confined to a church building. True worship takes place in daily spiritual living for Jesus Christ. True worship takes place anywhere and everywhere we go.

PRAYER THOUGHTS: Father, may my life always be pleasing worship in Your eyes. Help me to realize that true worship occurs not in a "church building," but everywhere Your people go. Make me truly a part of Your church. In Jesus' name, amen.

"SPLAIN!"

SCRIPTURE: John 4:25-30

VERSE FOR TODAY: Jesus answered, "I am the way and the truth and the life. No one comes to the Father except through me" (John 14:6, *New International Version*).

HYMN FOR TODAY: "The Way of the Cross Leads Home"

I love to watch old reruns of television programs. My favorite one has to be "I Love Lucy." Lucy and Ricky really get to my funny bone! You remember how Lucy would always get into trouble and drag her friend, Ethel, into the project with her. It was always some far-out scheme to make money or get into show business. Like the time that they dressed up as women from Mars and did a publicity stunt on the top of the Empire State Building for a "B" movie opening. My favorite part of those old Lucy shows is when Ricky caught her and said in broken English, "Splain!" What he meant was, "Explain to me what in the world got into you that caused you to do this." But, in his frustration, all that he could get out was, "Splain."

Explain is exactly what Jesus did to the woman at the well. Jesus clearly told her that He was the Messiah, the Savior of the world. And, He still is!

Looking for someone to "splain" the way to Heaven? His Word will guide you to the truth. Go to Jesus the Savior. He will not only explain it; He *is* the way!

PRAYER THOUGHTS: Lord God, Your Son, Jesus, is the way to Heaven. Help me to stay on the right road. Father, help me to always look to Your Word to guide, direct, and light my path. In the name of the Savior, Jesus, amen.

NOW IS THE TIME

SCRIPTURE: John 4:31-38

VERSE FOR TODAY: "Do you not say, 'Four months more and then the harvest'? I tell you, open your eyes and look at the fields! They are ripe for harvest" (John 4:35, *New International Version*).

HYMN FOR TODAY: "So Send I You"

I am a "frustrated farmer." I keep a medium-sized garden in the backyard. Because of the size of the garden, I have decided not to grow crops that take up a lot of space. So I grow mostly beans, tomatoes, and strawberries (I like strawberries).

Yesterday I went out into the garden to see if any beans were ready to pick. They were! I picked and picked until I had a "trash can" and a half full of beans. A trash can corresponds to a bushel or so. But the bad thing about beans is that they must be snapped. It takes at least four times as long to snap them as it does to pick them. Then they must be canned. That's my wife's department. By the end of the season she does not want to look at another bean!

Gardening has taught me an important lesson. When a crop is ready to be harvested it is ready to be harvested *then*—not the next day or week! Jesus said, "Look at the fields! They are ripe for harvest." Now is the time for reaping souls for Jesus. Go labor in the harvest fields!

PRAYER THOUGHTS: Lord of harvest, may I always be a faithful worker in Your harvest field. Give me eyes that see the labor needing to be done, and a heart that is willing to work. Lord, strengthen me for the task at hand. Help me to realize that the harvest time is today. I can not wait until tomorrow. In the name of Jesus, amen.

BEING THERE

SCRIPTURE: John 4:39-42

VERSE FOR TODAY: They said to the woman, "We no longer believe just because of what you said; now we have heard for ourselves, and we know that this man really is the Savior of the world" (John 4:42, *New International Version*).

HYMN FOR TODAY: "Come, We That Love the Lord"

They say being there is half the fun! I wouldn't really know, though. I've never really "been there." The closest that I have been to an important college or pro football game is when Yale played William and Mary at the Oyster Bowl! Neither team is a football power any more! Both schools are better known for brain power than sports brawn. Being there was important!

A few years ago, Georgia Tech and Nebraska played for the national championship for college football at the Citrus Bowl in Orlando, Florida. I minister in Tech country! Two men in the church are "big" Tech fans. They traveled to Orlando "just" to see the game! For them, being there was important. The excitement of the crowd, the thrill of actually seeing the team score, the electricity of being in the midst of thousands of other fans all make personal experience important!

Being there is important in your Christian walk, also. Group worship, mutual encouragement, Bible study, exhortation, fellowship, and communion with the saints all are great faith-builders! Being there and personally experiencing faith in action are important!

PRAYER THOUGHTS: Father, help me to realize the true importance of group worship. Help me to encourage my brothers and sisters. May I always try to build up and encourage Your children. Help me to be there when needed. In the name of Jesus, amen.

May 15

WHICH SIGN DO I FOLLOW?

SCRIPTURE: John 4:43-48

VERSE FOR TODAY: "Unless you people see miraculous signs and wonders," Jesus told him, "you will never believe" (John 4:48, *New International Version*).

HYMN FOR TODAY: "Guide Me, O Thou Great Jehovah"

I love directional signs! To hear me talk, you might not believe that because I hate the way that most of them are displayed. You know, the stop sign that is covered by the "spreading chestnut tree." Or the "exit only" signs on the interstate that are just a few feet before you get to the exit. I always get forced off into some of the "most scenic" parts of town. But the signs that I love the most are the directional signs on I-285 around Atlanta! They say the road goes east and west, but I want to go south!

Life can be that way, also. If we are always looking for a sign from God, we may be like the young man who saw P. C. in the clouds and thought it meant "Preach Christ." After a life of failure in the ministry, at the pearly gates he complained to Saint Peter: "But I had a clear sign," he said. "P. C.—Preach Christ!" Peter replied, "P. C. meant plant corn!"

Don't go through life frustrated, looking for signs from God. Look to His Word, the Bible, for guidance. It contains all the guidance you need.

PRAYER THOUGHTS: Father, may I always look to Your Word, the Bible, for guidance for my life. Help me to make Your truth a "light unto my path" (Psalm 119:105). Help me to take Your truth and let its light shine on others. In the name of Jesus, amen.

A HANDSHAKE WILL DO

SCRIPTURE: John 4:49-54

VERSE FOR TODAY: Then the father realized that this was the exact time at which Jesus had said to him, "Your son will live." So he and all his household believed (John 4:53, *New International Version*).

HYMN FOR TODAY: "Trust and Obey"

A friend and church member who is a lawyer was lamenting one time, "I wish we could go back to the time when a handshake was good enough and a man's word was his bond." We have a trust problem these days. People often don't do what they promise. So everyone wants a contract or a release from liability. A sign in an old general store says, "In GOD we TRUST—all others pay CASH!"

But what about the church? Some teachers say that they will teach, then fail to show up for class on Sunday morning. Some elders and deacons say at their ordinations that they will faithfully serve God and His church, but they only serve when they are not doing something else. Some preachers promise to be faithful to their calling and then get caught up in some scandal. You can name many more!

It's no wonder that people don't want to trust Jesus! We can't trust anyone anymore! But Jesus *is* trustworthy! "Then the father realized that this was the exact time at which Jesus had said to him, 'Your son will live.' So he and all his household believed" (John 4:53, *New International Version*). God's Word is always good!

PRAYER THOUGHTS: Father, strengthen my faith and trust in You. Help me to depend on Your promises, for they are true. Help me to commit to Your way, for it is right. Help me to be true to my word as You are true to Yours. In Jesus' name, amen.

THE MAN OF GALILEE

SCRIPTURE: John 7:1-9

VERSE FOR TODAY: And leaving Nazareth, he came and dwelt in Capernaum, which is upon the sea coast, in the borders of Zebulun and Naphtali (Matthew 4:13).

HYMN FOR TODAY: "The Stranger of Galilee"

Jesus felt at home in Galilee. There was a human part of Him that enjoyed living and ministering to the people in that northern part of Israel. Though born in Judea, He had been raised in Nazareth of Galilee. He was a native Galilean. When His ministry began, He left Nazareth and made His home in Capernaum, the little fishing village on the shores of the lake—the area where Peter, James, and John had been living when He called them. Yet He knew He had a destiny in Jerusalem. It was there that a dreadful encounter awaited Him.

Actors and actresses in a drama must know when to go on stage. They have a part to play. They are to appear no sooner and no later than the time assigned to them.

The ministry of Jesus in Galilee was part of His assigned task. But the "main performance" was to take place in Jerusalem. At the proper time, when it came time for Him to die, He would leave Galilee. He would go south to the "big stage on the mountaintop." Pilate would say "Behold the Man!" and Jesus of Nazareth would die on a cross just outside the city. When the time came, the Man of Galilee would go.

PRAYER THOUGHTS: Father, thank You so much for sending Your only begotten Son to deliver us from our sinful ways. Amen.

May 17-23. **Donnie Mings** and his wife, Charlotte, serve the Hauula Church of Christ in Hawaii. They have two grown children, Sheri and Jeffrey.

THE RABBI

SCRIPTURE: John 7:10-15

VERSE FOR TODAY: And the Jews marvelled, saying, How knoweth this man letters, having never learned? (John 7:15)

HYMN FOR TODAY: "Teach Me Thy Will, O Lord"

For many centuries a spiritual leader of Judaism has been called a "rabbi," one who teaches the Jewish people how to live and worship God under the Mosaic law. Some modern Israeli rabbis are predicting the imminent arrival of the promised Messiah, not realizing that the Messiah came upon the scene long ago. His name was Jesus of Nazareth. And He, too, was known as a rabbi.

People at the time thought of Him as just another teacher of the law. A good one, to be sure. And quite controversial. Not many rabbis claimed to be the Son of God. They liked the miracles. They liked the loaves and fish He multiplied and served them when they were hungry.

There was great expectancy in Jerusalem at this particular feast of Tabernacles. Would the rabbi show up? Would He have the courage? The people were well aware of the attitude of the authorities toward Him, and they spoke of Him in hushed tones, afraid to say anything openly.

Then suddenly there He was! Yes! And boldly lecturing in the temple courtyard. With amazing clarity. With eloquence. With authority. The Teacher had arrived.

PRAYER THOUGHTS: Dear Father, I thank You that Your Son, Jesus, gave us His precious teaching. Thank You that we have it preserved and made available to us today, and that it is just as powerful now as then. I commit to live as He taught us to live. Amen.

WONDERFUL WORDS OF LIFE

SCRIPTURE: John 7:16-24

VERSE FOR TODAY: The officers answered, Never man spake like this man (John 7:46).

HYMN FOR TODAY: "Wonderful Words of Life"

Take an ordinary man. Give him some training. Get him in good shape physically. Put a smart blue or black uniform on him. Put a badge on him. Give him the right kind of hat. Put him in a car with red or blue flashing lights. Make him swear in a short ceremony to uphold the laws of the city. You can do the same with a woman. Now you have a police officer. Behind that person stands all the power and authority of the city. When officer Smith says to stop, you stop.

When Jesus spoke to the crowds, the people were immediately struck by the realization that He spoke as one with authority. Not like the other teachers; he looked rather ordinary. But the message was powerful. And He obviously knew what He was talking about. Only God knew the things of God that well.

When the Creator came down and lived and walked among men, things began to happen. When He spoke, people listened. When He touched lives, they changed. His authority was the personal authority of God the Son delivering a message for God the Father.

PRAYER THOUGHTS: Father, thank You for the powerful way in which Your Son spoke to the people when He was down here in the flesh. I receive His words today as powerful and full of authority for me. I want my life to be daily guided by those words. Help me to live by Your Word. In the name of Jesus Christ, my Savior, I pray. Amen.

A QUESTION OF IDENTITY

SCRIPTURE: John 7:25-31

VERSE FOR TODAY: And it came to pass, as he was alone praying, his disciples were with him: and he asked them, saying, Whom say the people that I am? (Luke 9:18)

HYMN FOR TODAY: "Who at My Door is Standing?"

Recent surveys taken in the United States still show a remarkably high percentage of Americans believing in God. For that we are thankful. A majority of the people also believe in Jesus as the Christ. But not so many Americans translate their beliefs into commitment to the Lord. Many are asking why they should serve this God. Why should they worship Him in whom they seem to believe?

The Jewish people have a different kind of problem with regard to Jesus Christ. While many Jews at present do not believe in God at all, the problem the devout have is one of the identity of the Person. When Christ was here on earth, the lack of motivation to follow Him centered around their confusion about who He was.

There were two known personalities. One was the glorious promised Messiah, who would redeem His people and who would live forever. On the other hand there was Jesus of Nazareth. Jesus brought God's love and compassion. He worked miracles. But He looked so ordinary. Bringing the two together as one was the big challenge they faced. They must equate Jesus of Nazareth with the Messiah of the Scriptures.

PRAYER THOUGHTS: Dear Lord Jesus, I am sorry that when You walked on this earth many years ago, there was so much blindness and confusion as to who You are. I am determined that there will be no such confusion in my life. Amen.

May 21

HE IS THE SOURCE

SCRIPTURE: John 7:32-39

VERSE FOR TODAY: In the last day, that great day of the feast, Jesus stood and cried, saying, If any man thirst, let him come unto me, and drink (John 7:37).

HYMN FOR TODAY: "Springs of Living Water"

When you want food, where do you go? When you want water, where do you go? When you need clothes, where do you go to get them? Where do you get gas for the car? Where do you get building materials? In our modern, urban life-styles we increasingly depend on someone to sell us just about everything we need. Not many can go to the cow for milk, or to the mine for coal these days. Most people have very little connection with the real source of anything in our society.

God is the source of all good things in life. One way or another He gives us what we need. Our job or profession should be seen merely as a tool or channel through which God supplies what His children need. The job is not the source of income. He uses people and things to bless us.

In our passage today Jesus lets it be known that He is the source of living water. He, Jesus of Nazareth, is inviting the crowds there in Jerusalem to come to Him and receive. It means that He is God, the creator and sustainer of life. And even though He was going away somewhere mysterious, He was offering to them the precious gift of God's Holy Spirit. He is the Source.

PRAYER THOUGHTS: Dear Lord, I know all good things come from You. Thank You so much for providing for me. I look to You as my Source. And I claim Your Holy Spirit for my life. Amen.

JESUS OF NAZARETH IS THE MESSIAH

SCRIPTURE: John 7:40-44

VERSE FOR TODAY: And Simon Peter answered and said, Thou art the Christ, the Son of the living God (Matthew 16:16).

HYMN FOR TODAY: "Praise Him! Praise Him!"

On a recent trip to Israel I had the privilege of meeting with a group of Jewish Messianic believers. Along with my brother Lonnie and several Japanese Christians, I was taken by car out to a new Jewish settlement. There, in a private home, perhaps sixty or eighty people gathered to worship the Lord—not on Sunday, but on a Saturday morning.

The service was all in Hebrew. I didn't understand the words of the unfamiliar hymns they sang. But they praised Jesus of Nazareth as the Messiah. They prayed in His name. God was the Father, and Jesus was the Son. They read from both Old and New Testaments. These brothers and sisters in Christ do not call themselves Christians, for a couple of reasons. One is that the title Christ is Greek, not Hebrew. The other reason is that the Jewish people often point to persecution that was visited upon them by people calling themselves Christians. Therefore they prefer to be called Jewish Messianic believers.

But to them there is no question as to who Jesus is. He is the Messiah. He is the Christ. He is the Son of God, their Savior. The ancients, whether Jewish or Roman, had crucified their promised Redeemer. Now they pray for the redemption of Israel by the same Messiah that redeems the Gentiles. Jesus of Nazareth is the One.

PRAYER THOUGHTS: Father, thank You for opening our eyes to recognize who Jesus is. We know He is the Savior of the world. Amen.

BUCKING THE TREND

SCRIPTURE: John 7:45-52

VERSE FOR TODAY: For whosoever shall be ashamed of me and of my words, of him shall the Son of man be ashamed, when he shall come in his own glory, and in his Father's, and of the holy angels (Luke 9:26).

HYMN FOR TODAY: "Who is on the Lord's Side?"

The chief priests and Pharisees were obviously frustrated. The people were impressed with Jesus. Even the guards that were sent to arrest Him were amazed. They returned empty-handed. The power of His words had stunned them.

It takes courage to speak out against a dominant trend in society. Democracy gives us the privilege of voicing our opposition to wrongs in our government and community. We have the right to say which way things should go. More than just the right, we have the responsibility. The tragedy is that so many people in society do not exercise their rights. They do not fulfill their responsibilities. They do not discern right and wrong. They go with the flow. They do not buck the trend.

Nicodemus had courage. He saw the wrong. He had earlier gone personally to speak to Jesus, though secretly. Now he courageously opposed the blindness of the leaders of Israel. Later, he and Joseph of Arimathea would take the body of Jesus and lay it in a tomb, just outside the walls of Jerusalem. Nicodemus believed. He spoke up. Hopefully, we who believe today, would do the same.

PRAYER THOUGHTS: Father, give us the courage to speak up on Your behalf today. Help us to witness to others of Your power and saving grace. Help us to boldly be Your messengers of truth to our world. In the name of Jesus. Amen.

A PLACE TO CELEBRATE LIFE

SCRIPTURE: John 14:1-7

VERSE FOR TODAY: And I heard a loud voice from the throne saying, "Now the dwelling of God is with men, and he will live with them. They will be his people, and God himself will be with them and be their God (Revelation 21:3, *New International Version*).

HYMN FOR TODAY: "O That Will Be Glory"

Erna is the gracious owner-hostess of the widely acclaimed "Elderberry House," an expensive restaurant nestled in the lovely foothills of central California's Sierra Nevada mountains. Recently she fulfilled a long-held dream of building a "mini-chateau" behind the restaurant, patterned after the magnificent castles she knew in her native countries of France and Austria. Now restaurant patrons may stay overnight in her chateau for a "mere" $400. Each room in the inn is named after a French flower or herb, and all are filled with exquisite period furniture. On opening day, Erna proudly exclaimed, "This is a place to celebrate life."

Some day Erna's castle, like other earthly structures, will crumble and decay. Jesus promises us something better and more permanent than anything on this earth. His Father's house has many beautiful rooms prepared and ready for Christian travelers who have remained faithful through their spiritual journey of life. No weariness, pain, sorrow, hunger, or disappointments will mar our experience in that glorious place. Nothing *here* compares with our celebration of eternal life *there*.

PRAYER THOUGHTS: "When by the gift of His infinite grace, I am accorded in heaven a place, Just to be there and to look on His face, will through the ages be glory for me!" (from Today's Hymn).

May 24-30. **Kenneth Brooks** lives in Tulare, California. Though retired, he continues to preach and write at a more leisurely pace, enjoying a variety of activities.

LIKE SON, LIKE FATHER

SCRIPTURE: John 14:8-14

VERSE FOR TODAY: The Son is the radiance of God's glory and the exact representation of his being, sustaining all things by his powerful word (Hebrews 1:3, *New International Version*)

HYMN FOR TODAY: "Children of the Heavenly Father"

"His father was a well-known and loved doctor, and his son has followed in his steps. He, too, is a fine doctor, and you will like him." These were the rather unusual words shared with us by the nurse a few moments before we were to consult a prominent physician whom we had never met before. Her assurances were well-founded. Though we had not known the father, we became acquainted with the son's credentials and capabilities. Did the son resemble the father in physical appearance, mannerisms, style of medical practice? We do not know. We had never met the father. But our confidence in the son's competence was confirmed in his medical "know how."

Think then of this parallel in today's lesson. Philip asked Jesus, "Show us the Father and that will be enough for us!" (John 14:8, New International Version). Then Jesus correctly pointed out to him, in effect, "Like Son, like Father," demonstrated by His authority over all things, in healing power, miracles, and in His declaration of eternal truth.

Granted, we today are separated by many centuries since Jesus walked and talked among men. Yet we, too, who through eyes of continuing faithful obedience to the Son may see the glorious magnificence of our Heavenly Father, will some day be privileged to see Him face-to-face.

PRAYER THOUGHTS: Dear God, we ask that You will bless us with a deeper, lovelier acquaintance with Your Son, and in so doing be more willing, productive workers in Your kingdom. Amen.

FROM HOROSCOPE OR HOLY SPIRIT?

SCRIPTURE: John 14:15-20

VERSE FOR TODAY: I will ask the Father and he will give you another Counselor to be with you forever—the Spirit of truth (John 14:16, 17, *New International Version*).

HYMN FOR TODAY: "Holy Ghost, With Light Divine"

In a bulky packet of advertising received in the mail, we found an array of offers from several enterprising companies —all with one common appeal "Call our 900-number and you will receive. . . ." One ad caught my attention. It read, "Simply pick up your phone, enter this 900-number for your personal astrological sign, and your horoscope—updated daily, created by skilled astrologers—will be waiting for you." Remarkable, isn't it? Living in a revolutionary era of enlightened scientific and Biblical knowledge, many gullible people apparently still take stock in these concocted creations of man's imaginations!

We have, according to Jesus Christ in today's Scripture, a far more reliable source of counsel—God's Holy Spirit. Jesus further informs us elsewhere in John's Gospel (John 16:8) that the Holy Spirit will convict the world of guilt in regard to sin, righteousness, and judgment. He also will guide us into all truth, coming not from self-serving men, but from God himself! Pronouncements and predictions of fallible prophets are usually in error. So, do we rely on a horoscope or the Holy Spirit for the decisive directions our life should take? The safe course is God's Holy Spirit speaking through the holy Scriptures, directed to those who would be holy.

PRAYER THOUGHTS: Dear God, thank You for sending us Your Holy Spirit to dwell in our hearts, enlightening, encouraging, enriching us every moment of every day. In Your Son's name, amen.

"I DON'T HAVE TO MIND YOU, GRANDPA"

SCRIPTURE: John 14:21-24

VERSE FOR TODAY: Whoever has my commands and obeys them, he is the one who loves me. He who loves me will be loved by my Father (John 14:21, *New International Version*).

HYMN FOR TODAY: "I Will Serve Thee Because I Love Thee"

"I don't have to mind you, Grandpa. You are not my daddy!" Those were startling, shocking words spewing out of our three-year-old grandson's mouth when I attempted to persuade him to do what I had asked. Later, in discussing his defiance with his parents, we came up with a list of appropriate rules and consequences, posting them in a prominent place on the kitchen wall. Granted, he couldn't read them. But after that, when a problem arose, we went to the wall to point out what his mamma and daddy—primary authorities—had to say on the subject.

We bump into authority at every turn of life—personal, family, community, world, and the kingdom of God. Attitudes toward authority range from out-and-out defiance, like my grandson's, to eager compliance.

To us, Jesus' appeal to keep God's commandments lifts us up to the very highest level, and our obedience is anchored in God's love for us and our love for Him and His Son. God created us with a power of choice—we don't *have* to mind Him. But when we do, we'll make the glad discovery of the wonderful treasures God has reserved for those who love Him.

PRAYER THOUGHTS: Dear Father-God, sometimes like little children we disobey, talk back, ignore, or break Your commandments—then sadly discover the consequences. Lift us up to Your love today, so we may *gladly* submit to Your will, through Christ our Lord. Amen.

LASTING PEACE

SCRIPTURE: John 14:25-31

VERSE FOR TODAY: "I have told you these things, so that in me you may have peace. In this world you will have trouble. But take heart! I have overcome the world" (John 16:33, *New International Version*).

HYMN FOR TODAY: "Sweet Peace, the Gift of God's Love"

Jesus spoke truth when He said that in the world we will have trouble. Not too long ago, cooperating countries of the United Nations waged a fierce, devastating war against Iraq in the mideast. Many lives were lost. Much property was destroyed. The misery of war's aftermath lingers with us to this present moment. The Secretary of State, like his predecessors before, attempted to intercede to bring peace among the nations who have been at each other's throats for centuries. A temporary end to the conflict might be achieved, but there's no guarantee at all of lasting peace when war and hate remain in the heart.

As long as Satan, the prince of this world, presides supremely among people, he will unleash his destructive weapons of greed, lust, and selfish ambition every where.

In contrast, just as Jesus is not of this world, so, too, His peace is not of this world, This world's peace seems always to be temporary, conditional, capricious, and cunning, always seeking out and seizing the advantage. Christ's gift of peace always aspires to our highest good, not only for time but for all eternity. When this spiritual conflict is finally over, Christ will emerge the victor, for He has won the battle already.

PRAYER THOUGHTS: Dear God, You have given us the peace which passes all understanding. May we therefore be confident this day and always that it will guard our minds and hearts in Christ Jesus. Amen.

WE ARE GOD'S CHILDREN

SCRIPTURE: Romans 8:12-17

VERSE FOR TODAY: Those who are led by the Spirit of God are sons of God (Romans 8:14, *New International Version*).

HYMN FOR TODAY: "Jesus Loves Even Me"

At least twice each year, Oprah Winfrey, popular TV hostess, features programs in which adopted children are reunited with their birth mothers and other family members. A national search organization specializing in this service has had a remarkable success rate. Not all contacts and reunions are happy ones, however, especially where troubling problems have accompanied previous home life or the adoption itself.

"Adoption" is one of the great Bible words significant in our Scripture today. When we sin, we become part of Satan's family and are called "children of wrath" (Ephesians 2:3). But when we become Christians through faith and obedience to God's commands, we are adopted into His family with all the rights, privileges, and responsibilities that relationship implies. In God's family the Holy Spirit now becomes our guide, instructor, and encourager so that we want to love and respect our Father-God. We also desire to obey and follow the leading and example of Jesus Christ, our Savior. In God's family we learn to love, appreciate, and help our brothers and sisters around the world so that some day we may lay claim with them of that wonderful inheritance in Heaven.

PRAYER THOUGHTS: Dear Father, we recognize our fellowship with You as Your children today. We ask that we may have the wisdom to enjoy life thankfully, labor each day honestly, bear whatever disappointments and difficulties we encounter without bitterness or resentment, because we have learned to love You completely and joyously. Amen.

AN "A" ON OUR REPORT CARD

SCRIPTURE: Romans 8:18-27

VERSE FOR TODAY: And he who searches our hearts knows the mind of the Spirit, because the Spirit intercedes for the saints in accordance with God's will (Romans 8:27, *New International Version*).

HYMN FOR TODAY: "Fill Me Now, O Holy Spirit"

A hot, humid summer in the midwest found me in a classroom with other seminary students sweltering through an intensive study course, "The History of Philosophy" (as though the weather was not agony enough!). Unfortunately, too, it seemed only three students "knew" enough on the subject to engage in a four-way exchange of ideas with the professor, practically excluding us of lesser knowledge. Final exams were a disaster. Firmly convinced I had flunked the course, I was trying to be philosophical about it. Imagine my and other students' surprise when report cards stated that most of us received "A's!" As I look back on that summer's study, I am led to believe the professor possessed a great measure of the Holy Spirit, whose "groanings" about our weaknesses and inadequacies words cannot express, even in a classroom situation.

The good news is that the Holy Spirit intercedes for us time and time again throughout our spiritual learning experiences. And we, too, are in for a glad surprise when God issues His report card on our efforts in faith, hope, and love. The "A's" we find there must be credited to the good and gracious work of the Holy Spirit in our behalf.

PRAYER THOUGHTS: O Spirit of God, thank You for Your daily help in our prayers, our Bible study, and our witnessing to others. Through Christ our Savior, amen.

THANK YOU, GOD, FOR YOUR GRACE

SCRIPTURE: Philippians 1:1-11

VERSE FOR TODAY: But by the grace of God I am what I am, and his grace to me was not without effect. No, I worked harder than all of them—yet not I, but the grace of God that was with me (1 Corinthians 15:10, *New International Version***).**

HYMN FOR TODAY: "Amazing Grace"

One of the most wonderful things in the whole world is to have someone not make you suffer as much as you should for a wrong that you have done. When mankind had fallen so deeply into sin, God sent His Son, and we received His amazing grace through Jesus!

Some time ago a very unusual wedding took place in England. The groom was blind from an accident when he was only ten years old. He was now marrying a very beautiful woman. A short time before the wedding, William Dyke had eye surgery. On his wedding day the bride walked down the aisle with her father. Standing with the groom at the front of the church was one of Britain's most famous surgeons. In an unusual addition to the ceremony, the surgeon removed the bandages from the young man's eyes. For the first time, he looked into the beautiful face of his beloved bride. With a surge of indescribable joy, he cried, "At last! At last!"

We must not be blinded to the beauty of our God. We need to spiritually remove the bandages from our eyes and thank God for His grace.

PRAYER THOUGHTS: Heavenly Father, You are so good to us. Thank You that when we deserved much punishment for our sins, You took them all away with the precious blood of Christ! Amen.

May 31—June 6. **Kenneth Meade** has ministered to the Church of Christ at Manor Woods in Rockville, Maryland, for the past 37 years. He and his wife, Jan, have two children and four grandchildren.

DEVOTIONS

JUNE

photo by Luoma Photos

TELL THE WORLD ABOUT JESUS

SCRIPTURE: Philippians 1:12-18

VERSE FOR TODAY: He said to them, "Go into all the world and preach the good news to all creation" (Mark 16:15, *New International Version*).

HYMN FOR TODAY: "I Love To Tell The Story"

Have you ever been so excited about something that you just couldn't wait to tell someone? Isn't that a great feeling when you find a person with whom you can share?

In his book, *Fresh Bait for Fishers of Men,* Louis Albert Banks writes about something that clearly illustrates what it means to obey God. On one occasion while Sir Henry Brackenbury was a military attache in Paris, he was talking with the distinguished statesman Gambetta, who said to him, "In these days there are only two things a soldier needs to know. He must know how to march, and he must know how to shoot!" The Englishman quickly responded, "I beg your pardon, Excellency, but you have forgotten the most important thing of all!" "What's that?" asked the Frenchman. Brackenbury replied, "He must know how to obey."

Christ asked us to go into all the world and tell others about Him. We must not only know the facts from the Bible and live the Christian life ourselves, but we also must obey Him and share the gospel with every person we possibly can. This news is too good to keep to ourselves. Let's truly sing, "I love to tell the story."

PRAYER THOUGHTS: Lord Jesus, give me the courage to tell others about You and Your holy Word. I thank You for those who taught me the truth, and I rejoice that I am Your child. In Jesus' name, amen.

LIVING A LIFE THAT HONORS GOD

SCRIPTURE: Philippians 1:19-30

VERSE FOR TODAY: As a prisoner for the Lord, then, I urge you to live a life worthy of the calling you have received (Ephesians 4:1, *New International Version*).

HYMN FOR TODAY: "Living For Jesus"

How often have we heard a parent say to a child, "Why did you do that? You know better than that!" Parents are concerned about their children doing the right things and being good people. God also is concerned that we live good Christian lives.

A young janitor was hired to sweep the floors of a large bank. One day he found a roll of bills buried beneath some wastepaper under a table. No one had mentioned the loss, so he was greatly tempted to keep the money. He took it home at the noon hour, telling himself he would not use it selfishly but would give his mother a well-needed vacation. His Christian training soon prevailed, however, and he experienced some sharp pangs of guilt. Breathing a prayer for strength, he returned to the bank, placed the currency on the desk of the president, and explained how he had obtained it. The executive looked up in surprise and asked, "Why did you bring the money back?" The young man replied, "Sir, the Bible says we must be honest at all times. Besides, I just wouldn't be comfortable living with a thief!" The janitor went home with a spring in his step and a smile on his face. He knew that what he had done had honored the Lord and was a testimony to his faith.

PRAYER THOUGHTS: O Lord, we desire to do those things that are right in Your sight. May we live the kind of lives to make You proud of us as our Heavenly Father. We pray in the wonderful name of Jesus, amen.

CARING ABOUT OTHERS

SCRIPTURE: 2 Corinthians 1:3-11

VERSE FOR TODAY: And do not forget to do good and to share with others, for with such sacrifices God is pleased (Hebrews 13:16, *New International Version*).

HYMN FOR TODAY: "Pass It On"

Everyone needs a friend who cares. When Lou Little coached football at Georgetown University in Washington, D.C., he had on his squad a player of average ability who rarely got into the game. The coach noticed this player often walking arm-in-arm with his dad on campus. A few days before the big game with Fordham, the boy's mother called the coach and said her husband died that morning of a heart attack. "Will you break the news to my son?" she asked. "He'll take it better from you." The student went home with a heavy heart that afternoon, but three days later he was back. "Coach," he pleaded, "will you start me in the game against Fordham? I think it's what my father would have liked most." After a moment's hesitation, the coach said, "Okay, but only for a play or two." True to his word, he put the boy in—but he never took him out. For sixty action-packed minutes, that inspired youngster ran, blocked, and passed like an all-American. After the game the coach praised him. "Son, you were terrific! You've never played like that before. What got into you?"

"Remember how my father and I used to go arm-in-arm?" he replied. "Well, few people knew it, but he was blind. I like to think that today was the first time he ever saw me play!"

That boy cared about his father. Do we care about others?

PRAYER THOUGHTS: Our loving Heavenly Father, we thank You for caring about us. Help us to be caring. In Jesus' name, amen.

WE ARE GOD'S ANOINTED

SCRIPTURE: 2 Corinthians 1:12-22

VERSE FOR TODAY: But you have an anointing from the Holy One, and all of you know the truth (1 John 2:20, *New International Version*).

HYMN FOR TODAY: "Higher Ground"

Our hymn for today says, "I'm pressing on the upward way, New heights I'm gaining ev'ry day." As God's anointed people, we must always strive to become more like Him every day.

Recently I read about two men who worked on a large oceangoing vessel. One day the mate, who normally did not drink, became intoxicated. The captain, who did not like him, entered in the daily log: "Mate drunk today." He knew this was his first offense, but he wanted to get him fired. The mate was aware of his evil desire and begged him to change the record. The captain, however, replied, "It's a fact, and into the log it goes!" A few days later the mate was keeping the log, and concluded it with: "Captain sober today." Realizing the implications of this statement, the captain asked that it be removed. In reply the mate said, "It's a fact, and into the log it goes!"

As God's anointed, we must be truthful and kind but never do things intentionally to hurt other people. Our main goal is to realize that we belong to God and everything we do reflects upon Him.

PRAYER THOUGHTS: Heavenly Father, I will always be grateful th
You want me to be Your child. The greatest desire of my life is to se
You and do whatever You want me to do. I pray that many people wil
low You and accept You as their God. In Jesus' name, amen.

June 5

CHRIST WANTS US TO BE SUCCESSFUL

SCRIPTURE: 2 Corinthians 2:12-17

VERSE FOR TODAY: I can do everything through him who gives me strength (Philippians 4:13, *New International Version*).

HYMN FOR TODAY: "Victory in Jesus"

Do you have a personal desire for Jesus Christ to live in your heart and control everything about your life? The only success that is really important is where Christ leads. We don't want our lives to bring shame to Christ.

Recently I read about an incident that happened in 1775. The manager of Baltimore's largest hotel refused lodging to a man dressed like a farmer, because he thought this fellow's lowly appearance would discredit his inn. So the man left and took a room elsewhere. Later, the innkeeper discovered that he had turned away none other than the Vice-President of the United States, Thomas Jefferson! Immediately he sent a note to Mr. Jefferson asking him to return and be his guest. Jefferson replied: "Tell him I have already engaged a room. I value his good intentions highly, but if he has no place for a dirty American farmer, he has none for the Vice-President of the United States."

We often push the Lord aside in our lives because we want to look good in the eyes of the world. It's more important what God thinks of us than what others think. Always desire to be ͜ful and do your very best, but only in the way that

TS: Almighty God, there are times in my life when I
ower over me. Help me to keep my eyes centered on
ire the kind of success where He leads me. In the pow-
s, amen.

WE SERVE A WONDERFUL SAVIOR

SCRIPTURE: 2 Corinthians 4:1-6

VERSE FOR TODAY: Whoever serves me must follow me; and where I am, my servant also will be. My Father will honor the one who serves me (John 12:26, *New International Version*).

HYMN FOR TODAY: "The Longer I Serve Him"

One of the definitions the dictionary gives to the word "serve" is "to work for." We ought to think of the things we do in life as working for the Lord.

A friend of mine was telling me that when he was a boy, he lived next door to a kind old gentleman who did everything with skillful precision. After school one day, my friend stood watching him put the finishing touches on his carpentry work. Turning to him with a smile, the old gentleman said, "Perhaps you think I'm spending more time on this than necessary. Some might say, 'Who will know how well the house is put together once the walls are plastered and everything is covered up?' Shoddy work, however, reveals itself over the years; therefore, speed must always play second fiddle to quality. My boy, years from now when I am gone and people examine what I'm building today, no one will ask, 'How long did it take him?' But many will probably inquire, 'Who did this?' If you learn nothing else from me, remember, always do your best!" My friend said he had never forgotten those words.

We are serving a wonderful Savior, and we must always do our best for Him!

PRAYER THOUGHTS: Dear God and Creator of life, I'm thankful to be Your servant. Help me to not complain about life but look at the blessings and opportunities it holds for me. When I'm tempted to not do my best, may I remember that Jesus gave His best for me. In His name, amen.

MIRRORING JESUS' LIFE

SCRIPTURE: 1 Peter 2:18-25

VERSE FOR TODAY: To this you were called, because Christ suffered for you, leaving you an example, that you should follow in his steps (1 Peter 2:21, New International Version).

HYMN FOR TODAY: "O To Be Like Thee, Blessed Redeemer"

God has called us to salvation and to reflect the image of Christ in our lives. Our lives are to mirror the life of Jesus.

The Greek word used for *example* means "writing under." It was a writing copy which was used for children. It served as a writing exercise and a means of teaching values. The idea was for the child to reproduce the writing copy. The apostle Peter easily changes from this idea to that of "following in His steps." Just as the disciples could have literally walked in the footprints Jesus left in the sands of Palestine, all believers are to figuratively follow in His steps daily.

Jesus is our example and model for every aspect of life. He was sinless and free of all deceit. He bore the injustices that were heaped upon Him, especially in connection with His trials and crucifixion, without becoming retaliatory or vindictive. He showed compassion, concern, and forgiveness as He gave His life in our behalf. He is our Savior.

By being our Savior, Jesus frees us from our sins and gives us new life that we may "mirror the life of Jesus."

PRAYER THOUGHTS: Heavenly Father, thank You for calling us to be followers of Jesus. May our lives duplicate His example, and may we emulate His Spirit. In Jesus' name, amen.

June 7-13. **Merle Melton** ministers with the University Christian Church in Coralville, Iowa. He and his wife, Martha, make their home in Iowa City, Iowa.

LIGHTS IN THE WORLD

SCRIPTURE: Philippians 2:12-18

VERSE FOR TODAY: "You are the light of the world. Let your light shine before men, that they may see your good deeds and praise your Father in heaven" (Matthew 5:14, 16, *New International Version*).

HYMN FOR TODAY: "Make Me a Blessing"

God placed the sun, moon, and stars in the expanse of the sky to give light on the earth. The sun, moon, and stars are called lights or luminaries. Paul uses the same word in Philippians 2:15 to describe the nature and effective influence of the lives of Christians.

The apostle Paul uses contrasts as a means of expressing truths. Christians are luminaries in the world. The world is crooked, depraved, and is in darkness. Christians are to be blameless and pure. Our lives are to be straight in the midst of a warped, twisted, and distorted generation.

The purpose for living this quality of life is to have an influence upon others, and, by our example, show them the way to life in Christ.

The apostle Paul presents the Christian life quite differently from today's accepted view. Our emphasis is upon "my" salvation and how it benefits "me." Paul teaches "my salvation" as a means to bring Christ to others. We are to hold forth the Word of life, which is life-giving, life-sustaining, and life-eternal. When we so live, we fulfill the function of "lights in the world."

PRAYER THOUGHTS: Heavenly Father, today is mine to live for You. May I not use this day selfishly or to follow worldly pursuits. May I live today for Your honor and to Your glory. May my life influence the lives of others for You. In Jesus' name, amen.

TRUE FELLOW WORKERS

SCRIPTURE: Philippians 2:19-30

VERSE FOR TODAY: I am sending to you Timothy, my son whom I love, who is faithful in the Lord. He will remind you of my way of life in Christ Jesus, which agrees with what I teach everywhere in every church (1 Corinthians 4:17, *New International Version*).

HYMN FOR TODAY: "I Want to Be a Worker For the Lord"

The apostle Paul, Timothy, and Epaphroditus were fellow workers in establishing the church in Philippi. They were bound by mutual love, concerns, and goals. Paul was the leader, and Paul's co-workers accepted his leadership. The qualities exhibited by these prominent workers demonstrate the nature of a healthy, productive, and cooperative relationship.

Paul recognized the intrinsic qualities possessed by each of his fellow workers and acknowledged their commendable labors. In this non-threatening environment, competition was absent, and mutual concern prevailed.

After commending Timothy, Paul proceeds to write regarding Epaphroditus, "My brother, fellow worker and fellow soldier, who is also your messenger, whom you sent to take care of my needs" (Philippians 2:25, *New International Version*). "My brother, fellow worker and fellow soldier," is the epitome of commendation.

The example of these laborers should help us to see the benefit of having mutual respect, giving honest praise, accepting directives from our leaders, and working cooperatively in the church of Jesus Christ.

PRAYER THOUGHTS: Father in Heaven, thank You for salvation. May our work be to Your honor. In Jesus' name, amen.

JESUS RESTORES HARMONY

SCRIPTURE: 2 Corinthians 5:16-21

VERSE FOR TODAY: For he himself is our peace, who has made the two one and has destroyed the barrier, the dividing wall of hostility (Ephesians 2:14, *New International Version*).

HYMN FOR TODAY: "To God Be the Glory"

Prior to the apostle Paul's conversion, he knew Christ as the ringleader of a sect and the opponent of true religion. He now sees Christ as the universal Messiah redeeming and restoring obedient believers to the Father. Jesus restores harmony. Harmony expresses peace, accord, and oneness.

The apostle Paul states that, "God was reconciling the world to himself in Christ" (2 Corinthians 5:19, *New International Version*). Reconciliation stresses a barrier to be removed, enmity to be destroyed, and harmony to be restored.

In the vertical relationship, sinners are reconciled to God in Jesus Christ through His blood. This brings to the sinner forgiveness and restoration to the favor of God. He is at peace with God and is in a harmonious relationship with Him.

The second aspect of reconciliation is the horizontal. In the horizontal relationship, Christ is the center. The closer that we come to the center, the closer we come to each other. Harmony is in Christ. This is true vertically and horizontally. The parable of the prodigal son teaches that the father is grieved over both sons, the profligate son and the irreconcilable son and brother. Let's work and pray for the restoring of harmony both vertically and horizontally.

PRAYER THOUGHTS: Father, help us to bring the unsaved to You. Father, help us to restore harmony in the body of Christ. May we be peacemakers. In Jesus' name. Amen.

EXAMINE YOURSELVES

SCRIPTURE: 2 Corinthians 13:5-14

VERSE FOR TODAY: Examine yourselves to see whether you are in the faith; test yourselves. Do you not realize that Christ Jesus is in you—unless, of course, you fail the test? (2 Corinthians 13:5, *New International Version*).

HYMN FOR TODAY: "Search Me, O God"

There is wisdom in physical, dental and visual examinations. We should also realize the importance of a spiritual examination.

Christians have no reason to fear spiritual self-examinations. We are in Christ.

Self-examination accomplishes several positive things. It points out what we are doing right, what we are doing wrong, and qualities that need strengthening or improving.

The areas of self-examination are the spiritual, social, and attitudinal. In regard to the spiritual self: Are we submissive to God's will? Are our lives characterized by purity? Do we delight in the things of God?

Examining the social self: Do we practice and promote fair-mindedness, understanding, harmony, and cooperation?

Testing the attitudinal self: Are we free of harsh, and unjust motives? Are we governed by love, kindness, and forgiveness?

Allow the apostle Paul to speak to us: "Aim for perfection, listen to my appeal, be of one mind, live in peace. And the God of love and peace will be with you" (2 Corinthians 13:11, *New International Version*).

PRAYER THOUGHTS: Father, may we be sincere in our faith. May we have as our goal to be complete in Christ, to be of one mind, and to live in peace. In Jesus' name, amen.

FREE IN THE SPIRIT

SCRIPTURE: Galatians 5:13-25

VERSE FOR TODAY: If we are now living by the Holy Spirit's power, let us follow the Holy Spirit's leading in every part of our lives (Galatians 5:25, *Life Application Bible*).

HYMN FOR TODAY: "Father, I Adore You"

Freedom in Christ is a priceless blessing. Freedom is so often misunderstood, misused, and abused. Freedom does not mean unrestrained liberty. This principle is enunciated by the apostle Paul in Galatians 5:13.

Being free does not mean that we may use our freedom to destroy the character of another person. Rather, we are to love our neighbor as ourselves.

Being free in Christ does not mean that we can escape the conflict that goes on between the sinful nature and the Spirit's will. But the victory is in being under grace and not under law. Under grace the Spirit enables us to be victors, but He does not remove the conflict.

Freedom does not mean that we may practice the acts of the sinful nature. Read Galatians 5:21. The warning of this verse is sufficient reason not to participate in the sordid deeds of the flesh. A study of the root meanings of these sins reveals a striking similarity to our day.

We are to exercise our freedom in Christ to bear the fruits of the Spirit in a full, meaningful, worthwhile life. Our destiny is eternal life.

PRAYER THOUGHTS: Heavenly Father, You have created us and You know all about us. You know of the struggles we have with the flesh. Father, help us to accept and trust Your Word, crucify the flesh with its desires and be led by your Spirit. In Jesus' name, amen.

"LOVE ME"

SCRIPTURE: John 14:12-17

VERSE FOR TODAY: "A new command I give you: Love one another. As I have loved you, so you must love one another" (John 13:34, *New International Version*).

HYMN FOR TODAY: "Pass It On"

These two words say it all. Love is the essence of Christianity and of all acceptable obedience. Love draws and welds us to Him.

The love of which Jesus speaks is one of understanding, comprehension, and corresponding purpose. This is the quality of love that the Father had for the world.

Jesus gives the instruction of our text upon the eve of His death. He is saying, "If ye love me, keep my commandments." We are to obey, protect, and guard the instructions He has given. We are to keep, guard, and protect them as a sacred trust.

We are promised that we will do greater works than He. This does not mean that we will do something greater than raise the dead, which He did. The greater works are proclaiming the completed gospel, taking the gospel into all the world, and being used by God to effect conversions. These are the greater works.

Since we love Him, the promise of John 14:14 is ours. Anything we ask of Him, in keeping with His will, He will grant unto us.

Let us love Him who first loved us.

PRAYER THOUGHTS: Our Heavenly Father, Your love for us is so far beyond our comprehension. We cannot fathom the greatness of Your love. May we love You with our total being. May our love be sacrificial. May we have a burning desire to reach the unsaved and to edify the saints. In Jesus' name, amen.

KNOWING CHRIST IS THE BOTTOM LINE

SCRIPTURE: Philippians 3:1-11

VERSE FOR TODAY: But whatever was to my profit I now consider loss for the sake of Christ (Philippians 3:7, *New International Version*).

HYMN FOR TODAY: "Jesus Is All the World to Me"

Life is filled with opportunities where decisions must be made, where choices require deliberation, where a personal jury demands a verdict. We must examine carefully the pros and cons, the good and the bad, the alternatives.

Faith is an affirmative judgment based on evidence. We become a Christian when we have carefully considered the facts involved in the life, death, and resurrection of Jesus. On the basis of that evidence we make a positive decision that He is who He said He was, the Son of God and the Savior of the world.

Once that decision is made, then we must stake our lives on that choice. If Christ Jesus merits our loyalty then we must be loyal. If He deserves our love then we must love Him. If He has earned our trust then we must trust Him.

In Christ we have everything to gain. In Him we find a friend and companion. In Him we possess the power of His resurrection and our hope is fulfilled. In Him we have the fellowship of His suffering, for we know that to die is gain. What more do we need?

PRAYER THOUGHTS: Dear Lord and Savior of mankind, forgive our foolish ways. Accept our thanks for the joy that is ours in possessing Christ our Lord, in whose name we pray. Amen.

June 14-20. **Dan Lawson** is Director of Development at Emmanuel School of Religion in Johnson City, Tennessee. He and his wife, Linda, have two children.

June 15

MY HOME IS IN HEAVEN

SCRIPTURE: Philippians 3:12-16

VERSE FOR TODAY: But seek first his kingdom and his righteousness, and all these things shall be yours as well (Matthew 6:33, *Revised Standard Version*).

HYMN FOR TODAY: "I've Got a Home in Glory Land"

Several years ago I went to visit a lady from our congregation who was in the hospital. She had been ill for several weeks, and I thought that she was probably on the mend and ready to go back home. It was always my practice in hospital calling to be positive about life. A happy smile was the least I could offer.

It always seemed better to turn a hospital patient's thoughts to any good word concerning their condition. Therefore I always asked, "What's the good news?" As I visited this lady, I asked, "What's the good news?" She responded, "I'm going home!" *Well*, I thought, *that's great.* She had been at the hospital long enough. She could sleep in her own bed. Eat around her own dining table, and enjoy the familiar noises from her own family.

She began to describe home in the best of glowing terms, as I would have expected. But then with a smile on her face and a tiny tear in her eye, she said, "I am looking forward to being with my father." That caught my attention, because her father was no longer living. I responded, "You don't mean home, home, do you?" She responded with an obvious glow sparked only by Heaven, "Oh, no, I'm going to be with my Father in Heaven."

PRAYER THOUGHTS: Dear Lord, we look forward to being with You, eternal in the Heavens, made possible through Jesus our Savior. Amen.

FROM EARTH TO HEAVEN

SCRIPTURE: Philippians 3:17-21

VERSE FOR TODAY: For the trumpet will sound, and the dead will be raised imperishable, and we shall be changed (1 Corinthians 15:52, *Revised Standard Version*).

HYMN FOR TODAY: "Higher Ground"

Change is not easy! We get accustomed to our ways and do not look kindly to our patterns and places being altered. Especially when one has lived in the same place all his life, change is not viewed through grateful eyes.

Throughout the generations we develop customs. Many of those traditions have special meaning that can be appreciated only through history. Among the most difficult of changes is the moment required to move elderly persons from the homestead where they have lived for 75 years, where all of their children were born, and where the grandchildren like to play on holidays. That change is not easy for any of the generations involved, for it seems to tamper with history and memories.

Sometimes we fear change. We do not like to experience changes in our body. When our waistline expands from thin to wide, when our eyesight weakens from clear to fuzzy, when our health changes from good to bad, then change is feared.

The Savior will change us, and the change will be good. He will change all that is weak to become like His Heavenly power. He will change our place from the limitation of earth to the wide expanse of Heaven. He will change us from the years of old to the eternity of youth.

PRAYER THOUGHTS: O Creator of the beginning and Father of our hope, we look forward to that change that shall come in the twinkling of an eye, that will enable us to be with You. Amen.

YOUR GIFTS FOR SERVING OTHERS

SCRIPTURE: Romans 12:1-8

VERSE FOR TODAY: Until I come, devote yourself to the public reading of Scripture, to preaching and to teaching. Do not neglect your gift (1 Timothy 4:13, 14, *New International Version*).

HYMN FOR TODAY: "There Is Joy in Serving Jesus"

Christ taught us through parables. In the parable of the talents (Matthew 25), a master gave three servants differing amounts of talents or money, and then he went on a journey. Upon his return, he called his servants to account for what he had entrusted into their care. The first two servants had succeeded in investing their talents.

The third servant in the story holds an interesting lesson for us. The servant said to the master, "I was afraid, and went and hid thy talent in the earth" (Matthew 25:25). Why did the third servant not use his talent? Why do we not use our gifts and talent to serve the Lord?

Our fears cause us to reject God's call to do His work. Often our fears can simply paralyze us. We fear what others are saying; we fear having to move where God is calling us to serve; we fear the unknown territory; we fear darkness; we fear being alone and serving alone; we fear failure.

King David, who wasn't afraid to take on the giant Goliath, wrote in the Psalms, "The Lord is my light and my salvation; whom shall I fear?" (Psalm 27:1).

PRAYER THOUGHTS: O Lord, You are our light and our salvation; whom shall we fear? You are the stronghold of our lives; of whom shall we be afraid? Take away our fear of serving You. In Jesus' name, amen.

ACTIONS SPEAK LOUDER THAN WORDS

SCRIPTURE: Romans 12:9-20

VERSE FOR TODAY: Don't let anyone look down on you because you are young, but set an example for the believers in speech, in life, in love, in faith and in purity (1 Timothy 4:12, *New International Version*).

HYMN FOR TODAY: "Living for Jesus"

As very young children, we played games such as "Follow the Leader" and "Simon Says." We are most familiar with the pressure to conform to our peers. The names of "Guess" and "Nike" are important terms on the school campus.

When I was 10 years old, a college boy came to my church to be our summer youth minister. I idolized that young minister. I thought, *When I grow up, I want to be just like him.* Younger children look up to older youth.

When Christ Jesus preached his "Sermon on the Mount," He said, "You are the light of the world. Let your light shine before men, that they may see your good deeds and praise your Father in heaven" (Matthew 5:14, 16, *New International Version*).

Our good deeds are meant to draw attention, not to ourselves, but to God. Christianity is something which is meant to be seen.

We must be sure that our light is seen not only at the door of the church, but even more so in the ordinary activities of each day. We must live and move and have our total being in the Christ. That kind of life should be easily seen by those about us. May God receive the glory for the life we exhibit.

PRAYER THOUGHTS: Dear Master, may the lives we live day in and day out point those with whom we come in contact to You. May others see You living within us today. In Jesus' name, amen.

LOVE ONE ANOTHER . . . BEAR BURDENS

SCRIPTURE: Galatians 6:1-5

VERSE FOR TODAY: This I command you, to love one another (John 15:17, *Revised Standard Version*).

HYMN FOR TODAY: "Is Your Burden Heavy?"

The word "burden" describes an object that is heavy and oppressive. When we face a burdensome problem such as a death in the family, a devastating financial situation, a teenage runaway, a divorce, or a job loss, we must not be too proud to allow others to help us carry the burden.

On the other hand, we must be sensitive to others and be there to help when they have a burden. The way life usually goes, each of us will have a few times when others must help us with the difficult situations of life. But there are times when we are free enough from our own burdens, and in those times we must help those who are under heavy pressure.

Paul seems to make a contradiction in Galatians 6:5. He says "For each should carry his own load" (*New International Version*). Here the word "load" is different than "burden." It simply means an object that is to be carried. We all have responsibilities that we are expected to carry. We shop for our own groceries; we do our own homework; we earn a living; we devote ourselves to our children. We are capable under normal circumstances to do these things for ourselves.

But for that which is truly our brother's burden, we are to express our love by bearing his burden. This fulfills the law of Christ to "love one another."

PRAYER THOUGHTS: Dear Lord, thank You for carrying our burden of sin to the cross. May our love for You cause us to bear the burdens of those about us. In Jesus' name, amen.

LOVE IN THE CHURCH

SCRIPTURE: Galatians 6:6-10

VERSE FOR TODAY: Therefore, as we have opportunity, let us do good to all people, especially to those who belong to the family of believers (Galatians 6:10, *New International Version*).

HYMN FOR TODAY: "In Heavenly Love Abiding"

In the church family we do experience tensions and conflicts. We have different opinions; we come from different backgrounds; we are aimed toward differing goals and we have different strengths and weaknesses.

This tension can cause us to react and do evil instead of good. We can gossip; we can say hateful things; we can give the silent treatment and ignore; we can openly oppose and try to destroy; we can keep one out of our group or clique; we can use others for self gain; we can be angry. Paul says that those who do such things shall not inherit the kingdom of God.

Instead, let us do good as we have opportunity. In fact, let us make opportunities for doing good to our family in Christ.

Where there is gossip, let us sow words of kindness. Where there is hate, let us sow love. Where there is a silent wall of exclusion, let us have open arms. Where there is destruction, let us sow edification. Where there is evil silence, let us be aggressive to speak to a brother. Where there is self-gain, may God receive the glory. For the fruit of the Spirit is love, joy, peace, patience, kindness, goodness, gentleness, faithfulness, and self-control.

PRAYER THOUGHTS: Dear Lord, forgive us when we as Christians in the church do more evil than good toward people. Forgive us when we act like people who do not believe in You. Please be patient with us, Lord. Use us today to sow good seeds expressing Your love in the world. Amen.

MY FATHER'S WORLD

SCRIPTURE: Psalm 33:1-12

VERSE FOR TODAY: Blessed is the nation whose God is the Lord (Psalm 33:12).

HYMN FOR TODAY: "This Is My Father's World"

Long ago I built a house. It was a little house, but I was proud because I made it with my own hands—and some tools, of course.

I meant to build some cabinets in the kitchen and bookshelves in the living room, but I never did. I meant to paint the outside, too, but I didn't even do that. I got a job in another town, so we moved away and left the house unfinished.

Aren't you glad God finished the job when He built this great big, beautiful, wonderful world? He had other jobs, too—the sun and moon and millions of stars. But He built the earth just right, with high mountain peaks and low places for the oceans. He planted fruit trees, wheat for our bread, and beautiful flowers. He made fish and birds and animals. And when the wonderful world was done, He gave it to us to enjoy.

David was so glad that he sang a song to the Lord. He said everybody ought to praise God because He made the world and still rules it. David's song is not so singable in our language as it was in his, but we do have songs we can sing. One of them is "This Is My Father's World."

PRAYER THOUGHTS: Let your mind dwell on the part of the world that you know best. Think of several things that are useful and several that are beautiful. Thank God for them, one by one. Ask God to help you use them as He intended them to be used.

June 21-27. **Orrin Root** is a former editor at Standard Publishing Company. He resides in Cincinnati, Ohio, where he enjoys gardening and writing.

GOD RULES

SCRIPTURE: Psalm 96

VERSE FOR TODAY: Say among the nations, "The Lord reigns" (Psalm 96:10, *New International Version*).

HYMN FOR TODAY: "O Worship the King"

Tim thought he was pretty smart when he smuggled some beer into a party and shared it with a few friends. Later they saw a neat convertible in a driveway and decided to go for a ride. Tim knew how to start it without a key, but he didn't know how to stop it quickly when it went off the road. Now Tim is in jail for drunken driving as well as theft. It is a strong reminder that we have a government, and laws are to be obeyed.

There are no policemen whose badges read "Kingdom of God," and so some people forget that God is in charge and His rules are to be obeyed. He puts us on our honor, letting us choose to obey or disobey, and dishonorable people ignore His rules. They think it is smart to do as they please.

But God does rule. At the proper time "he shall judge the world with righteousness" (Psalm 96:13). Then everyone will know that the wise thing to do is to live by His rules, to love your neighbor as yourself, to be unselfish, kind, and helpful. The wise people are those who learn this and do it before Judgment Day. They are also the happiest people in the world.

PRAYER THOUGHTS: Thank God for the people who help us do right—parents, teachers, policemen. Thank Him for the Bible that tells about His rules. Promise to study the Bible carefully, and ask God to help you understand it and live by its rules.

GOD PROVIDES

SCRIPTURE: Psalm 104:24-35
VERSE FOR TODAY: I will be glad in the Lord (Psalm 104:34).
HYMN FOR TODAY: "Trust in the Lord"

How many living things are there in the sea? A hundred ton whale eats plankton, creatures so tiny that we can't see them without a microscope. How many of them does he need? And the zooplankton eat phytoplankton, microscopic plants that float in the sea.

The song we are reading says the sea creatures are innumerable. We can't even count the whales, and certainly we can't count the plankton that we can't see. But God can. He knows how many plankton it takes to feed a whale, and how many bugs it takes to feed a bird. He provides food for all those creatures, and for us too.

God provides our food, but He doesn't feed it to us with a spoon. The song says the animals gather what God provides for them. So do we. Some of us gather food from a garden. More of us gather it from a grocery store, and work five days a week to get the money to pay for it. But still God provides it. Not one cabbage would grow without His soil and sunshine. The song ends with a very good idea: "Praise ye the Lord." We praise Him in our songs and prayers; we praise Him by living as His Word teaches us to live.

PRAYER THOUGHTS: Thank God for the foods you like best. Thank Him for foods that are good for you, even if you don't like them so well. Think of other things God provides—for your clothes, house, and furniture, your toys, tools, and books.

JESUS SAVES

SCRIPTURE: Psalm 118:19-29

VERSE FOR TODAY: O give thanks unto the Lord; for he is good (Psalm 118:29).

HYMN FOR TODAY: "A Shelter in the Time of Storm"

Gordon Davis was repairing the fence at the back of his farm when he saw the black funnel. He ran for the house, half a mile away, praying for the Lord to save him and his family. As he ran, he saw his wife gather the children and go to the storm cellar. She beckoned to him to hurry. He waved for her to go on into the cellar, and she did.

Then the tornado struck. Gordon lay flat on the ground. The wind took his hat and pulled at his clothes, but did not lift him. When it was over, he found that it had torn the roof from the house and put it firmly on the door of the storm cellar. If he had run fast enough to be inside with his family, none of them could have gotten out of that dark prison.

The Lord saves His people in a surprising way. Psalm 118 tells of a stone the builders would not use, yet it became the main cornerstone. That is a poetic prophecy of Jesus. The rulers of His country rejected Him, but God made Him the Savior of the world and the cornerstone of the church (Acts 4:1-12). "O give thanks unto the Lord; for he is good; for his mercy endureth for ever" (Psalm 118:29).

PRAYER THOUGHTS: Have you lost anything in a tornado or flood or earthquake? Thank God for what you have not lost, including your life. Thank Him especially for Jesus, who can save your life forever. Promise to do what Jesus wants you to do.

BLESSED ARE THE PEACEMAKERS

SCRIPTURE: Philippians 4:1-7

VERSE FOR TODAY: The peace of God, which passeth all understanding, shall keep your hearts and minds through Christ Jesus (Philippians 4:7).

HYMN FOR TODAY: "Dear Lord and Father of Mankind"

Agnes and her sister Lucy were the best of friends until their mother died. Then Lucy quickly had the precious cherry bedroom suite moved to her place. "Mom wanted me to have it," she said.

"Oh, no!" Agnes protested. "Mom said I should have it." The two quarreled bitterly, and now they haven't spoken to each other for 30 years.

We don't know what Euodias and Syntyche quarreled about, but Paul didn't want them to be enemies for 30 years. He urged them to make peace, and he urged other Christians to help them. Our Scripture mentions several things that can help to make peace. One is to "stand fast in the Lord," to put Him first. We know He wants us to be at peace with each other. Another is to "rejoice in the Lord." With all He has done for us, aren't we too happy to be quarreling? Then we ought to be known for "moderation" or gentleness. Quarreling doesn't fit with that. "Be careful for nothing" means don't be anxious and worried. If we ask God, He will give us what we need. Why should we worry about more than that? If we follow all this advice, we can rest in "the peace of God."

PRAYER THOUGHTS: Have you had a quarrel that you are ashamed of? Ask God to forgive you and help you make peace with the one you quarreled with. Thank Him for blessing the peacemakers, and ask Him to help you be one of them instead of one of the quarrelsome.

THINKING AND DOING

SCRIPTURE: Philippians 4:8-13

VERSE FOR TODAY: I can do all things through Christ which strengtheneth me (Philippians 4:13).

HYMN FOR TODAY: "Where He Leads I'll Follow"

What have you been thinking about today—or yesterday, if you are reading this early in the morning? Recall two or three specific things that have been on your mind. Are they the kinds of things that Paul advises us to think about? (Philippians 4:8).

Thinking leads to doing. If we think of good things, we are more likely to do good things—things such as Paul and other Christians teach and do. What have you been doing today, or yesterday?

Philippians 4:10 gives an example of a good thing to do. The Philippians had sent an offering to a good missionary, Paul. They could not send it earlier because Paul had been at sea and then on an isolated island for months (Acts 27:1—28:10).

Now Paul was under house arrest in Rome (Acts 28:16). He had to pay rent and buy groceries, and he welcomed the offering. Still he had no complaint before it came. The Lord gave him strength to get along without enough food and keep on with his preaching (Acts 28:30, 31).

Can we also learn to be happy doing our jobs and worshiping God even when we are short of money?

PRAYER THOUGHTS: Have you had a really beautiful thought today or yesterday? Thank God for it. Thank Him for all the fine and lovely things in His world. Think how you can help a missionary or someone else, and promise to do it.

June 27

ENOUGH FOR ALL

SCRIPTURE: Philippians 4:14-23

VERSE FOR TODAY: My God shall supply all your need according to his riches in glory by Christ Jesus (Philippians 4:19).

HYMN FOR TODAY: "Trust and Obey"

Most of us don't have money to burn. When we buy something, we want to be sure to get full value for every cent we spend. But we also know there are values that can't be measured in dollars and cents. That's why we do some giving as well as spending.

The Philippians sent an offering to Paul when he was a prisoner. They had sent him offerings before, just as we send offerings to missionaries. They got no merchandise for that money, and they got no refund. They were making a sacrifice, doing without some good things they could have bought. But Paul said the gift would be put to their account. By doing without some things on earth, they were gaining treasure in Heaven (Matthew 6:19-21). How much was that worth?

But that was not all. They did without some things, but Paul was sure God would give them all they really needed. God does that for us too, doesn't He? When we share with a missionary, or with someone whose house has burned, or with the starving, and homeless, we still have enough to live on, and treasure in Heaven besides. Isn't it wonderful?

PRAYER THOUGHTS: Talk with God about your money today. Thank Him for it and all the good things you can buy. Think about how much you have spent for yourself this week, and how much you have used to help others. Do you want to promise any changes?

TELLING THE TRUTH

SCRIPTURE: Colossians 1:1-8

VERSE FOR TODAY: Let the word of Christ dwell in you richly as you teach and admonish one another with all wisdom, and as you sing psalms, hymns and spiritual songs with gratitude in your hearts to God (Colossians 3:16, *New International Version*).

HYMN FOR TODAY: "More About Jesus Would I Know"

The Vietnam tragedy claimed many casualties. In recent years doctors have noted numerous cases of blind Cambodian women who have no physical reason for their condition. Theirs is a psychosomatic response to the horrors of war. Many of these women saw their families tortured and murdered before their eyes, and the suppressed pain they felt is the cause of their blindness.

For these innocent victims, hiding the truth became a means of survival. Unfortunately, it now seriously handicaps their lives and prevents them from enjoying life to its fullest.

Without the gospel of Christ, people are blind to the truth that frees them from sin. They search unsuccessfully for satisfaction, but never experience the peace that comes from a cleansed heart and a right relationship with God.

Today, you are God's representative to a lost and hurting world. Some individual shared God's Word with you. Before that, another individual shared the gospel with the one who reached out to you. This is the way the message of Jesus touches lives. Let's share the Lord freely.

PRAYER THOUGHTS: God, thank You for sending a messenger to tell me about Your Son. Help me to share this good news with others. Amen.

June 28-30. **Larry Jones** is Associate Minister with the First Christian Church in Clearwater, Florida. He and his wife, Jane, have two children, Nathan and Laura.

June 29

SECOND-ORDER CHANGE

SCRIPTURE: Colossians 1:9-13

VERSE FOR TODAY: For we are God's workmanship, created in Christ Jesus to do good works, which God prepared in advance for us to do (Ephesians 2:10, *New International Version*).

HYMN FOR TODAY: "Lord Jesus, I Long to be Perfectly Whole"

Psychologists sometimes speak of two orders of change. The first order really involves no change at all. This might be compared to a thermostat as it turns on and off to maintain a constant temperature. Slight variations in the atmosphere take place, but in the end, no change has occurred. Second-order change is different. If the temperature in a room is undesirable, the thermostat can be altered, creating permanent change.

Many organizations exist for the sole purpose of improving lives. Some help those suffering from chemical dependency. Others deal with all forms of codependency. Often, there will be an immediate change in life-style and behavior, but as time progresses, the old pattern returns. When success occurs, people learn new ways of coping with life's struggles and, in effect, experience a change of heart and mind.

A true conversion in Christ always involves change of the second order. The difference is seen in attitude and action. Jesus provides a perfect example and His commandments give clearly defined instructions for living. Beyond this, Christians are "strengthened with all power according to his glorious might" (Colossians 1:11, *New International Version*). Today, let God continue His renovation of your heart as you strive to reach your potential as His creation.

PRAYER THOUGHTS: Father, thank You for Your Word and the daily guidance it provides. Amen.

JESUS ABOVE ALL

SCRIPTURE: Colossians 1:14-20

VERSE FOR TODAY: Let us fix our eyes on Jesus, the author and per-fecter of our faith (Hebrews 12:2, *New International Version*).

HYMN FOR TODAY: "All Glory to Jesus, Begotten of God"

Not long ago, developers at Max Factor introduced a new line of "Invisible Cosmetics." The goal was to help a woman look as though she was not wearing any makeup. *Forbes* listed this invention in its yearly list of top-ten products. Customers praised the cosmetics because they were easy to use in touch-ing up, and if someone were in too big a hurry to put the makeup on, no one would know the difference.

God is invisible to mortal man, but He has never intended to go unnoticed. His creation bears witness to His glory, and His people praise Him for His greatness. He has been made most visible through His eternal Son who existed before all creation and holds absolute supremacy and power in the world.

When we serve Christ, Satan taxes our patience with unex-pected trials and temptations. He tries to distract us by focus-ing our attention on problems and unrealistic expectations of ourselves. In the midst of these distractions, our preeminent Savior reminds us of His place in all of creation. Because He holds all things together, we are certain to overcome any ob-stacle in life.

Today, free yourself from discouragement by remembering the authority of Christ, your Savior. No situation is too large or too complicated for Him to conquer.

PRAYER THOUGHTS: God, thank You for putting me above my prob-lems through Your Son. Teach me to turn to Him when my world over-whelms me. Amen.

My Prayer Notes

DEVOTIONS

JULY

July 1

COME SWEET DEATH

SCRIPTURE: Colossians 1:21-29

VERSE FOR TODAY: To them God has chosen to make known among the Gentiles the glorious riches of this mystery, which is Christ in you, the hope of glory (Colossians 1:27, *New International Version*).

HYMN FOR TODAY: "Faith Is the Victory!"

Come Sweet Death is the title of a small book in my library. It came out of the mid 60s when despair literature was taught in the schools and existentialism was the prevailing theological wind. This book reflects that mood by suggesting that death is to be preferred to boredom, unfairness, and the social tragedies of this life. What a sad view of our culture!

On the other hand, a friend of mine lost his father to cancer. His death came after a full lifetime of devoted ministry to Christ and the church. My friend, who himself was a minister, told me of the close, happy, Christian family in which he was reared.

When the doctors indicated nothing more could be done, they brought the elder statesman of God home where he could die in the presence of his family. The family gathered around the bedside to pray and sing hymns of victory and joy in the Lord as they often had done around the family piano. With a smile on his face, the ailing saint slipped away to be with the Lord even as the family sang a favorite hymn of victory. Christ was indeed his hope of glory!

PRAYER THOUGHTS: Jesus, my hope of glory, fill my life with joy each day, and may I ever anticipate going home to be with You forever. Amen.

July 1-4. J. **David Lang** is a minister and founding editor of the senior adult magazine, *Alive.* He and his wife, June, have four children.

LET'S GET TOGETHER

SCRIPTURE: Romans 5:6-11

VERSE FOR TODAY: You see, at just the right time, when we were still powerless, Christ died for the ungodly (Romans 5:6, *New International Version*).

HYMN FOR TODAY: "Wounded for Me"

Years ago an old "preacher story" made the rounds among evangelists who wanted an emotional tug to close their sermons. It went something like this:

A young man sought the pleasures of this life to the frustration and disgust of his father. Finally in anger and exasperation the father kicked his son out of the home and told him never to return. He never wanted to see him again. The boy's mother grieved until finally she became mortally ill. A family friend had kept in touch with the boy and wrote to him about his mother's terminal illness and that she wanted to see him before she died.

When the boy arrived at the hospital, he found his mother very weak and frail. In the hospital room, the father stood on one side of the bed with his back to the son who stood on the other. The mother took the hand of each man, and with her last strength pulled their hands together. With this final effort she died. The men fell across her bed and wept. Finally the father said, "To think, it took her death to bring us together." With that he embraced his son, and both wept tears of sadness and joy.

Indeed, we have been separated from our Heavenly Father. To think it took the death of His Son to bring us together!

PRAYER THOUGHTS: Thank You, Jesus, for bringing us back together with God. Let us live in Your presence. In Your name, amen.

"JUSTIFIED"

SCRIPTURE: Romans 5:12-16

VERSE FOR TODAY: The gift of God is not like the result of the one man's sin: The judgment followed one sin and brought condemnation, but the gift followed many trespasses and brought justification (Romans 5:16, *New International Version*).

HYMN FOR TODAY: "Redeemed"

Theological words mean little or nothing to most people. In fact, many are turned away from Christianity because Christians tend to talk in a kind of religious jargon. It sounds almost like a foreign language to those who don't understand.

"Justified" is one of those words. It simply means that a person is considered to be without sin or wrongdoing, even when he actually has sinned. Someone suggested to think of its meaning as "just as if I had not sinned." Not bad. Scholars might find fault with this definition, but it is generally accurate and easy to grasp.

When your son or daughter totals your new car, you say, "That's OK, you're forgiven;" then he or she is treated as if it didn't happen. That's justification. Or when a spouse is unfaithful, the innocent mate forgives and accepts the wayward partner back. That's justification—being made righteous as if the wrong had not occurred.

Of course, more is involved. The damage on the car must be paid. The sinful mate may have caused serious problems that neither mate can fully resolve. However, when Christ justifies us—makes us righteous—He has already paid the whole price with His death. Our debt is paid. We are justified.

PRAYER THOUGHTS: Dear Father, take away my sins as if they had not occurred. Remove them as far as the East is from the West as You promised. In the name of Jesus. Amen.

BIRTH OF FREEDOM

SCRIPTURE: Romans 5:17-21

VERSE FOR TODAY: For just as through the disobedience of the one man the many were made sinners, so also through the obedience of the one man the many will be made righteous (Romans 5:19, *New International Version*).

HYMN FOR TODAY: "Under His Wings"

Today is the birthday of the United States of America! Over 200 years ago this nation declared herself to be free from the tyranny of the mother country. It was like a new birth accompanied with the usual birth pangs and suffering.

Freedom did not come with built-in righteousness or sinless perfection. No nation on the face of the earth, past or present, had such significant founding principles. But we made mistakes. As the years passed, it seemed our nation forgot some of those principles. We learned the meaning of Romans 3:23: "All have sinned and fall short of the glory of God," (*New International Version*). This could refer to both the people and the nation. We thought of ourselves as pretty good, but righteousness can only come from God. He alone can declare us, or our nation, to be righteous.

When we sin (we have and we do), we are instructed to repent and turn to God (Acts 3:19) or "confess our sins" (1 John 1:9) in order to be forgiven. It can be true of our nation as it is personally. Jesus is the Righteous One. He is the Way, the Truth, and the Life. In Him is our freedom and our righteousness.

PRAYER THOUGHTS: O God, make our nation free and righteous in Your eyes. Forgive her sins as You forgive our personal sins. In the name of Jesus, I pray. Amen.

HIDDEN TREASURES

SCRIPTURE: Colossians 2:1-7

VERSE FOR TODAY: In whom are hidden all the treasures of wisdom and knowledge (Colossians 2:3, *New International Version*).

HYMN FOR TODAY: "Jesus Is All the World to Me"

A treasure is anything we hold or keep as precious. Children are noted for their treasures. I have had the grubby little hands of some of the most poverty-stricken children open to show me a "treasure." Often it was a pretty rock or other seemingly insignificant object picked up on the way to school and guarded carefully throughout the day. Some of my most cherished treasures are Christmas gifts given to me by these same children. They are precious because I know the sacrifice made by the families to provide the gifts.

Paul tells us in Colossians 2 that we have available to us treasures of such magnitude that they can combat all of today's problems. These mighty treasures of wisdom and knowledge required a far greater sacrifice than those of my gifts. These treasures were bought with the blood of Christ. They are hidden in Christ, but revealed to those who are joined to Him, drawing each day's direction from that union.

Whether we are faced with false doctrines as were the Colossians or with problems unique to our personal circumstances, Christ wants to guide us. His treasures can be ours if we seek them.

PRAYER THOUGHTS: Thank You, Father, for Your Word. Help us to cherish and use the treasures You have so graciously provided. Keep us rooted in Your Word, open to Your guidance, and always seeking Your will. In His name, amen.

July 5-11. **Dr. Martha Melton** is an administrator in public education. She and her husband, Merle, make their home in Iowa City, Iowa.

COMPLETE IN CHRIST

SCRIPTURE: Colossians 2:8-15

VERSE FOR TODAY: You have been given fullness in Christ, who is the head over every power and authority (Colossians 2:10, *New International Version*).

HYMN FOR TODAY: "A Mighty Fortress"

Today's world abounds with unbiblical philosophies, cults, and sects. Numbered among our friends and acquaintances in our university city are Hindus, Buddhists, Muslims, Bahais, people embracing various forms of Christian doctrines, as well as agnostics and atheists. Although this can be partly attributed to our jet age and modern world, Paul faced philosophies based on human ideas and experiences in the first century. His admonition to the Colossians was that the fullness of God lives in Christ and in Him they had everything. As Christians today, so do we. Our only purpose in investigating other religions should be to better equip ourselves for sharing Christ.

I am challenged and humbled as I observe my young Indian friend, Sonatina, sharing Christ with her Hindu friends. She is loving and kind, never denigrating their beliefs. Yet she takes advantage of every opportunity to speak of her love for Christ and how He has changed her life, and to include these friends in her Christian activities. She shares her faith in warmth and love, prays for them and trusts God for the rest.

We are complete in Christ, and like Sonatina, we need to lovingly share Him with others.

PRAYER THOUGHTS: Father, as we face the many false doctrines of today's world, help us to remain firm in the knowledge that You alone are the source of truth. May we never be tempted by contemporary philosophies that conflict with Your Word. In Jesus' name, amen.

FREEDOM FROM LEGALISM

SCRIPTURE: Colossians 2:16-23

VERSE FOR TODAY: These are a shadow of the things that were to come; the reality, however, is found in Christ (Colossians 2:17, *New International Version*).

HYMN FOR TODAY: "Buried with Christ"

The church has always been plagued with legalism. In the first century, it was Old Testament laws, holidays, and feasts being carried over into the church. Today it is often man-made rules and traditions that impede the work of Christ. Tenacious self-discipline, living by a strict moral code, or adhering to a set of exacting rules may make us feel righteous or appear righteous to others, but our salvation is dependent upon our life in Christ. To make our salvation dependent on self-discipline and rules limits the power of Christ in our lives.

Paul told the Colossian Christians that the Old Testament laws were only shadows of the real thing—Christ himself. When we unite ourselves with Christ, the Head of the body, He frees us from legalistic rules and invites us to a life of righteousness centered in Him. The changing of our thoughts and attitudes are a by-product of that relationship.

Although the exactness of legalism may be appealing, it cannot compare with acting in response to a loving God and living the Christian life as an ongoing process. May we enjoy our freedom in Christ.

PRAYER THOUGHTS: Thank You, Father, for freeing us from the legalism of the law. Father, it is so easy to be attracted to rules that seem to give us answers to our problems. Help us to realize that legalism today can keep us in bondage just as surely as the law kept the Colossians in bondage. In Jesus' name, amen.

FREE IN CHRIST

SCRIPTURE: Galatians 5:1-12

VERSE FOR TODAY: No longer as a slave, but better than a slave, as a dear brother. He is very dear to me but even dearer to you, both as a man and as a brother in the Lord (Philemon 16, *New International Version*).

HYMN FOR TODAY: "He Lifted Me"

In Belinda Hurmence's novel, *A Girl Called Boy*, Blanche Overtha Yancey (Boy), an 11-year-old pampered black girl, wants no part of any family traditions that associate her with her slave ancestors. Then she is mysteriously transported back in time to the 1850s and slavery. There she learns to appreciate her heritage and her freedom. As she returns to the 20th century, she pleads with her friends to come with her: "We can all be free. . . ."

This longing for freedom is innate within each of us. Even very young children assert themselves and non-verbally demand freedom. True freedom is responsible and balanced with respect. The birth of Christianity gave new importance to this concept. The very essence of Christianity, with its regard for the worth and dignity of each individual and its emphasis on a loving family relationship within the church, promotes freedom. Paul often uses slavery as an antithesis to illustrate our freedom in Christ. He tells us in Galatians that we are free in Christ—free from sin, free from the bondage of the law, and free to love and serve.

To quote the motto of a dear Christian friend, Leroy Trulock, "Isn't God wonderful?"

PRAYER THOUGHTS: Father, how grateful we are that You grant us true freedom—freedom to love and to serve in Your kingdom. We are grateful that You love us and accord worth and dignity to each of us regardless of our station in life. We praise You in Jesus' name, amen.

WE BELONG TO HIM

SCRIPTURE: 1 Corinthians 15:3-8

VERSE FOR TODAY: For we are God's workmanship, created in Christ Jesus to do good works, which God prepared in advance for us to do (Ephesians 2:10, *New International Version*).

HYMN FOR TODAY: "Now I Belong to Jesus"

Years ago I heard a minister tell a story that went something like this: A little boy designed and built a small sailboat. He constructed it with loving care. When it was finished, he took it down to the river for its first sail. The boat drifted away from him, and he was devastated. Sometime later in the little town where he lived, he saw the boat in a store window for sale. He collected all of his money, went to the store and purchased the boat. Then he said, "Little boat, you're mine, all mine. First I made you, then I bought you, and now you're mine!"

This describes our relationship with God, our Father. First, He created us in His own image. Then we alienated ourselves from Him by our transgressions. But God had already provided the sacrifice to buy us back through the blood of His Son. The Son had sealed our hope of eternal salvation by His resurrection from the dead, thus fulfilling Old Testament Scriptures.

As Christians, we have been created, bought with the blood of Christ, and then recreated in His likeness. Now we belong to Him.

PRAYER THOUGHTS: As a people purchased with a great price, we thank You for Jesus' death, burial, and resurrection. May our lives show forth to the world that we belong to Him, and that He is Lord of our lives. In the name of our Savior, amen.

GOD SPEAKS THROUGH HIS SON

SCRIPTURE: Hebrews 1:1-13

VERSE FOR TODAY: Therefore God exalted him to the highest place and gave him the name that is above every name (Philippians 2:9, *New International Version*).

HYMN FOR TODAY: "God Hath Spoken by His Prophets"

Jesus Christ is the glory of the person of God. His superiority is the theme of the book of Hebrews. He is superior to the angels. This one who is the glory of God is also the one who died to cleanse us and clear our record of all sin. He then sat down at the right hand of God the Father in the place of highest honor.

In the Old Testament era, God spoke to His people in many different ways—in visions (Isaiah), in dreams (Jacob), and personally (Abraham and Moses). In the New Testament era, He speaks through His Son. Not only is Jesus God's spokesman, He is the revelation of God.

The writer of Hebrews speaks of God's creative power as being the same power that clears our record of sin. Sometimes in an intimate moment with nature, when we view a breathtaking scene for the first time, the realization that we are a part of God's indescribable universe is overwhelming. The knowledge that this same power removes our sins, and that the source of that power is our Savior and high priest, makes us bow in humble gratitude and adoration.

PRAYER THOUGHTS: Thank You, Father, for speaking to us through Your Son. Thank You for His power, His glory, and His unchanging nature. Help us, Father, to keep our eyes focused on Him, because it is through Him that we come to know You. In the name of Your Son, amen.

THE PERFECT MEDIATOR

SCRIPTURE: Hebrews 7:23-28

VERSE FOR TODAY: My dear children, I write this to you so that you will not sin. But if anybody does sin, we have one who speaks to the Father in our defense—Jesus Christ, the Righteous One (1 John 2:1, *New International Version*).

HYMN FOR TODAY: "Come Every Soul"

The term mediator is a familiar one in today's society. It means someone who arbitrates between parties at variance. We find these mediators negotiating between groups, such as labor and management, and between individuals in various settings. These mediators have been professionally trained, but have not necessarily experienced the circumstances of the parties at variance.

The writer of Hebrews tells us that Jesus Christ is our mediator, intercessor, and high priest. Unlike the world's mediators, He has perfect understanding of our circumstances. When our transgressions put us at variance with the Father, Jesus Christ goes into His presence as the sinless one who has already paid the price for our forgiveness.

Our spiritual life is a practical one that is lived daily. Because we are human, we sin and constantly need our lives fine-tuned in order to reflect God's love. The more frequently we approach our mediator for this fine tuning, the more we are united in an intimate relationship with God. Christ makes it possible for us to live each day in the presence of the Father. We can then say with Paul, "Nothing can ever separate us from His love" (Romans 8:38, 39).

PRAYER THOUGHTS: Father, as we live in a covenant relationship with You, may we realize that we are never alone but that we live continuously in Your presence through our Savior and mediator, Jesus Christ. Help us to be totally joined to You through Your Son, in whose name we pray. Amen.

THROW OUT THE OLD

SCRIPTURE: Colossians 3:1-11

VERSE FOR TODAY: You have taken off your old self with its practices and have put on the new self (Colossians 3:9, *New International Version*).

HYMN FOR TODAY: "Take My Life and Let It Be"

I was looking over the clothes my children had outgrown. Although they were still in good shape, they were of no value now. These clothes did not fit the children's bigger bodies, and we had had to buy new clothes.

Paul tells us that, like clothes we have outgrown, we must put off some of the things we did before we became Christians. Paul wants us to "put on the new self" that is the Christian us.

Sometimes it is hard to give up old things that we have enjoyed. Even after we have died to the world through Christ, we cling to it and the things we liked about it. It is hard not to pass along the latest gossip or tell a good, but off-color, joke. It is hard not to use the four-letter words we hear all around us. It is hard not to go with the crowd to the places we used to enjoy. Yet these are the "old" that no longer fit us as Christians. These are the things we have put off like outgrown clothes.

We will still make mistakes and sin. But we also know that one of the "new" things we have put on in Christ is the certainty of His forgiveness when we humbly ask for it in a spirit of repentance.

PRAYER THOUGHTS: Please help me, Lord, to put off my old self so that I can serve You only with all my talents and abilities. Please forgive me when I fail, and thank You for dying for me. Amen.

July 12-18. **Betty Steele Everett** is a freelance writer who has authored numerous articles. She makes her home in Defiance, Ohio.

LOVE! LOVE! LOVE!

SCRIPTURE: Colossians 3:12-17

**VERSE FOR TODAY: We love because he first loved us (1 John 4:19,
New International Version).**

HYMN FOR TODAY: "Love Divine"

A Sunday-school teacher once described the perfect family.
"The parents love the children so much they will do anything
for them. They want only the best for them. The children love
each other too much to fight. They love their parents so much
they obey all rules without arguing, because they know the
parents would never make a rule that was not for their safety
and benefit."

One man laughed. "Sounds great! But how do I get my kids
to go along with it?"

The teacher shook his head. "I don't know. God's always
had the same problem with His children."

We laugh uneasily because we know that is true!

As God's children we have not loved Him or each other as
we should. We have been impatient, we have held grudges,
and we have wanted to be the "stars" of the church. We have
not greeted strangers with love, preferring to keep the group as
it is.

Love, Paul says, is the essential ingredient that binds all
other Christian virtues together in perfect unity. It is the one
thing necessary for happy families, growing churches, and effective Christians who can change the world around them.

**PRAYER THOUGHTS: I am sorry I have not loved You or those around
me as I should, dear Father. I will try harder to remember Your love for
me—and to copy it in my own life. In the name of Jesus. Amen.**

WHO ARE WE SERVING HERE?

SCRIPTURE: Colossians 3:18-25

VERSE FOR TODAY: Whatever you do, work at it with all your heart, as working for the Lord (Colossians 3:23, *New International Version*).

HYMN FOR TODAY: "My Jesus, I Love Thee"

A friend complained about the first words of today's Scripture. "Male chauvinism! No woman has to be 'submissive' to her husband!"

Her argument is not new, but it is not what Paul had in mind. Nor does verse 22 mean that God approved of slavery, as some slave owners argued in the 1800s. You have to read to the end of the chapter to understand what Paul is really saying.

Paul says it is not husbands, wives, parents, children, or even employers we are serving here each day. It is the Lord Jesus!

If we were speaking to Jesus instead of each other, would we shout and get angry? Would we bark out orders as we often do now? Would we demand our "rights" in every situation? Would we refuse to be "submissive?"

Or would we speak quietly and politely, deferring to Jesus and His wants and desires instead of our own? Would we be so happy to be with Him that our own ego would take a far back second place?

Paul knew that if Christians behaved in all their associations as though the actions were for Jesus, happy families and good relationships with those we work for and with would come easily and naturally.

PRAYER THOUGHTS: I want to remember it is You I am serving each day, Lord Jesus, but sometimes it is hard. Give me the ability to see You in all my relationships, and the strength to act accordingly. Amen.

MORE TIME FOR PRAYER

SCRIPTURE: Colossians 4:1-6

VERSE FOR TODAY: Devote yourselves to prayer, being watchful and thankful (Colossians 4:2, *New International Version*).

HYMN FOR TODAY: "Sweet Hour of Prayer"

I am a "link" on our church's "prayer chain." When a member or friend of the church is sick, faces family problems, or needs special prayer, that name is telephoned from one "link" to the next, so that many will soon be praying for that person.

This kind of prayer is good, but it still falls short of Paul's directions for Christians to "pray without ceasing" (1 Thessalonians 5:17).

Praying without ceasing is not easy. It may even seem impossible. But it is the goal for which we are to aim. We can be thankful by looking for things to thank the Lord for throughout the day. It can be a big thing, like a neighbor finally agreeing to go to church with us. It can be a small thing, like getting a telephone call from a friend.

We can be watchful for times to pray while doing dishes, walking, or jogging, riding the bus, or mowing the lawn.

We can use "signals" from the world around us to pray. Students can pray when class bells ring; we can pray when we hear an ambulance siren.

However we add to our prayer time, we will be working toward Paul's instructions to "devote" ourselves to prayer.

PRAYER THOUGHTS: Hear my prayers, O Lord—even the ones that are voiced quietly, privately, and quickly. Bless those who are also praying in Your name. Amen.

HANG IN THERE!

SCRIPTURE: Colossians 4:7-11

VERSE FOR TODAY: I am sending him to you . . . that he may encourage your hearts (Colossians 4:8, *New International Version*).

HYMN FOR TODAY: "For You I Am Praying"

A friend had written a book about her experiences as a Christian professional woman. She had confidently sent it to an editor who had seemed interested in publishing it. Then the manuscript came back. My friend was discouraged by the rejection, but even more so by the letter the editor wrote her.

The editor said she would tell my friend some things "in love." Then she went on to harshly criticize both the manuscript and my friend's Christian life.

We all have moments of discouragement. As Christians we know we have the Lord to lean on, but we also need encouragement from earthly friends to "hang in there!"

We can encourage Christian friends by praying with and for them. We can keep in close touch through visits, telephone calls, and letters. We can ask other Christians to help.

"Encouragement" is one of the gifts Paul lists in Romans 12. Some people are obviously better at it than others, but we can all do something to uplift our brothers and sisters in Jesus.

And if mistakes must be pointed out, we can do it gently and at a proper time without being critical of them as people or Christians.

PRAYER THOUGHTS: Show me, dear Father, which of my brothers and sisters needs special encouragement today. Lead me in saying and doing the right things to help them. In the name of Jesus. Amen.

GET TO WORK!

SCRIPTURE: Colossians 4:12-18

VERSE FOR TODAY: Tell Archippus: "See to it that you complete the work you have received in the Lord" (Colossians 4:17, *New International Version*).

HYMN FOR TODAY: "Work For the Night is Coming"

During the summer, my children would often ask, "What can I do now?" I could not understand their problem. I could see many activities and opportunities around them.

I sometimes wonder if God doesn't feel that way about us, His children. We live in a world, country, town, and even home that needs many things done for Him, yet we don't seem to see them.

The workers who were with Paul had no trouble finding God's will and doing it. Apparently, though, they did not all do the same work. One was always "wrestling in prayer" for the churches. Another held church meetings in her house. By asking that his letter be read to other churches as well, Paul laid the groundwork for a "networking" among the Christians of different churches.

What does God want you to do this week? It may be as ordinary as writing to a missionary. It could be something as obvious as helping in the Sunday church service or teaching Sunday school.

We will not all be doing the same kind of work for God, but we all have work to do. Paul's warning to Archippus applies to us, too!

PRAYER THOUGHTS: Lead me to the work You want me to do this week for You, O God. Please give me the strength to complete it as it should be done. In the name of Jesus. Amen.

WHAT'S YOUR GIFT?

SCRIPTURE: 1 Corinthians 12:1-11

VERSE FOR TODAY: Now to each one the manifestation of the Spirit is given for the common good (1 Corinthians 12:7, *New International Version*).

HYMN FOR TODAY: "Blest Be The Tie That Binds"

When I was a teen and we needed someone to pray in our youth group meeting, my brother was always called upon to pray. He seemed to have the gift of talking aloud to the Lord and telling Him what the group needed. Yet my brother was never asked to sing a solo! That would have been a disaster! He definitely did not have that gift!

It's easy to forget that every church member has some gift. It is easy to think only about those who do things that stand out—like praying, singing solos, or leading Bible studies.

It's harder to think of the woman who quietly takes a loaf of homemade bread to every new family, or the teenager who comes early to help set up chairs and layout songbooks as having "gifts."

Yet Paul assures us that the same Spirit gives all these gifts to whomever He chooses. We do not know why some people's gifts stand out more than others' do, but we do know that to God all gifts are of the same value because they were all given by His Spirit. Our job is to recognize our gift, then use it as best we can and not worry about whether it is the one the world considers "outstanding."

PRAYER THOUGHTS: Show me, Father, what my special gift from You is and how You want me to use it this week. Help me to be willing to use it, whether it is "great" or "small," for Your glory. In the name of Jesus. Amen.

THE MAN WITH A MUSTACHE

SCRIPTURE: Philemon 1-7

VERSE FOR TODAY: For we have great joy and consolation in thy love, because the bowels of the saints are refreshed by thee, brother (Philemon 7).

HYMN FOR TODAY: "Make Me A Blessing"

I waved as the gray van approached, but too late I realized that it was not my daughter-in-law behind the wheel. We usually passed each other at this time of the morning; she, on her way to work, and I, on my route as a school bus driver. Now I felt sheepish as the man with the black mustache, who drove a van that looked like hers, passed by. Several days later, I again waved at the same man mistakenly; and the next day it happened again.

This went on two or three days a week for the next several weeks. Each time I waved, the man with a mustache returned my wave with a peculiar, puzzled glance. I'd laugh to myself, realizing he must think I was nuts. Finally, one day he returned my wave with a slight smile, and the next time with a grin. Eventually he even waved. My mistaken communications with the stranger with a mustache gradually relaxed his aloofness. Perhaps it wasn't a mistake after all.

The apostle Paul commended Philemon for his love and faith toward others. Even when unintended, expressing a simple Christian grace may make someone's day. See if you can provoke someone to smile today.

PRAYER THOUGHTS: Father, I don't always feel like communicating Your love. Help me to elicit from others a glad response because of Your presence in my life. In Jesus' name, amen.

July 19, 20, 21, 24, 25. **Penny Smith** is a Christian writer who contributes to many publications. She lives in Harrisburg, Pennsylvania.

CHOICES

SCRIPTURE: Philemon 8-14

VERSE FOR TODAY: I beseech thee for my son Onesimus, whom I have begotten in my bonds (Philemon 10).

HYMN FOR TODAY: "Wonderful Grace of Jesus"

The young man stood before the sober judge who presided over the juvenile probation court. "What makes you think you should be discharged?" the judge asked.

Dennis answered unhesitatingly. "I know I am eligible for discharge, but I would like to remain in the program until I graduate from high school."

The judge, noticeably shaken by this response, looked to me for an explanation. Dennis had chosen to forfeit his freedom in order to continue practicing the Christian disciplines which had enabled him to overcome a history of deviant behaviors.

"If funding is not available, I'm willing to take Dennis into my home," I offered.

The judge acted in his behalf, and Dennis "freely" entered another phase of his rehabilitation. Because of his strong commitment to the Lord, I was proud to plead his cause. He would honor the judge's decision, I knew.

Bondages are broken when we allow the grace of God to work in our lives. Paul realized that position and status matters not. God's grace reaches to master and servant alike, for when we are bound to Him, we find out what freedom is all about.

PRAYER THOUGHTS: Father, I sometimes forget about the people who are enslaved by sin. Will you lead me to that one who is open and ready to receive the gift of salvation? Then help me to properly represent You, for Jesus' sake. Amen.

THE PRICE

SCRIPTURE: Philemon 15-25

VERSE FOR TODAY: If he hath wronged thee, or oweth thee ought, put that on mine account (Philemon 18).

HYMN FOR TODAY: "Jesus Paid It All"

A friend and I recently went to a restaurant for breakfast. While we were eating, a couple from our church greeted us as they left. Later, when we took our check to the cashier, she informed us it had already been paid by the couple. Perhaps you have had a similar experience. If so, you will recall the desire to thank your benefactor.

The familiar gospel account known as the story of the good Samaritan illustrates the apostle Paul's treatment of the runaway servant, Onesimus. Paul was willing to settle any unpaid account for this one who had become his brother in the Lord. Likewise, the Samaritan, filled with compassion, cared for the wounded man who fell prey to thieves on the Jericho road; he paid for his care in the inn.

I believe that Onesimus was grateful and served Paul in every way possible. The wounded man of the good Samaritan story surely must have tried to find the one who had helped him in order to thank him.

What can compare with the debt that Jesus has paid for our redemption? How can we thank Him?

PRAYER THOUGHTS: Lord Jesus, You paid a debt You did not owe, and I thank You. I give You the right to my life and to all that I possess. If I should attempt to take control, please show me Your cross again. In Your holy name, amen.

FAMILIES

SCRIPTURE: 1 Corinthians 1:1-9

VERSE FOR TODAY: He that built all things is God. . . . Christ as a son over his own house; whose house are we, if we hold fast the confidence and the rejoicing of the hope firm unto the end (Hebrews 3:4, 6).

HYMN FOR TODAY: "The Church's One Foundation"

Although I live alone, I belong to a large family, numbering close to three hundred. I have a close relationship with most of them; others live too far away, and so we correspond; others I do not know. Still we are family, bound together by our family name and our blood line. For a family that size, our love for each others is remarkable.

I also have a church family, and this is even larger. Many members are scattered worldwide, so I don't know them; others live far away and we correspond; but with the members within my sphere of activity and service I have a close relationship, not so much different from my biological family. The church is indeed a family, bound by one name—Christ. We are bound also by a blood tie—the atoning blood of our Savior. And our love for each other sets us apart (John 13:35).

Whoever you are, reading this, we may or may not know each other; but if you are a child of Christ, you are my brother or sister. One day we all shall know each other, when we gather around the Lamb's marriage supper, our Lord at the head of the table. What a terrific feast that will be!

PRAYER THOUGHTS: Our Father, You have given us numerous family members to help and encourage us, to rebuke and comfort us. May we continue in a spirit of caring and cooperation so that Your kingdom may grow. In the name of Jesus. Amen.

July 22, 23. **Jacqueline Webster** is a Christian writer from Cincinnati, Ohio.

IS YOUR SHADE PULLED?

SCRIPTURE: 1 Corinthians 1:10-17

VERSE FOR TODAY: Is Christ divided? was Paul crucified for you? or were ye baptized in the name of Paul? (1 Corinthians 1:13).

HYMN FOR TODAY: "Crown Him With Many Crowns"

My friend's neighbor told of getting up in the morning and looking out the window to discover a fog so thick that she couldn't even see the patio. She knew she wouldn't be able to drive in those conditions, so she decided not to report to work. When she put on her eyeglasses to phone her office, however, she discovered that the *white window shade* covered the window. She hadn't noticed without her glasses! Some fog, huh?

That is probably what happened to the Corinthian believers addressed in our passage today. They had foggy vision. Division had come into the church because they followed personalities rather than keeping their focus upon Christ. They had "pulled the shade," so-to-speak, and couldn't see beyond Paul, Apollos, or Cephas.

I can imagine the scenario. "Who baptized you? Apollos? Well, I was baptized by Cephas." Paul came along and said, "Well, thank God I didn't do it!"

In our generation we've made a fuss over televangelists. The true minister of God points the flock to the Lord and not to himself. If you're a born-again Christian, you are a minister of the gospel. Do you pass the acid test or is the shade pulled?

PRAYER THOUGHTS: Father, I want to be faithful to point others to You and not to myself or any other personality. You alone have the answers to life. You are altogether lovely. Help me to communicate You and to reflect You through every part of my being. In Jesus' name, amen.

BLUE ROCKS

SCRIPTURE: 1 Peter 2:4-10

VERSE FOR TODAY: Ye also, as lively stones, are built up a spiritual house, an holy priesthood, to offer up spiritual sacrifices, acceptable to God by Jesus Christ (1 Peter 2:5).

HYMN FOR TODAY: "Redeemed"

I worked my way around my mobile home as I applied the fresh new paint to the trim. All at once, the gallon can of paint toppled from the ladder to the ground. Blue paint spread over the mountain rocks below, creating an ugly mess. As I wiped up the globs of paint, I found myself rearranging the blue rocks which now matched the trim on the mobile home.

That's what I've done with you, the Lord seemed to say. I've washed away your sins, covered your blemishes, and placed you *in* my body as a lively stone. Now I'm rearranging your priorities and making you acceptable to me.

Today's Scripture passage describes us as lively stones which are built upon the chief cornerstone, Jesus Christ. Once our blood-washed lives are rearranged into a spiritual house, we will reflect His honor and praise. We will sing praises to Him because He has brought us out of darkness into a wonderful light. We, as lively stones, will bear the royal robes of our heavenly Bridegroom.

PRAYER THOUGHTS: Thank You for the times You speak to my heart, dear Father, even through the messes that I cause. Most of all, I'm grateful for the rearrangement You've made of the messy life that I've given to You. Thank You. Amen.

GO TO THE SOURCE

SCRIPTURE: 2 Corinthians 9

VERSE FOR TODAY: And God is able to make all grace abound toward you; that ye, always having all sufficiency in all things, may abound to every good work (2 Corinthians 9:8).

HYMN FOR TODAY: "My Anchor Holds"

The missionary couple to India had raised financial support through faith promises before leaving the United States. Several months later, they were destitute. It seemed their friends had forgotten them.

The missionary described his frustration and anger with God. "I obeyed You," he cried. "I brought my wife halfway around the world, and I can't care for her. You let me down. Those people made promises they didn't keep, and You don't care."

Suddenly he heard the chain rattle on the gate, indicating someone had come. He regained his composure and went to the gate as he wiped tears from his eyes. A young Indian boy handed him an envelope containing rupees equivalent to one hundred dollars, with this message: "I was praying and the Lord said to send this to you immediately."

As a new flood of tears filled his eyes, he felt the Lord reminding him, I am able to make all grace abound toward you, for I don't need the promises of your friends back home to meet your needs. I can meet them here.

The couple never lacked for support again, for they learned to trust the proper Source for their support.

PRAYER THOUGHTS: Thank You, Father, for divine provision. When I have doubts or fears, will You "rattle my chain" and remind me that You are the divine source for all that I require? In Jesus' name, amen.

THE WALKING DEAD

SCRIPTURE: Ephesians 2:1-5

VERSE FOR TODAY: As for you, you were dead in your transgressions and sins (Ephesians 2:1, *New International Version*).

HYMN FOR TODAY: "Christ Receiveth Sinful Men"

Ghosts. Haunted houses. Moving lights and clanking chains in the night. For some people these are not simply Halloween games or stories to frighten children, but are things believed to be very real. Some of the religions of the world are based on such things. Ghosts and harmful spirits become so powerful that death seems more significant than life.

Are there really ghosts? Do people walk around after they die to cause harm and to inhabit buildings? According to our Verse for Today, the Christians at Ephesus were once "dead" people going about their daily tasks. But they were not ghosts; they were "dead" because of their sins and transgressions. In fact, Paul considered all people who were not Christians as being "dead." We see them every day. They are on T.V., they are at work, school, or walking around in the mall. They look quite alive, but from the spiritual perspective they are the "walking dead."

It is so good to be alive. "God, who is rich in mercy, made us alive with Christ even when we were dead in transgressions" (Ephesians 2:4, 5, New International Version). We never knew life until we met Jesus. Share the gift of life by sharing Jesus Christ.

PRAYER THOUGHTS: Father, may we enjoy the fullness of life today. May we not complain or fear or be depressed, but be open to Your Son in whom we pray. Amen.

July 26—August 1. **David Grubbs** is a medical missionary who served in Zimbabwe for many years. He and his wife, Eva, have four children.

GRACE, EXPRESSED IN KINDNESS

SCRIPTURE: Ephesians 2:6-10

VERSE FOR TODAY: . . . the incomparable riches of his grace, expressed in his kindness to us in Christ Jesus (Ephesians 2:7, *New International Version*).

HYMN FOR TODAY: "Amazing Grace"

An African woman came to our door one day, saying, "There is something the doctor needs to know. His dogs are coming to my village early in the morning to eat my goats. I know he doesn't know about it, so I have come to tell him." We were very surprised but had no reason to doubt her story. When asked if she would accept a payment for the loss of the goats, she refused, saying, "Our family once had a serious problem and the doctor came to help us. I am now repaying his kindness."

We may be impressed with power, but we are moved by kindness. There has always been enough violence among us to satisfy our need to see human power in action. Men like to use force and threats to accomplish their temporal goals. What the Rambos of the world have achieved temporarily, Jesus, in His kindness, has accomplished eternally.

There is no other way for us to clearly see the value (riches) of the grace of God except to see it in the kindness of Jesus. There is no better way for us to demonstrate it to others than by our kindness. We all respond to the grace of kindness. To be a Christian is to reflect the kindness of God by showing them Christ Jesus.

PRAYER THOUGHTS: May I control myself today, Lord, and show kindness. Help me to see the need of another person today and, in kindness, respond to that need. Amen.

TEMPORARY BEAUTY

SCRIPTURE: John 15:1-9

VERSE FOR TODAY: If anyone does not remain in me, he is like a branch that is thrown away and withers (John 15:6, *New International Version*).

HYMN FOR TODAY: "Draw Me Nearer"

Zimbabwe is a country blessed with great natural beauty. The Victoria Falls, the many game parks with their wild animals, and the mountains of the Eastern Highlands draw tourists from all over the world. They come to see, but once they cut themselves off from the source of the beauty, they have only pictures and memories of the beauty.

Zimbabwe is also the third largest exporter of cut flowers in the world, following the Netherlands and Israel. Selling cut flowers for export is a difficult business. Once a flower is cut, it is soon destined to end in the trash bag. Cut from its source, the beauty of the flower is fragile and temporary.

Human beauty is a reflection of God, and it is only lasting when it is under the control of God. Physical attraction must never be confused with beauty. That which is of the earth fades, but that which is from God is eternal. Many popular singers began using their talents in praising God in worship. Later, their love for the gift became greater than their love for the Giver, and the gift of music was used to please the world. The songs sung around the throne are eternal songs, sung with eternally beautiful voices.

The branch that is cut off soon withers and becomes ugly. Only the memory of what it once was is beautiful.

PRAYER THOUGHTS: O Father help me not to cut myself off from Jesus, or I will wither and die. Keep me in His strength. Amen.

CHOSEN TO PRODUCE

SCRIPTURE: John 15:10-17

VERSE FOR TODAY: You did not choose me, but I chose you and appointed you to go and bear fruit—fruit that will last. Then the Father will give you whatever you ask in my name (John 15:16, *New International Version*).

HYMN FOR TODAY: "Give of Your Best to the Master"

In traditional African society, marriages were arranged for the benefit of the families. Some people were married before birth! The woman's most important role in the marriage was to bear children, and as many children as possible. In an environment where disease or famine could wipe out an entire clan in a season, there was little room for marriages based on romance.

One day at Mashoko Mission Hospital we visited with two elderly sisters. During the conversation we asked how many children they had produced. One had had eighteen pregnancies and still had eighteen living children. The other had sixteen living children from sixteen pregnancies. They were very respected mothers to have produced and preserved thirty four children for their families. Certainly they would have been given anything they requested from their husbands. They were chosen for production, and they had produced!

Jesus has chosen us to bear fruit that will last. We must produce what is durable and eternal. Think of how much of our time is spent on temporary things. That was the criticism Jesus had for Martha (see Luke 10). Her energy was devoted to the temporary. He has promised, "Then the Father will give you whatever you ask in my name."

PRAYER THOUGHTS: Father, help me to produce what is eternal. May the fruit of today's labors be lasting. In Jesus we ask these things. Amen.

ON WINGS LIKE EAGLES

SCRIPTURE: Isaiah 40:28-31

VERSE FOR TODAY: But those who hope in the Lord will renew their strength. They will soar on wings like eagles (Isaiah 40:31, *New International Version*).

HYMN FOR TODAY: "Blessed Assurance"

Our children brought home a fuzzy ball of feathers one day. It was a young eagle that had been rejected from the nest by its dominate sibling. It was an education watching it grow. We agreed it would not be caged but would grow up with freedom. Watching it learn to fly was very exciting for us all. It would patiently stand, waiting for a strong breeze. Then it would stretch its wings and test the strength of its wings against the flow of the wind. At last, after days of hope with assurance, it launched itself into the wind and soared into the heavens. It was born to fly in freedom.

We have a destiny. It is to enjoy eternity with God. We were born for freedom and for soaring in the heavens. It is our human nature to grow tired, to become discouraged, to weary in well-doing. Many of us never learn how to stretch our wings and test the wind. We do not know that our strength is in the Lord. So we never enjoy flying.

Our eagle was seriously injured one day. It decided to walk among men. It was not designed to walk, and certainly not among people. But we had also taught it to be "human." Its salvation was to behave after its design. God has designed us to live in His strength.

PRAYER THOUGHTS: Lord, renew our strength. Let us test our wings in Your wind today, and may we soar like eagles. Help us to let go of the world today. Amen.

LIMITS OF KNOWLEDGE

SCRIPTURE: Ephesians 3:14-19

VERSE FOR TODAY: and to know this love that surpasses knowledge—that you may be filled to the measure of all the fullness of God (Ephesians 3:19, *New International Version***).**

HYMN FOR TODAY: "Love Lifted Me"

There is an African proverb that says, "A baboon is not injured by falling from a tree." It reflects a parallel truth that a person is the most secure when he is in the area of his greatest knowledge. That is one of the benefits of limiting ourselves to our area of expertise. We avoid insecurity.

It is enjoyable to teach African nursing students and watch them gain confidence as their ability and knowledge grows. When they first begin giving injections, their hands shake so badly that, at times, the patients faint with fear. But as the weeks and months of training pass, they handle problems that increase in difficulty, and they do it with confidence. However, a situation often arises where they need to call for help. There is always a limit to one's knowledge.

New situations bring both a blessing and an insecurity. The blessing is that what was old and harmful, or shameful, can be put aside. The insecurity is due to our limited knowledge decreasing our confidence. Paul's prayer was that the Ephesians (and we) will come to grasp the dimensions of God's love and will understand that His love will carry us beyond the limits of our knowledge.

PRAYER THOUGHTS: Father, grant us the security of Your love. May we not trust our own understanding but hope in Jesus. Fill us with Your love today. We pray through Him. Amen.

DEVOTIONS

AUGUST

AN UNLIMITED HEAVEN

SCRIPTURE: Galatians 6:11-16

VERSE FOR TODAY: Neither circumcision nor uncircumcision means anything; what counts is a new creation (Galatians 6:15, *New International Version*).

HYMN FOR TODAY: "A New Name in Glory"

Question: How do you divide four pieces of cake among ten children? (**Answer**: You can't. You must bake more cake.)

Question: What if you cannot bake more cake? (**Answer**: Then the children will fight, and some of them will not eat cake.)

The world has a limited supply of material wealth. It is perpetually being redistributed among the peoples of the earth. Empires and individuals have been known for their accumulation of that wealth, but in the end it has been passed on to others in following generations. How very hard we work for that which we cannot keep. It is the way of the world.

God has intentionally limited the resources of the earth. He put enough here to sustain us, but He wants to remind us that eternal security does not remain here. God has an additional plan for a new creation.

God also has intentionally limited religious practices. Jewish religious practices were designed to prepare people for the first coming of Jesus. Christian religious practices are designed to prepare us for His second coming. The practices are not eternal. The new creation is. Get ready! He is coming with enough Heaven for everyone forever!

PRAYER THOUGHTS: Creator, help us to conserve what You have given for us to use, but let us not hoard or trust in it. We look for our newness in Your new creation. Through Jesus we pray, amen.

HE DESTROYED THE WALL

SCRIPTURE: Ephesians 2:11-17

VERSE FOR TODAY: His purpose was to create in himself one new man out of the two, thus making peace, and in this one body to reconcile both of them to God through the cross, by which he put to death their hostility (Ephesians 2:15, 16, *New International Version*).

HYMN FOR TODAY: "Draw Me Nearer"

"Something there is that doesn't love a wall, /That wants it down." Echoing the apostle Paul, Robert Frost, in his poem, "Mending Wall," recounted how he and his neighbor repaired the stone wall between their farms each spring. They would walk along the wall, each on his side, and lift the boulders that had tumbled his way.

Why did they rebuild the wall? If asked, the neighbor would simply repeat his father's adage, "Good fences make good neighbors." For his part, Mr. Frost saw no need for the wall: "Before I built a wall I'd ask to know /What I was walling in or walling out. /And to whom I was likely to give offense."

Keeping a "safe" distance may be an old New England recipe for neighborliness, but it is not God's will for His creation. Through the blood of Jesus, He brought down the wall that separated Gentiles from Jews and separated us all from Him.

PRAYER THOUGHTS: Thank You, God, for sending Jesus to break down the wall of guilt that separates me from You. Through His death and Your Spirit, You have made it possible to enjoy intimacy with You and others. Amen.

August 2-8. **Robin Smith** is a lawyer who lives with his wife, Lois, in Baltimore, Maryland.

August 3

ADOPTED INTO GOD'S FAMILY

SCRIPTURE: Ephesians 2:18-22

VERSE FOR TODAY: God raised us up with Christ and seated us with him in the heavenly realms in Christ Jesus, in order that in the coming ages he might show the incomparable riches of his grace, expressed in his kindness to us in Christ Jesus (Ephesians 2:6, 7, *New International Version*).

HYMN FOR TODAY: "O Happy Day"

Tom Canty was born into a family of paupers in sixteenth-century London during the reign of Henry VIII. His father "was a thief, and his mother a beggar." In due course his parents made a beggar of him. When Tom "came home empty-handed at night, he knew his father would curse him and thrash him." To forget his aches and pains, Tom often dreamed of leading "the charmed life of a petted prince." As Mark Twain tells the tale, Tom Canty realized his dream by trading places with the young Prince of Wales.

According to Ephesians, we realize our dream—indeed, more than we can dream of—by the grace of God, who is uniting His chosen people into a dwelling where He lives. The apostle Paul describes a life infinitely superior to that envisioned by Mark Twain's preadolescent pauper—a life of union with Christ in the heavenly realms, of community with others in God's own household, of adoption into God's family as heirs to inconceivable wealth.

PRAYER THOUGHTS: We praise You, O God, for You have blessed us with every spiritual blessing in Christ. We worship You for bringing us into Your family, where we can be of use to You. Amen.

OF COURSE

SCRIPTURE: Romans 6:1-14

VERSE FOR TODAY: Don't you know that all of us who were baptized into Christ Jesus were baptized into his death? (Romans 6:3, *New International Version*)?

HYMN FOR TODAY: "I'll Live for Him"

"As a man thinketh in his heart, so is he." The proverb reminds me that my very identity is determined by what I think. What I think about myself, my situation in life, and my prospects for the future deeply influences how I respond to life's blessings, disappointments, and vagaries.

If I think, *I can never do anything right; that's why I'm stuck in this rotten job,* I'm vulnerable to depression. Thinking *I'm only human* or *Everyone does it* fosters sinfulness. Telling myself *To err is human* just leads me to sin more and more.

Focusing on biblical truths can counter and displace this wrong perspective. If I remember that God cares for me and is at work in me, transforming me into Christ's likeness, then I'm likely to find opportunities for good wherever I am. If I focus on the Biblical truth that my old self was crucified with Christ and I am dead to sin, I will of course sin less. Today, then, I will concentrate on telling myself this truth: "I am dead to sin and alive to God in Christ Jesus!"

PRAYER THOUGHTS: Dear God, when I think of my baptism I think of the wonderful change it made in my life. My union with Christ made a change, is making a change, and will make a wonderful change in my life. Thank You, Lord. Amen.

INTERNAL WARFARE

SCRIPTURE: Romans 7:13-25

VERSE FOR TODAY: But he said to me, "My grace is sufficient for you, for my power is made perfect in weakness." Therefore I will boast all the more gladly about my weaknesses, so that Christ's power may rest on me (2 Corinthians 12:9, *New International Version*).

HYMN FOR TODAY: "Grace Greater Than Our Sin"

"I want to do good, but instead I do evil." Perhaps nowhere is the poignancy of this struggle depicted more starkly than in Graham Greene's novel, *The Power and the Glory.* Facing a government intent on eradicating the church, a lone priest does his best to maintain his ministry. He is not a good priest, however. He is a bad priest, and he knows it. Years of persecution have taken their toll, and he now leans on the bottle for support. A whiskey priest—that's all he is. But as the soldiers search for him village by village, he refuses to flee. And though he despairs of life itself, he will not willingly be captured.

Like Greene's anonymous whiskey priest, I see the rubble of my failures and wonder, as it accumulates, whether it will one day altogether choke up the source of grace. "Who will rescue me," I ask, "from this body of death?" And then I think: "Thanks be to God—through Jesus Christ our Lord!"

PRAYER THOUGHTS: Forgive me, O Lord, for my failures; sanctify me in Your Spirit that I may resist the devil. Thank You for Your marvelous grace, which is greater than all my sins. Amen.

SET FREE BY GRACE

SCRIPTURE: Romans 8:1-10

VERSE FOR TODAY: Therefore, there is now no condemnation for those who are in Christ Jesus (Romans 8:1, *New International Version***).**

HYMN FOR TODAY: "Redeemed"

Having just uttered the gut-wrenching cry, "What a wretched man I am!," the apostle juxtaposes the equally true irony that he has been set free from sin and death. Victor Hugo dramatized the redeeming power of grace in his novel, *Les Miserables*. Recently released after nineteen years in prison, Jean Valjean experienced nothing but condemnation until he met Monseigneur Bienvenu, the Bishop of Digne. The bishop invited Jean Valjean into his house. He set a place at his table for the stranger and prepared a bed. The criminal repaid this kindness by stealing the bishop's silverware and fleeing into the night. When the gendarmes stopped him the next morning, he claimed that the bishop had given him the cutlery. They returned him to the bishop's house. Upon Jean Valjean's appearance at his door, and before the policemen could speak, Monseigneur Bienvenu hailed him and asked why he had not also taken the candlesticks, which, he said, he had given him as well. The bishop dismissed the gendarmes. Handing the candlesticks to the stunned thief, the bishop gave grace and forgiveness, not condemnation.

PRAYER THOUGHTS: O Lord, I praise You for the wonder of what You have done. Even though I continue to struggle with sin, I know what it means to be free from the power of sin. You do not condemn me but instead give me Your Spirit. Thank You. Amen.

POWER IN HIS LOVE

SCRIPTURE: Romans 8:35-39

VERSE FOR TODAY: In all these things we are more than conquerors through him who loved us (Romans 8:37, *New International Version*).

HYMN FOR TODAY: "In Heavenly Love Abiding"

Christians face opposition every day of their lives. The opposition sometimes appears openly. People whose deepest love is love of self may be unsettled by one whose deepest love is love of God. People whose highest loyalty is to their country may fear one whose highest loyalty is to the kingdom of God. More frequent, perhaps, than open opposition is the devil's internal opposition. When I want a day off from my job, the devil tempts me to tell my employer I'm ill. When I'm stopped by a policeman on the highway, the voice of evil suggests that a lie might keep the officer from issuing a citation. When I lose my job or see my son or daughter fall prey to serious illness or injury, Satan tries to get me to believe that God must not care.

How reassured I then am to hear Paul say that nothing can separate me from the love of Christ. Nothing. Not my "friends." Not my enemies. Not the government. Not demons. Not even the devil himself. The Creator of the universe loves me. And this incontrovertible fact sustains me against every assault. Because of His love I am able to rise above my circumstances and glory in the ultimate victory that is assured.

PRAYER THOUGHTS: I praise You, O God, for Your loving-kindness. You are indeed a rock upon which I can lean in times of testing and trouble. Thank You for showing me in Christ how much You love me and for demonstrating Your faithfulness throughout history. Amen.

LIVING FOR LOVE

SCRIPTURE: Galatians 2:15-21

VERSE FOR TODAY: I have been crucified with Christ and I no longer live, but Christ lives in me. The life I live in the body, I live by faith in the Son of God, who loved me and gave himself for me (Galatians 2:20, *New International Version***).**

HYMN FOR TODAY: "Jesus, Rose of Sharon"

Perhaps the hardest part of being a Christian is coming to grips with the means of my salvation. Even though I say the words "saved by grace, not by works," I find within myself a tendency to try to justify myself by doing good things. And, if that weren't bad enough, I tend to set up rules, or standards of behavior, by which to judge myself and others. That I base my rules on the Bible provides no consolation.

Happily, when I catch myself thinking in terms of rules and of being good enough (or not good enough!), I can remind myself that "it just ain't so." God loves me just as I am. When I focus on His love, the law loses its power over me. I know that who I am is not defined by any set of standards. I am not defined by how completely I conform to any code of conduct.

I'm glad I was crucified with Christ. I have a new life now, a life based on my faith in the Son. That's what matters now; not rules. What's more, I can stop looking at other people from a worldly point of view, too.

PRAYER THOUGHTS: O Lord, I believe You love me because You gave Your Son over to death for me. Your wonderful act gives my life a new focus. Now it's possible for me to live for You. Amen.

LOOKING BACK OR WALKING FORWARD?

SCRIPTURE: Romans 6:15-23

VERSE FOR TODAY: It is for freedom that Christ has set us free. Stand firm, then, and do not let yourselves be burdened again by a yoke of slavery (Galatians 5:1, *New International Version*).

HYMN FOR TODAY: "My Faith Looks Up To Thee"

The children of Israel were slaves in Egypt. Then God sent Moses as their deliverer and led them across the wilderness to the place where they could live the lives God wanted them to live—as His chosen people. But they were barely out of Egypt when they began to look back. They forgot the bitterness and despair of their lives in Egypt and said, "There we sat around pots of meat and ate all the food we wanted" (Exodus 16:3, *New International Version*). They were ready to return to slavery just to satisfy their physical desires for a moment.

We, too, have been slaves—slaves to sin. God sent us a deliverer in His Son, Jesus Christ. Now we are free. But sometimes when our walk in God's way gets tough, we look back on our enslavement to sin and that life looks easy and satisfying. We forget that that kind of life leads only to eternal death. The freedom God gives us is the freedom to live the lives He wants us to live—as His loving, faithful people. Just like the children of Israel, only when we are obedient to the will of God are our lives truly free.

PRAYER THOUGHTS: Father, as we go through each day, help us to keep our eyes on You and our hearts turned toward Your will that we may live the lives You want us to live, both now and eternally. In Jesus, our deliverer's name, amen.

August 9-15. **Denise Buhr** is housing coordinator for the Christian Student Fellowship at Indiana University. She lives in Bloomington, Indiana, and is pursuing a career as a children's author and storyteller.

IN HIS FOOTSTEPS

SCRIPTURE: 1 John 2:3-11

VERSE FOR TODAY: And this is love: that we walk in obedience to his commands. As you have heard from the beginning, his command is that you walk in love (2 John 6, *New International Version*).

HYMN FOR TODAY: "Let Us Ever Walk With Jesus"

Soldiers on parade want to look sharp. They must be in step, so each one follows the one in front of him; all of them follow the commands of their leader. Then everyone watching the parade cheers and applauds.

Christians are the soldiers of God. Jesus has given us our commands and has walked the path He wants us to follow, and He is still leading us day by day through His Word. We can also follow the examples of the Christians who have gone before us—the disciples, the apostle Paul, our pastors and teachers, our grandparents and parents. We probably won't get any cheers or applause from those around us. We might even receive jeers and insults instead.

For the soldiers on parade, it is easy to get out of step and confused, and to give a bad impression to those on the sidelines. It is critical for the soldiers to watch and follow the one leading them.

Christians can also get out of step and confused, and consequently turn people away from the Truth. Therefore it is crucial to watch, listen, and follow the only One who can lead us—Jesus Christ.

PRAYER THOUGHTS: Dear Lord, You gave us Christ's example to follow, and You lead us even now through Your Word. Help us to walk in Christ's footsteps so that others will know Who we follow and come to know You also. In Jesus' name, amen.

YOU HAVE ALREADY WON!

SCRIPTURE: Luke 16:9-13

VERSE FOR TODAY: Command those who are rich in this present world not to be arrogant nor to put their hope in wealth, which is so uncertain, but to put their hope in God. . . . In this way they will lay up treasure for themselves as a firm foundation for the coming age, so that they may take hold of the life that is truly life (1 Timothy 6:17-19, *New International Version*).

HYMN FOR TODAY: "Lord of Glory, Who Has Bought Us"

"You may have already won!" "You could be the next millionaire!" "Ed McMahon could be calling you!" Another sweepstakes letter has arrived. Do you rush your entry back the next day, believing you could win? Do you toss it in the garbage, saying, "I'll never win." Or are you skeptical but decide that since there's "no purchase necessary" you can afford a stamp—just in case.

There's no doubt with God. Christians are already winners. The prize is the biggest and best of all time, and the call comes to each of us personally from God. He has called us to be His children and offers us the gift of eternal life through faith in Jesus. We don't have to purchase anything, although the price He paid was high.

How sad that every day more people place their faith in a sweepstakes or lottery where the chances of winning big are so small. With God, everyone can win and no one gets less than the full prize, no matter how many people enter His kingdom.

Most of us will never have to think about what to do with all that money. What a joy to think about the greater prize that waits for us in Heaven.

PRAYER THOUGHTS: Dear Lord, thank You for the wonderful and free gift of salvation through Your Son, Jesus. Help us to share the news of that great gift with those around us. In Jesus' name, amen.

MAKE THE MOST OF EVERY OPPORTUNITY

SCRIPTURE: Ephesians 5:15-21

VERSE FOR TODAY: Whatever you do, work at it with all your heart, as working for the Lord, not for men, since you know that you will receive an inheritance from the Lord as a reward. It is the Lord Christ you are serving (Colossians 3:23, 24, *New International Version*).

HYMN FOR TODAY: "Hark! The Voice of Jesus Crying"

"What are you going to do with your life?" Sometimes the answer seems certain. The student studying for a particular career gives a confident reply based on his plans and dreams. The college graduate who can't find a job in his chosen field may have no answer. Each person will answer the question differently. Even the same person can give different responses at different times in his life. As Christians we have been given a very clear answer to what we should be doing with our lives.

Jesus tells of the faithful and wise servant who was put in charge of his master's house while his master was away. He was given certain duties to perform. Jesus says, "It will be good for that servant whose master finds him doing so when he returns" (Matthew 24:46, *New International Version*).

There are many passages in Scripture that give specific examples of the duties of the Christian. Most of all we ought to be "making the most of every opportunity" (Ephesians 5:16) to share the good news of salvation.

PRAYER THOUGHTS: Father in Heaven, You have given me life, both earthly and eternal. Help me, while in the world, to make the most of every opportunity to share Your love and mercy with others. In Jesus' name, amen.

LIGHTING THE DARKNESS

SCRIPTURE: Luke 11:33-41

VERSE FOR TODAY: In the same way, let your light shine before men, that they may see your good deeds and praise your Father in heaven (Matthew 5:16, *New International Version*).

HYMN FOR TODAY: "The Light of the World is Jesus"

Once I went on a tour of Wyandotte Cave in southern Indiana. This was not a casual walking tour on a well-lit path, but six hours of crawling and climbing that required several members of our group to carry lanterns. At one point the guide asked us to sit, and then one by one had those people carrying lanterns extinguish them. Then, very slowly, he turned down the flame on his lantern until it too went out. In the darkness, I held my hand just inches from my face and saw nothing. People spoke and their voices echoed out of nowhere. It was a relief when the lanterns were relit and we knew we could see our way to get out safely.

The world is also a very dark place because of sin. People are lost in that darkness, stumbling and falling and suffering. They need the light that shines out from Christian lives to help them find the way. For that light to burn brightly, we must fuel our faith with prayer, worship, and the study of God's Word, and always look to Jesus to be our guide.

PRAYER THOUGHTS: Almighty God who created light, help each of us to shine in the darkness of this sinful world that others may see the truth and come to faith. In Jesus' name, amen.

WHAT PLEASES THE LORD

SCRIPTURE: Ephesians 5:1-11

VERSE FOR TODAY: A good tree cannot bear bad fruit, and a bad tree cannot bear good fruit. Every tree that does not bear good fruit is cut down and thrown into the fire. Thus, by their fruit you will recognize them (Matthew 7:18-20, *New International Version*).

HYMN FOR TODAY: "Awake, My Soul, and With The Sun"

One year my "green thumb" seemed to turn brown. I had planted a dozen different kinds of flowers from seeds, bulbs, and shoots. But for weeks, all I had around my patio were three dozen pots of dirt. I watered and weeded and kept turning the pots for the best sunlight. Finally, tiny green shoots pushed their way up and grew and grew. But still, there were no flowers.

One day I went out for a couple of hours. I returned and was coming up the sidewalk when something on the patio caught my eye. There it was—a very small but very bright pink flower! Just one where none had been a few hours before. And over the next several weeks more and more flowers of all different varieties blossomed, and my patio became a rainbow of living color. I was delighted!

God is delighted, too, when people's lives grow out of the darkness and dirt of sin and blossom with the beauty of Christ-filled living.

PRAYER THOUGHTS: Dear Lord, thank You for lifting me out of my sins and giving me new life. May the love and joy I have in Christ show to those around me. In His most beautiful name, amen.

BE A LIVING SACRIFICE

SCRIPTURE: Romans 12:1-8

VERSE FOR TODAY: I have been crucified with Christ and I no longer live, but Christ lives in me. The life I live in the body, I live by faith in the Son of God, who loved me and gave himself for me (Galatians 2:20, *New International Version*).

HYMN FOR TODAY: "Take My Life and Let It Be"

Two friends were brought before the king. One was accused of some misdeed and sentenced to death. He asked for time to settle his affairs, but promised to return. His friend offered to stay in prison, and if need be, to die in his place. The king agreed and the first man went home.

The day appointed had arrived. The man had not returned, so his friend was taken to the executioner. Suddenly there was a commotion at the gate. The first man rushed in. He had been delayed but had never forgotten his promise and had come back to fulfill it. The king was determined to uphold the law. Someone must die, and the two men had to decide which of them it would be. But the two men couldn't agree. They began to argue because each man wanted to die in place of the other. The king was so impressed by the love and loyalty of these two friends, he released them both.

Out of His great love, Christ willingly took our place and gave His life up to death for us. How can we offer Him anything less than to give our lives up to living for Him?

PRAYER THOUGHTS: Dear Jesus, You gave up Your life for us. Now we offer our lives to You. May the ways of our lives glorify You and the work of our lives help Your kingdom to grow. In Your name, amen.

THE PERFECT FAMILY

SCRIPTURE: Genesis 2:18-25

VERSE FOR TODAY: Every good and perfect gift is from above, coming down from the Father of the heavenly lights (James 1:17, *New International Version*).

HYMN FOR TODAY: "The Family of God"

Take the weather of Hawaii, add the tranquility of an isolated place far from the crowds, and eliminate all cares and woes of daily life. You now have what most of us would consider the perfect honeymoon setting and an ideal living environment. Adam and Eve had it all. Their life was like a continuous honeymoon. Adam worked in a garden free of weeds. He tended animals that were always friendly and content. He never worked up a sweat. Eve's role was to be his companion, to keep him company, ready to help in any way. Preparing the meals was a snap. With perfect conditions, the food practically fell into their laps.

Wouldn't it be easy to raise a family in this neighborhood? But it wasn't enough. Two perfect people in the perfect place, and they failed. We shouldn't be too surprised when we sometimes fail. However, we must remember that God didn't simply overlook that "one little weakness" of Adam and Eve. Sin has its price, and sin exacts its toll in family life today just as it did in the very first family. What a dreary life this would be without the hope we have in Jesus Christ.

PRAYER THOUGHTS: Father, thank You for the gifts You give to us each day. Fill our hearts with thankfulness. Amen.

August 16-22. **Wesley Bell** is a direct support missionary serving as Field Director for the El Paso office of Amor Ministries. He is a husband, father, grandfather, and writer.

THE PERFECT BEAUTY

SCRIPTURE: 1 Peter 3:1-6

VERSE FOR TODAY: Charm is deceptive, and beauty is fleeting; but a woman who fears the Lord is to be praised (Proverbs 31:30, *New International Version*).

HYMN FOR TODAY: "Turn Your Eyes Upon Jesus"

Are you familiar with the old saying, "Beauty is as beauty does"? That's the message Peter was trying to get across to his readers. A truly beautiful woman lives a life of beauty. A woman may gain a husband with outward appearances, but only inward beauty can win a husband to Christ.

Advertisers today try to convince women that beauty comes from a bottle, wearing the latest fashions, or a physical appearance that the latest diet or exercise machine will provide. At best, these provide only a temporary beauty.

Peter was selling an "unfading beauty," something that comes from "a gentle and quiet spirit." It's a permanent beauty that pleases God, and, best of all, it's free. However, wives must not forget that maintaining this spiritual beauty requires discipline and exercise just the same as physical beauty.

When people say, "Beauty may be only skin deep, but ugly goes all the way to the bone," they are stating, without intending to do so, a Biblical truth. There can be much ugliness beneath a beautiful exterior. True beauty comes from within. It is the only beauty that leads to lasting satisfaction in marriage. This type of beauty draws attention to the Creator, not the creation.

PRAYER THOUGHTS: Heavenly Father, author and creator of all things wonderful and beautiful, help us keep our eyes upon Your truth and look for the inward beauty in those around us. Amen.

THE PERFECT EXAMPLE

SCRIPTURE: Philippians 2:1-8

VERSE FOR TODAY: Once made perfect, he became the source of eternal salvation for all who obey him (Hebrews 5:9, *New International Version*).

HYMN FOR TODAY: "Blessed Assurance"

It doesn't come naturally to be submissive, especially for Americans who are known for their independent spirits. In demanding "our rights," we can overlook the rights of others. Democracy does not mean that each vocal and well-organized minority gets their way. Democracy, like Christianity, requires that we respect and respond to the needs of others.

This requires putting Jesus at the center of our lives. The very thought of considering others to be better than ourselves is an absurd idea to people molded by the philosophy of the "Me first" generation. Yet it is this servant attitude which we are commanded by Jesus to nurture, as He demonstrated by words and example (John 13:1-17).

Jesus never worried about His "rights." He came to earth to serve, in obedience to the wishes of His Father. Our Lord did not look to other human beings as His example. His eyes were always turned toward Heaven. Likewise, if we seek to be obedient to God's calling in our lives, we should never use other people as our measuring stick. Jesus, the perfect-example of an obedient son—even to the point of an undeserved death—is where we should keep our focus if we want to please God.

PRAYER THOUGHTS: Lord, we come to You with humble hearts, knowing how unworthy we are, yet accepting the truth that You loved us so much that You sent Your Son to earth to die in our place. Amen.

THE PERFECT MARRIAGE

SCRIPTURE: 1 Corinthians 7:1-7

VERSE FOR TODAY: We all stumble in many ways. If anyone is never at fault in what he says, he is a perfect man (James 3:2, *New International Version*).

HYMN FOR TODAY: "Make Me a Blessing"

Marriage is not a one-way street. Give-and-take has to go in both directions if the relationship is to be Scriptural. What must flow freely along this two-way street is communication. Failure to communicate is a leading cause of broken marriages.

In some cultures, the wife is expected to remain silent and walk one step behind her husband. Done willingly, this is an attitude of respect. When performed out of fear and repression, it becomes subservience, not submission. The Bible demands a mutual submission that comes out of love, not fear. It is a sad situation when a wife does not feel she can freely share her emotions or thoughts with her husband. It is an equally sad situation when a wife, through her actions and words, controls her husband and becomes the head of the family. While marriage is a partnership of equals, God has ordained the husband as the leader. As the leader, the husband is responsible to have love and respect as the standards by which to measure all his words and actions. The same is true for the wife.

As children, we may have said, "Sticks and stones may break my bones, but words can never hurt me." As adults we know that is not true. Words do destroy marriages, both the words that are spoken and those that are not but should be.

PRAYER THOUGHTS: Father, help us to lean on the Holy Spirit. Grant us peace and understanding in our relationships with those we love the most. Amen.

THE PERFECT HUSBAND

SCRIPTURE: Ephesians 5:25-33

VERSE FOR TODAY: But my dove, my perfect one, is unique (Song of Songs 6:9, *New International Version*).

HYMN FOR TODAY: "I Would Be Like Jesus"

Everyone wants respect. From the Christian perspective, we should be respected for who we are, an individual created in the image of God. From the viewpoint of society, however, we are judged by our visible achievements. A sports team may have players with talent, but in order to gain respect, they must win. It is not enough in the eyes of the world to simply do the best we can with the ability God gave us.

To gain respect, the world says a husband must have some recognizable achievement—like a title, a position of importance, or a job that pays well. Paul says the husband's goal in life is to follow the example of Jesus. This means leading a life without stain or blemish, a life that is holy and blameless. In order to accomplish this goal, a husband may have to make choices that will not allow him to gain that title, position, or money that the world values above everything.

The Verse for Today can apply to the husband as well as the wife, because we are each unique. Each individual is lovely in God's eyes. Our first goal in life must be to seek the approval of God. Only with this type of attitude can we gain the respect that produces eternal benefits.

PRAYER THOUGHTS: Thank You, Lord, for making me unique. Thank You for the cleansing blood of Jesus that will make me perfect in Your eyes on judgment day. Amen.

THE PERFECT CHILD

SCRIPTURE: Proverbs 23:15-25

VERSE FOR TODAY: Children, obey your parents in the Lord, for this is right (Ephesians 6:1, *New International Version*).

HYMN FOR TODAY: "I'm a Child of the King"

The child-rearing pendulum has swung from "Children should be seen, not heard" to "Every child has rights." The middle ground and not the outer extremes is usually the wisest choice when raising children. While children may have rights, they also have responsibilities, just as do adults.

Parents have the responsibility to give their children roots and wings. The child, as Solomon pointed out, has the responsibility to heed the wisdom and guidance of his or her parents if those roots are to be planted firmly in good soil. Sometimes a child has to learn the hard way, because being given the freedom to make mistakes is a part of developing the wings to fly. Too often, however, learning the hard way means that the child has ignored the advice of the parents. There are no new problems or temptations. The old ones simply come dressed up in new clothing.

Children face many decisions in their lives, but none has a greater impact on their future than the decision they make with regard to honoring and respecting their parents. This decision is so important that God made it the first commandment with a promise (Exodus 20:12). While times may change, God's law concerning the relationship between children and their parents has not, and never will, change.

PRAYER THOUGHTS: Father, we admit we are not perfect and we make mistakes. Let Your light and Your wisdom shine through us so that our children will choose to become Your children. In the name of Jesus. Amen.

THE PERFECT PARENTS

SCRIPTURE: Deuteronomy 6:1-9

VERSE FOR TODAY: Aim for perfection . . ." (2 Corinthians 13:11, *New International Version*).

HYMN FOR TODAY: "Pass It On"

The search for perfection begins early in life. Parents want their children to have perfect teeth, achieve A's on their report cards, find the perfect spouse, be hired for the ideal job, and then live happily ever after. This creates tremendous pressure on the parents as well as the children. Some parents go through life with guilt feelings for their child's shortcomings. Yet this is not to say that parents do not have responsibilities.

No matter how hard he tried, Moses could not get the children of Israel to faithfully follow God's instructions. No matter how hard we try, our children will not follow all our instructions either. From the day Adam was created, God gave humans the freedom to accept or reject His commands. Sin came into the world as a result of disobedience.

Only Jesus lived a perfect life. He was tempted and He suffered, yet He remained perfect (sinless) because He was always obedient to what God commanded. Paul challenges us to "Aim for perfection." Our first responsibility as a parent is to keep our eyes upon Jesus. Our faithfulness, not the faithfulness of our children, is the basis upon which God will judge us.

PRAYER THOUGHTS: Eternal Father, thank You for making us Your children. Thank You for the direction You give to our lives. Help us to be obedient to Your command to surrender our burdens into Your hands. We pray in the name of our Savior, Jesus Christ. Amen.

A DANGEROUS DISGUISE

SCRIPTURE: Matthew 4

VERSE FOR TODAY: Be sober, be vigilant; because your adversary the devil, as a roaring lion, walketh about, seeking whom he may devour (1 Peter 5:8).

HYMN FOR TODAY: "Yield Not to Temptation"

The six-foot, two-inch woman seen in a shopping center looked like many others who meandered through the stores. Her yellow cotton dress was fashionable for the summer. Short black hair framed her face which was partially concealed by sunglasses. But her appearance was deceiving. The reddish-purple lipstick failed to line a smile as this man who carried a butcher knife in his purse demanded money from a bank teller.

Being in disguise is typical of the enemy of Christianity. Viewing the appearance of evil, we are deceived by the camouflage presented by the devil. He offers the world an appealing way to discover fun, power, or wealth. But he never reveals the degradation of character, the pitfalls of emotions, the loss of self-respect, the alienation of loved ones, or the condemnation of the Lord which will result.

In the wilderness as he tried to pull Jesus into his snare, Satan's disguise was ineffective. Jesus saw him for what he is. Going through the trauma of wrestling with the enemy and experiencing the sweet taste of victory, Jesus paved the way for us. It is our choice to follow His example.

PRAYER THOUGHTS: Lord God, we thank You for the perfect example of the life of Jesus. We pray for wisdom to recognize the evil one and the courage to push him out of our lives. We pray in the name of Jesus. Amen.

August 23-27, 29. **Lillian Robbins** is retired and enjoys writing from her home in Tarboro, North Carolina.

CHOSEN WITH LOVE

SCRIPTURE: Ephesians 1:1-6

VERSE FOR TODAY: We are the children of God: And if children, then heirs; heirs of God, and joint-heirs with Christ (Romans 8:16, 17).

HYMN FOR TODAY: "The Family of God"

Martha was nervous. She held her hands together so she wouldn't bite her nails. She smiled and prayed that this would be the couple who would take her home with them. The orphanage was not bad, but more than anything else in the world, Martha wanted a family.

The decision was the same as always. They walked right past her and chose a blue-eyed blond with dimples. Martha's beautiful personality wasn't seen on the surface, and those who came to adopt never thought she was the little girl they wanted.

Oh, what a blessed Savior who never passes over one because of unfavorable appearances! The ugliest, most handicapped, and all others are invited to become a part of the family of God. We need not stand aside and watch while others are chosen. There is room for all. The Master's door is open, and He calls us to come in.

As children of God, you and I share with all the other members of God's family and dedicate ourselves to glorify His name. In no other place can there be found greater love, compassion, protection, and security than in the family where the Heavenly Father looks down and cares for us.

PRAYER THOUGHTS: Our loving Father in Heaven, help us feel the blessing of adoption and the privilege of sharing as brothers and sisters of our Lord. As we strive to be an asset in this relationship, may we gain the strength that is present in such a union. We pray in the name of our Savior, Jesus Christ. Amen.

NECESSARY CONNECTION

SCRIPTURE: Ephesians 1:9-23

VERSE FOR TODAY: I can do all things through Christ which strengtheneth me (Philippians 4:13).

HYMN FOR TODAY: "Power in the Blood"

Stacy called out in distress. The TV wouldn't come on, and it was time for her favorite show to begin.

Mom stopped her work and went to check it out. Wouldn't you know, the wall plug had been knocked loose. The connection was made, and the show came on. Electricity is a marvelous invention, but without the proper connection, its power is useless.

That's the way it is with the power of God and His subjects. Paul wrote that the gospel of Christ is the power of God unto salvation.

Just before He ascended back into Heaven, Jesus declared that all power was given to Him in Heaven and in earth. He is the source, and when the light of our lives shines in a dark and heedless world, it is only possible because we are plugged into our Savior, Jesus Christ.

As certain as the parable of Jesus reveals the necessity for branches to abide in the vine to produce fruit, we, as Christians, must be plugged into the power of Christ that we may be effective in our efforts. It is through our proclaiming the gospel in word and deed that His light shines every day.

PRAYER THOUGHTS: Our Father, help us to know that with power from on high, we can do all things that You would have us accomplish in Your name. Help us to be bold in proclaiming Your message and in living that which we proclaim. In the name of Jesus. Amen.

PREPARATION FOR BATTLE

SCRIPTURE: 2 Corinthians 10:1-6

VERSE FOR TODAY: God is our refuge and strength, a very present help in trouble (Psalm 46:1).

HYMN FOR TODAY: "The Fight Is On"

A young mother serving on the mission field was left alone with two small children while her husband went further into remote areas. Her baby became seriously ill. As she mopped the feverish brow and constantly cared for the sick child, there was no relief for her.

The days dragged on, and the young woman became so physically and mentally exhausted she had no energy to word a lengthy prayer for God's assistance. But she knew the Lord saw her predicament and could hear her plea as she repeatedly spoke to Him, "Lord, I have You for such a time as this."

Paul writes that the weapons of our warfare are mighty through God. The Lord is far above all principality, power, and might. Whether it be temptation to commit a carnal sin or the danger of permitting doubt to stifle our trust, the abiding faith within us can fight the battles we face.

Gaining knowledge of God's Word is preparation for battle. Hidden in our hearts, "The word of God is quick, and powerful, and sharper than any two-edged sword . . . and is a discerner of the thoughts and intents of the heart" (Hebrews 4:12).

PRAYER THOUGHTS: Dear God, help us to consider the importance of knowing Your Word. Give us an understanding of its meaning and its place in our lives so that we might have the exact weapon needed in any situation that may arise at any moment. Help us to be like our Master, Jesus Christ, in whom we pray. Amen.

LIFE'S CONTENTS

SCRIPTURE: 2 Timothy 2:1-7

VERSES FOR TODAY: Present your bodies a living sacrifice (Romans 12:1). If we live in the Spirit, let us also walk in the Spirit (Galatians 5:25).

HYMN FOR TODAY: "All To Jesus I Surrender"

The Sunday-school teacher set a jar on the table in front of the students. When asked what they saw, they responded, "A jar half full of water."

The discussion brought varied ideas. Because the jar was half empty, any number of good things could be added: tea, coffee, concentrated juice, more water. On the other hand, if one would add mud, tar, or poison, the water would be ruined and even dangerous.

We are much like that jar. Our lives are going to be filled with something. We can choose to be filled with good and allow no room for evil, or we may choose to be filled with evil.

Paul admonishes us to give ourselves to the Lord, not in death, but as living sacrifices. The fruit of the Spirit such as love, long-suffering, meekness, and gentleness can make Christianity run over in our lives and bless those around us.

When we are busy as servants of the Lord who are giving glory to His name, there will be no time or space for evils to reside in our hearts. Hatred, murders, drunkenness, and adultery have no place in the lives of those who are consecrated to the will of God.

PRAYER THOUGHTS: Thank You, Lord, for the opportunity to choose how we spend our time. Give us the courage to fill our lives with that which will honor Your name, and help us to dispel thoughts or actions which may lead to disobedience of Your will. In the name of our Savior, Jesus Christ. Amen.

SUITING UP

SCRIPTURE: Ephesians 6:13-17

VERSE FOR TODAY: I am thy God: I will strengthen thee; yea, I will help thee; yea, I will uphold thee with the right hand of my righteousness (Isaiah 41:10).

HYMN FOR TODAY: "Stand Up, Stand Up for Jesus"

Siegfried was a mythological warrior who was fearless and powerful. Since he always met his foes head-on, he never wore any armor to protect his back. Unfortunately, when his enemy learned this, he crept up behind the resting Siegfried and stabbed him fatally in the back.

Overconfidence is dangerous. Our enemy, Satan, is ruthless and clever in seeking to negate our armor. Today we must sift through a lot of miry distortion to reclaim a nugget of truth. Righteousness, or *right*ness, becomes whatever suits a person at any given moment. Disagreement beclouds the gospel of salvation, as to whether one has it or how to attain it. Faith, the shield that protects the whole body, is the main target of Satan's darts. Once that shield is destroyed, the rest is vulnerable. But Christians must attack as well as defend. Our sword is the Word of God, as Jesus used it against the tempter (Matthew 4:1-11). Our whole armor is *of God*, through our captain, Jesus Christ. We do not just keep it on hand; it is to be put on and worn at all times to give us constant protection.

So suit up and stand strong. Remember, you are not alone.

PRAYER THOUGHTS: Father, we know that our victory is in Christ, who provides us our armor, and we thank You. May we realize that when we resist the devil he will run the other way.

August 28. **Jacqueline Westers** is a Christian writer and former editor of adult literature at Standard Publishing. She makes her home in Cincinnati, Ohio.

VICTORY OF THE SOUL

SCRIPTURE: Hebrews 2:9-15

VERSE FOR TODAY: Then shall the King say unto them on his right hand, Come, ye blessed of my Father, inherit the kingdom prepared for you from the foundation of the world (Matthew 25:34).

HYMN FOR TODAY: "Victory In Jesus"

During the period before 1954, polio was one of the most dreaded illnesses in the United States. Death or crippling of individuals from all walks of life was everywhere. Jonas Salk worked with dedication to perfect a safe vaccine that could eliminate such fear. When he administered to himself the first test on humans, he was risking his life.

Victory over a fatal disease, whether it be whooping cough as in days of old, or polio, brings joy and thanksgiving to the hearts of people.

Sin is a more fatal condition than the most painful, debilitating disease of the body. Its destruction is prevalent throughout the world, and many people are not even aware of the cure provided by Jesus—who not only risked His life but gave it to provide a remedy for the sickness of the soul.

When Jesus conquered sin, our way to final victory was prepared. The fight with the devil is difficult, but what a wonderful blessing to know there is victory in Jesus. Joy and peace that passes all understanding is ours as we look toward that home in Heaven where there will be no more sickness or death.

PRAYER THOUGHTS: Thank You, Father, for providing a sure way for cleansing sin from our lives. Instill in our hearts the wonderful anticipation of the reunion when saints will gather with the Father and the Son in the Heavenly home where tears and sadness will have vanished from our lives. Thank You for giving to us Jesus Christ, in whom we pray. Amen.

WHERE ALL THINGS BEGIN

SCRIPTURE: Genesis 1:1-2; John 1:1-5

VERSE FOR TODAY: In the beginning God created the heavens and the earth (Genesis 1:1, *New International Version*).

HYMN FOR TODAY: "This is My Father's World"

Consider the plight of the atheist. He has no one to thank for this beautiful world. When he traces the chain of events, he comes to a dead end. For him, the world is a giant accident and the product of a series of random occurrences.

Not so for people of faith. Christians see a mind behind creation which gives it purpose. While the concept of God is beyond complete understanding, the idea that there is no God is ludicrous. Genesis begins not by arguing for God's existence, but assuming it. All nature is a testimony of God.

The apostle John reminds us that not only does nature bear witness to the existence of God, but even more so does Christ. Jesus was there in the beginning and was a participant in the creation of this world. When He came to this world, He was coming to a place that bears His artist's touch. That makes it all the more startling that the creation was allowed to rebel against the Creator. Two of God's greatest revelatory acts were the creation and the incarnation. That which He created, He visited, in His mercy.

PRAYER THOUGHTS: Lord, help me to notice Your brush strokes in every sunset. Let me recognize that every star stands as a silent but eloquent witness of Your creative genius. If I look carefully I will see Your fingerprints on all created things, but most of all I will see Your image in the face of Your only begotten Son, in whose name we pray. Amen.

August 30—September 5. **J. Michael Shannon** is a college professor and minister who lives in Cincinnati, Ohio.

August 31

BASKING IN THE GLOW

SCRIPTURE: Genesis 1:3-5; Jeremiah 31:35-37

VERSE FOR TODAY: God saw that the light was good, and he separated the light from the darkness (Genesis 1:4, *New International Version*).

HYMN FOR TODAY: "Fairest Lord Jesus"

We are children of the light, not children of the night. God's creative activity begins with the creation of light. This is because light is fundamental to creation. Even before there are "lights," like the sun, moon, and stars, there is the light of God's creative energy. For generations man has seen God's activity as a struggle between light and darkness. The light always wins. You can dispel darkness with light, but you cannot dispel light with darkness.

Light remains a mystery to us, almost as mysterious as God himself. We don't understand it, but we can enjoy it. The Bible teaches that God himself is light and in Him is no darkness at all. We need God in the same way we need light.

Without light there is no sight. Without light there is no warmth. Without light there is no growth. Without light there is no security. Without light there is no life.

God has given to us the light of the world. In Him, we have no need of fear. He lights our way. Darkness or death have no power over us. In Him, we have life.

PRAYER THOUGHTS: Like the sun You created, O God, I cannot look directly at You, but I can bask in the glorious rays of Your presence. You are like light itself—beyond comprehension—but a welcome and comforting presence. Just as the morning light dispels the darkness of the night, may Your presence dispel any darkness in my soul. Through Christ, Amen.

DEVOTIONS

· · · · · · · · · · · ·

SEPTEMBER

September 1

LOOK UP!

SCRIPTURE: Genesis 1:6-8; 14-19

VERSE FOR TODAY: And God said, Let there be lights in the expanse of the sky to separate the day from the night, and let them serve as signs to mark seasons and days and years" (Genesis 1:14, *New International Version*).

HYMN FOR TODAY: "How Great Thou Art"

The sky has lost much of its "poetry." It has been examined, studied, mapped, and explored. We no longer sing, "Twinkle, twinkle, little star; how I wonder what you are." We sing, "Twinkle, twinkle, little star; I know exactly what you are."

Yet on a summer's day, we still might lie on our backs in the grass and ponder the wonders of the sky. We use the sky to chart our course. We use it to calculate the seasons. We observe it to predict the weather.

Most of all, though, the sky delights. David declared that the "heavens declare the glory of God" (Psalm 19:1). They still do. We have the advantage of knowing that the firmament is far more vast and complex than our ancestors comprehended. If it communicated the glory of God to them, how much more should it communicate to us. Every twinkling star is a sun in its own right, placed in the firmament for us. So, the next time you experience any doubt whatsoever about the existence of God, just look up.

PRAYER THOUGHTS: When we look at the firmament, O God, we feel small and insignificant. We feel that way until we comprehend that all we see in the sky has been used by You for our blessing. Then we find our significance in You. Thank You for giving Your universe to us, and especially we thank You for giving us salvation through Jesus. We pray in the name of Jesus. Amen.

WATER!

SCRIPTURE: Genesis 1:9,10; Isaiah 40:21-26

VERSE FOR TODAY: And God said, "Let the water under the sky be gathered to one place, and let dry ground appear." And it was so (Genesis 1:9, *New International Version*).

HYMN FOR TODAY: "There's a Wideness in God's Mercy"

When astronauts first saw the earth from the perspective of outer space, they marveled at how blue the planet appeared. The pictures that have come back from such expeditions have caused some to label earth as "the blue planet." This is a testimony to how prominent water is on our planet. It is also a testimony to how crucial water is to the balance of nature and our survival.

The sea remains in many ways a mysterious frontier; we have yet to fully explore its depths. What is not mysterious is our need for water. Man can not live without water. The earth would dry up and die without water.

Water, like light, is essential for life itself. The taste of water refreshes us. The sound of water relaxes us. The splash of water can be invigorating as well as cleansing. The partnership of water, earth, and light produces growth. Both saltwater and fresh water provide food for the hungry.

With this in mind, it should come as no surprise that Jesus described himself as the "living water."

PRAYER THOUGHTS: O God, we thank You that You have provided the rain, the rivers, the lakes, and the seas to serve us. We are humbled by this great gift. We thank You even more for our Lord Jesus, the living water. Through Him I pray, amen.

September 3

CONSIDER THE PEANUT

SCRIPTURE: Genesis 1:11, 12; 29, 30

VERSE FOR TODAY: The land produced vegetation: plants bearing seed according to their kinds and trees bearing fruit with seed in it according to their kinds. And God saw that it was good (Genesis 1:12, *New International Version*).

HYMN FOR TODAY: "Fairest Lord Jesus"

George Washington Carver was an inspiration to all people, not just the black community. He had a great curiosity about nature, and his mind speculated about many diverse and nebulous subjects. One day Carver was being philosophical and he asked God to show him the meaning of the universe. He later recorded that he sensed God saying to him, "Why don't you ponder the mystery of the peanut? That is more your size." So, Carver did ponder the peanut and came up with some marvelous uses for this humble plant. He also came to appreciate the beauty of nature.

If we want to capture the mystery of the universe, all we have to do is look at one of God's simpler creations. Look at any plant; notice the beauty and craftsmanship. Notice how many plants give beauty as well as something for food. Even the tiniest blade of grass is a marvel.

Jesus told us to "consider the lilies" (Luke 12:27). He pointed out that if God takes a great interest in a plant, will He not much more care for His crowning creation? The lily is a wonder, but so is the peanut, and even more are you.

PRAYER THOUGHTS: O Father of life, even in the simplest of living things I see Your genius. I see the complex systems and I realize how much more complex is mankind. Thank You for making me in Your image. Through Your perfect Son I pray, amen.

UNDER THE SEA

SCRIPTURE: Genesis 1:20-22; Psalm 8:3-8

VERSE FOR TODAY: And God said, "Let the water teem with living creatures, and let birds fly above the earth across the expanse of the sky" (Genesis 1:20, *New International Version*).

HYMN FOR TODAY: "All Things Bright and Beautiful"

God created the sky, earth, and sea. For each He prepared inhabitants designed to live and thrive in that environment. God wasn't interested in just creating places. The places were prepared for life and living things.

God's creativity is particularly evident in the residents of the seas, lakes, and rivers. There are over 21,700 species of fish. They represent an incredible variety of design and appearance. Some time ago, I decided to start an aquarium. I had no idea what I really wanted, just some fish. I was amazed at all the choices available. The shapes and colors were absolutely stunning. This illustrates just a small part of God's marvelous creativity.

God didn't have to create so many different kinds of fish. He could have made them all one shape or all one color. The fact that He didn't gives us insight into His nature. He wasn't interested in making generic fish; He created many kinds, with enough variety and color to make a virtual living kaleidoscope.

PRAYER THOUGHTS: O God, so much of Your creative work is out of my sight. I am in awe of what I can see each day, but help me to recognize that far from human sight is a world of beauty and diversity. There is much in which to delight in this world. Help me to see that You have given us all things richly to enjoy. In the name of Christ Jesus, I pray. Amen.

ALL CREATURES GREAT AND SMALL

SCRIPTURE: Genesis 1:24-26

VERSE FOR TODAY: God made the wild animals according to their kinds, the livestock according to their kinds, and all the creatures that move along the ground according to their kinds. And God saw that it was good (Genesis 1:25, *New International Version*).

HYMN FOR TODAY: "All Creatures of our God and King"

We owe a lot to the animals. They have provided for the health and comfort of man. Some animals, like the sheep, give of themselves to provide the clothes that give warmth. Some animals, such as the cow, give butter, cheese and milk. Others, like the ox and horse have given of their strength to ease our labor. Dogs and cats can protect their masters and give affection and love.

God gave man dominion over the earth, including the animals. That responsibility implies care and respect. It is not wrong to accept what the living creatures can give us. However, it is wrong to be unappreciative and cruel.

A visit to the farm or zoo should bring people to a new level of worship. God is the creator of all these marvelous creatures. They bring so much into our lives. We are impressed by the animals, but we should be more impressed with the One who dreamed of them and gave them life.

This same God, the God of the Universe, has given us the gift of life and the gift of animals to make our life better.

PRAYER THOUGHTS: Help us to recognize, our God, that we share this planet with some amazing creatures. What is more amazing is how You have allowed them to serve us. All of this is part of Your plan and a reflection of Your love. For this we are grateful. Through Jesus, amen.

"WHO DOES THE BABY LOOK LIKE?"

SCRIPTURE: Genesis 1:26-28

VERSE FOR TODAY: So God created man in his own image, in the image of God created he him; male and female created he them (Genesis 1:27).

HYMN FOR TODAY: "Let the Beauty of Jesus"

We had just moved over a thousand miles to a town on the east coast. On our first Sunday there, I left our two-year-old son in the church nursery. When I went to pick him up after the worship service, a young father met me at the door. Before I could point out my youngster, he grinned and said, "I know which one is yours—he looks just like you."

Actually, he didn't look a bit like me, but I was thrilled that someone saw a resemblance between my son and me.

It's one of the first questions we ask when a baby is born: "Who does the baby look like?" We look for a behaviorism that will indicate who the baby's personality is like. We delight both in telling, and hearing, about the family resemblance.

No less does our Creator take pleasure in His children when they show a family resemblance to Him.

Do I "look" the least bit like the Heavenly Father? I was made in God's image. Is that image plain to see in my attitudes, speech, and actions? If not, how strong is my desire to "let the beauty of Jesus be seen in me"?

PRAYER THOUGHTS: I know Your image in me is marred, Lord, but with the help of Your Holy Spirit in me, may Your beauty shine through me. In the name of Jesus, my Savior. Amen.

September 6-12. **Wanda Trawick** is a physician who serves in the Watauga Presbyterian Church, Johnson City, Tennessee, as a Sunday school teacher and Missions Committee member.

September 7

THE BREATH OF LIFE

SCRIPTURE: Genesis 2:1-9

VERSE FOR TODAY: And the Lord God formed man of the dust of the ground, and breathed into his nostrils the breath of life; and man became a living soul (Genesis 2:7).

HYMN FOR TODAY: "Breathe on Me"

During my internship year at Charity Hospital in New Orleans, I rotated to different departments every month or two. From the obstetrical unit I went to Internal Medicine. What a difference!

In the delivery room we waited expectantly (and sometimes anxiously) for the newborn's first wail, signaling that first breath. On the Internal Medicine wards, we often waited with anxiety and dread for that last breath which signaled death.

Breath. We fight desperately for it when we can't get it. Just ask any asthmatic.

How appropriate is that Scripture which tells us that at our creation we were <u>energized</u> by the breath of God. We became <u>living souls</u>. As our bodies are nourished and sustained by the oxygen we breathe, our souls are nourished and sustained by the life-giving energy we receive from the breath of God. Physically and spiritually, we are created and sustained by the breath of God.

As children of God, that breath of God's Spirit is not optional for us. It is as necessary as the air we breathe.

PRAYER THOUGHTS: O God, do I "hunger and thirst" for Your energizing Spirit as much as I crave my next breath of air? Create in me a hunger for that Spirit which would make me fully alive. In the name of my Savior, Jesus Christ, I pray. Amen.

SO MUCH FOR RUGGED INDIVIDUALISM

SCRIPTURE: Genesis 2:15-20

VERSE FOR TODAY: And the Lord God said, It is not good that the man should be alone (Genesis 2:18).

HYMN FOR TODAY: "Blest Be the Tie"

A friend of mine works as a volunteer with Contact ministries in our city. Besides acting as a "hot line" for potential suicide victims and others with acute problems, the volunteers give daily "reassurance" to shut-in persons who live alone. If the shut-in doesn't answer, a relative or the police are contacted.

Fortunately, most of the time the shut-in does answer and, as the term "reassurance call" suggests, is reassured by the sound of another human voice.

Although I am far from being a shut-in, I do live alone. Actually, I like living alone—although my two cats might be insulted by my saying I live "alone." In spite of the companionable cats, however, I do need human contact. I rejoice in the sound of my little grandson's voice on the phone, a visit from the elderly widow across the street, the warm friendships of those in my church and Sunday school class.

God made us for each other. We were created for relationship, both with our Creator and His creatures. His plan for us includes family, community, and congregation. We were made to need each other.

PRAYER THOUGHTS: Thank You, Heavenly Father, for designing us not only with a need for You, but for each other. Give us wisdom to choose our human companions with discernment, and lead us to those who need us and to those whom we need. In the name of Jesus. Amen.

SOMETHING MISSING

SCRIPTURE: Genesis 2:21-25

VERSE FOR TODAY: And Adam said, This is now bone of my bones, and flesh of my flesh (Genesis 2:23).

HYMN FOR TODAY: "Love Divine"

We had company the day our fourth-grader came home from school with news he couldn't contain. On the other hand, he didn't want to share it with a roomful of people. He sidled over to me and whispered, "Come to my room."

I excused myself and followed him to his room where he carefully closed the door. I sat down on his bed and waited for his apparently momentous news. "Guess who sat next to me on the bus?" he asked, his eyes intense and his face as impassive as he could make it.

I hazarded a name (fortunately, the right one)—a girl in his class who lived down the road. "Yes," he breathed. "Don't tell anyone."

That was all. But I knew he had made a discovery that day—that his family, the animals on the farm, the boy across the road, and heroes in his books were not enough to make his life complete.

His little heart was as full that day as was Adam's must have been when his feeling of incompleteness was vanquished by the creation of one who was both like him and different from him.

PRAYER THOUGHTS: Dear Father, in spite of all the complications that have arisen in the relationships between men and women in the past few decades, help us to rejoice in the completeness You made possible by Your creation of both. In the name of Jesus. Amen.

THE AWESOMENESS OF GOD

SCRIPTURE: Job 36:22-33

VERSE FOR TODAY: Behold, God is great, and we know him not, neither can the number of his years be searched out (Job 36:26).

HYMN FOR TODAY: "Holy, Holy, Holy"

His father sat my two-year-old grandson on his shoulders as we entered the mechanized dinosaur exhibit in the science museum in San Francisco. He had been looking forward to the exhibit with great enthusiasm, telling me all about what we were going to see.

But as we stood before a replica of the tyrannosaur, he grew wide-eyed and silent. As the robotic dinosaur began to "roar," he clapped his hands over his ears and kept them there until we exited the large display room. The actual experience of being in the presence of the lifelike "monsters" was more awe-inspiring than he could ever have imagined.

Remember Isaiah's experience in the temple when he "saw the Lord, high and lifted up" (Isaiah 6:1)? We're not sure what Isaiah's relationship to God was before that experience, but we do know he was never the same after it. In the presence of the awe-inspiring greatness and holiness of God, he recognized his own sinfulness.

Like Isaiah, when we really behold Him, He is overpowering. We see Him and ourselves as we really are. Like the prophet, we recognize our sinfulness. Like young Elihu, we recognize our ignorance.

PRAYER THOUGHTS: Lord, help us to be humble enough to recognize the majesty of God and His "unknowableness" and yet maintain the intimacy in prayer that Jesus taught us when He addressed God as "Father." Amen.

MORE THAN WE KNOW

SCRIPTURE: Job 37:1-13

VERSE FOR TODAY: Great things doeth he, which we cannot comprehend (Job 37:5).

HYMN FOR TODAY: "To God Be the Glory"

My eighth-grade science class was laughing about some of the "scientific" ideas of the past. To them the alchemists' dreams of converting lead into gold were childish. They felt the same about the old "phlogiston theory" which posed the presence of a substance called phlogiston in all flammable substances. The phlogiston was supposed to be given off as the material burned.

And what about those scientists of long ago who believed in "spontaneous generation"—the view that living things were produced spontaneously from dead or inorganic material? The students shook their heads in disbelief that their ancestors could have been so foolish.

But when I asked them if they thought students 200 or 300 years from now might consider many of our own scientific ideas utter foolishness, they sobered up and gave the question some thought. Maybe their generation didn't have all the answers either.

We know more than our ancestors about some things, but we don't understand all there is to know about the creation or the Creator. We need to share Paul's admission, "Now we see through a glass, darkly" (1 Corinthians 13:12).

PRAYER THOUGHTS: O Father, keep us from laziness. Help us to learn all we can about You and Your creation. May we never overestimate our understanding of the way You and Your world operate. In the name of Jesus, Amen.

HOLD YOUR TONGUE!

SCRIPTURE: Job 38:1-11

VERSE FOR TODAY: Who is this that darkeneth counsel by words without knowledge (Job 38:2)?

HYMN FOR TODAY: "Take My Life and Let It Be"

The Sunday school lesson was on John the Baptist, and two of us were engaged in a spirited debate over some relatively minor point about the prophet's life. Suddenly in the middle of it all, one class member rose in tears and hurried out the door.

Later we learned that her husband had been diagnosed with inoperable cancer that week. Can you imagine how our prattling on about the eccentricities of John the Baptist must have grated on her raw nerves as she sat there contemplating her husband's impending death?

How many of our discussions, even at church, are just tossing out "words without knowledge?" And how much of the advice we offer is composed of well-meaning but empty words? How often do we look beyond the surface?

How much better off we and those we attempt to counsel might be if we simply held our tongues and listened more often—especially if we listened with our eyes as well as our ears. How important is it to be sensitive to those around us?

There are times when we should listen, and there are times when we should speak. But when we do speak, we need to remember that "words without knowledge" are worse than no words at all.

PRAYER THOUGHTS: Heavenly Father, give us sense enough to desire understanding more than glibness of tongue. Give us insight into our reasons for speaking, and help us to guard our tongues from hurting others or leading them astray. In the name of Jesus. Amen.

GODLY DECISIONS

SCRIPTURE: Genesis 3:1-6

VERSE FOR TODAY: The world and its desires pass away, but the man who does the will of God lives forever. (1 John 2:17, *New International Version*).

HYMN FOR TODAY: "Not What These Hands Have Done"

Decisions, decisions! Every person faces many decisions daily. Our decisions range from minor details to life-changing events. Some common decisions we make are how we spend our time, with whom we make friends, or moral choices.

In the Garden of Eden, Adam and Eve made a decision. They were faced with a temptation that appeared to have a reasonable, beneficial outcome.

Like Adam and Eve, we are responsible for our actions and must answer to God. God has given us the ability to think independently and make conscious choices. Later in Genesis 3, God states to Adam and Eve the consequences of their improper decision.

Unfortunately, we also make decisions that cause us to sin. It is important to know that we can guard ourselves from wrong decisions by seeking the will of God continually through His Word. We become more godly through submission to Him and by being obedient to the commands in His Word. We have assurance (1 John 2:17) that those who make godly decisions will live forever in a kingdom that will not be shaken.

PRAYER THOUGHTS: Lord, help me to seek Your Word daily. Reveal Your will to me and help me to make godly decisions. Give me strength to overcome my own weaknesses. Thank You for being a perfect example. In Jesus' name, amen.

September 13, 15-19. **Virginia L. McCabe** is a Christian free lance writer who resides in Cincinnati, Ohio.

EXPOSED

SCRIPTURE: Genesis 3:7-11

VERSE FOR TODAY: Whither shall I go from thy Spirit? Or whither shall I flee from they presence?

HYMN FOR TODAY: "Nothing Between"

When someone has done something wrong, the natural reaction is to run away or hide. On the TV news, when an offender is arrested, every attempt is made to cover his or her identity. This inclination makes it hard for some sinners to come to Christ. Even Peter, after seeing Jesus' miracle of the great catch of fish, fell down before Jesus, saying, "Depart from me; for I am a sinful man, O Lord" (Luke 5:8). "I am too wicked," or "I cannot change" are barriers.

There is no hiding from God, as Adam found out. Hiding from Him is impossible, for He knows everything about us, even our thoughts before we think them. We are exposed to Him. God "looketh to the ends of the earth, and seeth under the whole heaven" (Job 28:24). He takes away the need to hide because of His love and mercy. Read Psalm 103:1-14. This is great drawing power, fully demonstrated by Jesus, who said, "If I be lifted up from the earth, will draw all men unto me" (John 12:32). Thus God himself becomes a hiding place, to save us and shelter us from evil.

PRAYER THOUGHTS: We thank You, Father, that we have no need to hide from You, because Your Son has reconciled us to You. Keep us ever safe and secure in Your presence. We pray in the name of Jesus, Our Savior. Amen.

September 14. **Jacqueline Westers** is a Christian writer and former editor of adult literature at Standard Publishing. She makes her home in Cincinnati, Ohio.

CASTING THE BLAME

SCRIPTURE: Genesis 3:12, 13; Psalm 139:1-12

VERSE FOR TODAY: O Lord, you have searched me and you know me (Psalm 139:1, *New International Version*).

HYMN FOR TODAY: "Nothing But the Blood"

Has anyone ever made you their scapegoat? A scapegoat is someone who bears the blame for another person's wrongdoing. God does not expect us to blame others for our own sin.

God demands that we give personal account for our mistakes. Sin can bring us to such a low state that we make excuses and blame others for what we do.

This is illustrated by the first sin that was committed by Adam and Eve. Adam blamed God and Eve for his sin. Eve blamed the serpent for her sin. Our instinct is to try to escape the blame and hide from God.

God's omnipresence makes it impossible for us to hide from Him. God is personal and He wants to be active in our lives. He knows us better than we know ourselves (Psalm 139:1-6).

We cannot flee from God. Although our sin causes us shame and guilt, God continues to seek us through our failures (Psalm 139:7-12).

There will be times when we will fail. God expects us to take responsibility for our actions. We must daily ask Him to guard our hearts and provide us with guidance as we strive to lead righteous lives.

PRAYER THOUGHTS: Lord, forgive me when I fail, and help me to come to you in honesty. I am thankful that Jesus was willing to take my sins upon himself. Thank You for Your mercy and unconditional love. In the precious name of Jesus, amen.

PUNISHMENT FOR THE CRIME

SCRIPTURE: Genesis 3:14-19

VERSE FOR TODAY: In your struggle against sin, you have not yet resisted to the point of shedding your blood (Hebrews 12:4, *New International Version*).

HYMN FOR TODAY: "Let Jesus Come Into Your Heart"

Have you ever sat in a courtroom and observed the variety of cases before the judge? The law system addresses each crime and decides what punishment the criminal will receive. The severity of the crime committed determines the degree of punishment that will result.

Adam and Eve sinned and had to face the consequences for what they had done. God determined the personal punishment for their sin. He developed a punishment based on the type of crime that was committed.

Jesus endured opposition from sinful men and surrendered to the point of shedding His blood for crimes He did not commit. In the struggle against our sin, we will sometimes face punishment. We should not grow weary, but view the punishment as an opportunity to build our strength.

We should be encouraged because Jesus died for our sin. The cross takes away the pain and guilt of our crime. God's forgiveness and grace help us to overcome the shame. "Let's throw off everything that hinders and the sin that so easily entangles, and let's run with perseverance the race marked out for us" (Hebrews 12:1, *New International Version*).

PRAYER THOUGHTS: Dear Heavenly Father, thank You for Jesus. Help us to endure punishment. Make us strong so that we may share in Your holiness. Treat us as sons and daughters and train us in Your ways. Through Jesus Christ, amen.

MY FIRST LOVE

SCRIPTURE: Deuteronomy 6:4-14

VERSE FOR TODAY: Love the Lord your God with all your heart and with all your soul and with all your strength (Deuteronomy 6:5, *New International Version*).

HYMN FOR TODAY: "My Jesus, I Love Thee"

Who (what) am I putting first in my life? This is a challenging question that I continually ask myself. It helps me put my priorities into perspective, redefine my goals, and focus on a right relationship with the Lord. The answer is an unchanging one. The Lord should always be first.

In our Scripture passage today, God commands Israel to put Him first. He made it clear to them that He was the only One whom they should love, worship, and trust. God wanted the people of Israel to love Him with undivided attention. He expressed that Israel's obedience should be the result of a loving relationship with Him. It should not be a relationship based on duty or obligation.

God commanded Israel to love Him. He commands us to love Him. Love is an expression of loyalty and develops from devotion to God.

God expects us to love Him wholeheartedly and make Him first priority in our lives. "Whoever has my commands and obeys them, he is the one who loves me. He who loves me will be loved by my Father, and I too will love him and show myself to him" (John 14:21).

PRAYER THOUGHTS: Lord, thank You for Your unconditional love. Help me to love like You do in spite of my own weaknesses. Teach me to grow and be strengthened by Your Word. Let my heart be open to Your will and Your love. I love You. In Jesus' name, amen.

QUALITY COMMITMENTS

SCRIPTURE: Psalm 37:3-9, 27-31

VERSE FOR TODAY: Delight yourself in the Lord and he will give you the desires of your heart (Psalm 37:4, *New International Version*).

HYMN FOR TODAY: "Seek Ye First"

We live in a fast-paced world. We revolve around fast-food restaurants, self-serve gas stations, and while-you-wait services. The average person works a full-time job, attends school, has family responsibilities, and is involved in two or three other activities that he participates in regularly. Sometimes among our busy schedules, our commitments become overwhelming, even cumbersome.

We find ourselves overwhelmed and over-committed. We agree to fulfill obligations, but we stretch ourselves so far that we cannot effectively fulfill every commitment we have made.

Our commitment to the Lord is vital. Our commitment to Him should be first priority. We should not squeeze Him into our busy schedules or take the last few minutes of the day to study the Word or pray.

When we consider the commitments we make, we should decide which ones are the most valuable to the Lord and which ones we can fulfill most effectively. We should seek the Lord's will, evaluate the things we are committed to, and make changes if necessary.

Psalm 37 encourages us to strengthen our commitment to the Lord and put Him first in our lives.

PRAYER THOUGHTS: Lord, help us to be committed to You daily. Guide our decisions so that we can make quality commitments. Thank You for Your patience, and help us to do good. In Jesus' name, amen.

AN ATTITUDE OF GRATITUDE

SCRIPTURE: Psalm 119:1-8

VERSE FOR TODAY: In all your ways acknowledge him, and he will make your paths straight (Proverbs 3:6, *New International Version*).

HYMN FOR TODAY: "Heavenly Sunlight"

What makes you smile? Smiling is an outward expression that is based on an inward feeling.

"You were born with a smile," "You smile too much," and "You should be on a toothpaste commercial," are common phrases I have heard frequently throughout my life. I also have been called nicknames such as "Smiley" and "Grinny." When I was younger, I did not understand why people thought my constant smiling was so unique. Smiling has always been a natural way for me to communicate my happiness to others.

My senior year in high school, the class chose senior personalities, and I was chosen for the category of sweetest smile. Although this was done out of senior spirit and fun, there was some truth to these awards.

As an adult, I realize that I am able to smile so freely and naturally because my heart and spirit are in right relationship with the Lord. The inner happiness and peace I have developed produce outward fruit.

Our passage today tells us that if we walk with Him we will develop a foundation of inner peace and true happiness. A right relationship with God will be evident.

PRAYER THOUGHTS: Lord, thank You for the encouragement Your Word gives us daily. Give us continual strength to be who You want us to be. Help us to use our gifts wisely. Allow our hearts to be open to Your Word so we can walk upright before You. In Jesus' name, amen.

COMING OR GOING?

SCRIPTURE: Genesis 3:20-24

VERSE FOR TODAY: Therefore the Lord God sent him forth . . . to till the ground from whence he was taken (Genesis 3:23).

HYMN FOR TODAY: "He Leadeth Me"

"Mommy," a small boy once asked. "In Sunday school they said that God made man out of dust. Is that true?"

"Yes, it is," Mother agreed. "Why do you ask?"

"Because there's someone under my bed—and he's either coming or going!"

Adam's failure in the garden ended that part of God's plan for him, but it certainly wasn't the end of God's concern. For although Adam had fallen, God had alternate plans for him. He had to face something new—hard work—but he still had a relationship with God.

We, too, fail—and though we aren't banned from a paradise, it can mean a gap in our relationship with Him. Yet, as with Adam, God is always open to us as we seek to reestablish ties with Him. When we ask Him to, God lovingly accepts us into His arms and offers us new life, hope, and opportunities for service in a new atmosphere. So, like Adam, whether we're coming or going, God provides for us.

PRAYER THOUGHTS: Thank You, Father, that You have provided for us under all circumstances. May we stay within Your will. We thank You for making it possible for us to have a relationship with You. In Christ's name, amen.

September 20-26. **Anne Adams** is on the staff of St. Luke's United Church in Houston, Texas. She and her husband, Tom, have one daughter, Noelle.

THE PITY PARTY

SCRIPTURE: Genesis 4:1-7

VERSE FOR TODAY: And Cain was very wroth, and his countenance fell (Genesis 4:5).

HYMN FOR TODAY: "Have Thine Own Way, Lord"

"Hey, I hear that Jason didn't make the team," Mother said to Jeremy. "How's he taking it?"

Jeremy shrugged. "Okay, I guess. He's over the disappointment and now he's into a pity party."

"A what?"

"You know—feeling sorry for himself. But he'll snap out of it very soon."

Self-pity. A problem as old as man—and so wasteful!

Even so, we often do feel sorry for ourselves, particularly when we wish we'd done something differently. We brood and worry about it.

How do we avoid self-pity? Here's one way—we can accept whatever happened, forget the past, and then go on to new experiences and look for new challenges, having learned from what happened. The important thing not to do is to be trapped in the mire of self-pity and the bitterness of self-recrimination.

After all, God's loving provision is only operational in our lives when we're open to Him and not wallowing in a pity party! If you're having one, maybe it's time to get yourself dis-invited!

PRAYER THOUGHTS: Heavenly Father, we know that self-pity is actually seeing our problems as bigger than You are. Help us to keep our vision on You and not on our difficulties. In His name, amen.

LET GOD HANDLE IT!

SCRIPTURE: Genesis 4:8-16

VERSE FOR TODAY: The LORD said, "What have you done? Listen! Your brother's blood cries out to me from the ground (Genesis 4:10, *New International Version*).

HYMN FOR TODAY: "Oh, Master, Let Me Walk With Thee"

Though safety experts recommend drivers gently tap their horn as a warning to another driver who pulls too close in front, a Houston man recently found it wasn't good advice! He tapped his horn at a vehicle cutting too close to him, but the response wasn't exactly what he expected. The other car pulled alongside a few minutes later, the driver produced a gun, and he proceeded to fire at the horn-tapper—flattening one of his tires! Obviously the horn tap had angered the assailant, and he wanted to get even!

When someone offends us and we feel vindictive, we should not try to "get even." We will only hurt ourselves. Instead we should let God handle it. Seeking revenge always hurts our relationship with God. After all, we only know our part of the offense, while God knows all aspects and can handle it with loving objectivity.

There is an old saying, "Don't get mad—get even." The only way a Christian should "get even" is by letting God handle it!

PRAYER THOUGHTS: Dear heavenly Father, You handle our situations in the best way—with loving and proper justice. Teach us to know what is right and to act upon it. Let us not leave undone what You want us to do, but help us to remember that we can rely on Your Power to care for us in our daily lives. Give us wisdom to let you handle the problems. In Christ's name, amen.

GIANT-SIZED PROBLEMS

SCRIPTURE: Genesis 6:1-8

VERSE FOR TODAY: There were giants in the earth in those days (Genesis 6:4).

HYMN FOR TODAY: "God Will Take Care of You"

Folklore giants are supposed to be as strong as they are tall, but in Robert Wadlow's case that wasn't at all true.

Though he weighed an average eight pounds at birth, as he continued to grow (he was 5'4" by age 5) he was diagnosed as having a glandular abnormality. He eventually attained a full height of nearly nine feet.

Though Robert tried to live a normal life, his abnormal height caused him too many physical problems. His body simply grew too large to function properly. Foot problems forced him to drop out of college because he couldn't walk to class. And in 1940, at age 22 he was fitted with an ankle brace. The brace cut into his skin, causing an infection that killed him. He was a quiet, polite young man whose physical height was far greater than his physical strength.

We often think of our problems as being giant-sized and therefore beyond solution. They seem overwhelming from their size alone. Yet when we look beyond them to trust God to solve them, we see how small and weak they really are.

PRAYER THOUGHTS: Father, we so often see our difficulties as too large to be overcome. Help us remember that You are always ready to help us cut them down to size. May we, O Father, live holy before You. Help us to allow Your Holy Spirit to guide and direct our ways. Thank You for Jesus and for His love that covers all our sins. In His name, we pray. Amen.

WINDOWS OF ACCESS

SCRIPTURE: Genesis 6:11-22; 7:1

VERSE FOR TODAY: A window shalt thou make to the ark (Genesis 6:16).

HYMN FOR TODAY: "There's a Wideness In God's Mercy"

"Boy, is it dark and stuffy in here!" Chad gasped and coughed as he entered his college dorm room.

"Huh?" his roommate said drowsily from the bed. "Oh, I'm sorry—I guess I fell asleep. Open the window."

As Chad did so, light and fresh air streamed into the room, and within a few minutes the stuffy, stagnant darkness had been replaced by brilliant sunshine and cooling, crisp breezes.

Windows have always served as a point of access to the outside, and just as God provided a window in the ark for Noah to have access to himself, so does He today give us the same reassuring contact . . . even when we forget Him in the midst of our problems!

We may ignore Him, shutting the windows in our lives. Yet He waits patiently till we open them up again—to re-establish that access and contact where we again feel the bright light and welcome freshness of His constant, loving provision. God doesn't force His way in—He waits for us to open the windows from our side.

Indeed, with access readily available, why would we want to remain shut-up?

PRAYER THOUGHTS: Father, we know that we are able to come to You through Your Son, Jesus Christ. When we feel our lack of Your presence, help us to remember that the windows of access only operate from our side. Give us the desire to live righteous before You. In His Name, amen.

THE PERSON OF THE PROMISER

SCRIPTURE: Genesis 9:8-17

VERSE FOR TODAY: And I will establish my covenant with you (Genesis 9:11).

HYMN FOR TODAY: "Praise to the Lord, the Almighty"

"But Daddy, you promised!" I pleaded.

Dad sighed, but kept his word to take an earnest six-year old on a promised outing. He could have refused; after all, he was only human, and his ability to keep his promise was based entirely on his person and the decisions that went with it. Yet though he could have backed out, he didn't—because he was a person of integrity.

However, when God makes a promise, there's never a question as to His keeping it or not. After all, His ability to keep His promises—and everything else He does for us—is based on His perfect, infallible Person. Because He is a perfect divinity, therein lies the basis of our security.

Through our belief in Christ, we are related to the Supreme Being of the universe—the same one who made the promise to Noah—and yet with the ability to individually remember His promises to each of us.

And when our guidance and security—both temporal and eternal—depend on His Word, His person, and His promises, it is indeed comforting. We can be assured that our God will keep His promise.

PRAYER THOUGHTS: We praise You, O Father, that Your promises are as perfect as You. Help us to trust in You and Your ways. In our timorous times, that's a comforting thought—help us to remember it. In the name of our Savior, Jesus Christ. Amen.

PURE RELIEF!

SCRIPTURE: Psalm 32

VERSE FOR TODAY: Blessed is he whose transgression is forgiven, whose sin is covered (Psalm 32:1).

HYMN FOR TODAY: "To God Be The Glory"

A man once went to a shoe store and asked to see a selection of shoes in a size eight. The salesman proceeded to present him with a variety of styles, but as he tried them on, the customer would wince and squint at what was obviously a tight fit.

Finally the salesman measured his foot and found the man actually wore a size ten!

"If you wear a size ten, then why did you ask for a size eight?" the salesman asked.

"Oh, I always wear an eight," the man replied. "I don't mind the pain of wearing them when I think of how good it feels to take them off!"

We, too, can share a bit of that sense of relief when, like the psalmist describes, we experience the happiness and even sense of freedom that comes when we know our sins have been confessed and forgiven . . . and even forgotten! Then, when that happens, we are set free to continue growing in our spiritual walk, leaving our burden behind. No wonder the psalmist calls such a person blessed and happy!

PRAYER THOUGHTS: Father, our failures only hamper our relationship with You, but Your forgiveness removes all of that. Help us to remember to lay our failures at Your feet and live victoriously in our restored relationship with You. In His name, amen.

MY TOWER OF BABEL

SCRIPTURE: Genesis 11:1-9, 31, 32

VERSE FOR TODAY: Then they said, "Come, let us build ourselves a city, with a tower that reaches to the heavens, so that we may make a name for ourselves" (Genesis 11:4, *New International Version*).

HYMN FOR TODAY: "Glorify Thy Name"

I walked into an office supply store the other day and noticed rack after rack of books dealing with money, business, and personal success. Every conceivable area was covered: sales, management, dress, motivation, techniques, investments, and personal achievement. It was an interesting commentary on our culture today.

Our society has geared itself more toward financial and personal success rather than service. We build bigger companies, press toward climbing the corporate ladder, make more sales. Family and home take a backseat to the main priority—success. God is often considered a mystical figure far away in some cloudy realm. Our goal: to be #1.

Men do not possess this passion exclusively. In this new age of equal opportunity, women also have similar desires to reach "the top." Unfortunately, both men and women who seek this kind of goal often leave behind a trail of broken homes, scarred children, damaged friendships, and a personal emptiness—a terrible price to pay to build a personal "tower of Babel." God does not tolerate the worship of self or one's search for personal glory before Him.

PRAYER THOUGHTS: Lord, forgive me when my personal desires and striving for recognition get in my path of worshiping You. Amen.

September 27-30. **J. David Lang** is a minister and founding editor of the senior adult magazine, *Alive*. He and his wife, June, have four children.

SEEKING A FREE LIFE-STYLE

SCRIPTURE: Genesis 12:1-8

VERSE FOR TODAY: The Lord had said to Abram, "Leave your country, your people and your father's household and go to the land I will show you" (Genesis 12:1, *New International Version*).

HYMN FOR TODAY: "I'll Go Where You Want Me to Go"

Not everyone can do it or even desire it. A TV news special focused on a family who opted out of the big city "rat race" to settle in a small midwestern town of less than 2,000 population. There they built a modest home and lived a simpler life.

Another couple quit high-paying jobs in the investment community, purchased a large sailboat, and set out to cruise the oceans of the world. Still another family chose a wilderness area where they built a log cabin miles from civilization and lived partially off the land while they enjoyed nature.

One young man, a successful banker, chose to leave his profession and study in a Bible college to prepare himself for the Christian ministry. While in school, he accepted a call to serve a small, dying church in a tiny community. Within a few months people came to see why a banker would become a preacher in such a place. Soon the church began to grow, and they had to build a new building to handle the attendance. God blessed this man who, like Abraham, stepped out on faith not knowing where God would lead him.

Is God calling *you* to step out in faith?

PRAYER THOUGHTS: O Father, open my heart so that I may step out in faith to go where You want me to go, to be what You want me to be, to say what You want me to say. In the name of Jesus, I pray. Amen.

CHILDREN OF FAITH

SCRIPTURE: Galatians 3:2-9

VERSE FOR TODAY: Understand, then, that those who believe are children of Abraham (Galatians 3:7, *New International Version*).

HYMN FOR TODAY: "I Know Who Holds Tomorrow"

I remember a young couple in a church where I once preached who made a simple commitment to Christ. Dennis was baptized and his wife was already a Christian. They committed their home to the Lord. Dennis became a deacon and later an elder in the church. He grew rapidly in the faith. I remember their four little children sitting quietly in a church pew with their parents during worship.

Dennis soon accepted some supply preaching invitations and actually began to preach regularly for a little church in a nearby town. Fearing he might leave, his company offered him a significant increase in salary along with a responsible new position. But the church liked the young man and his family and asked him to move to their parsonage and become their regular minister. They said, "We will pay your salary, send you to school, and take care of your family during the week while you are away."

By faith, Dennis made that move to honor and serve his Lord. His faith has been richly rewarded. Today he preaches to a congregation of over 1,000, many souls have been won to Christ, and his family walks in the way of the Lord.

PRAYER THOUGHTS: O God, make us Your children to walk in faith. May we desire to serve You at all cost. In Jesus' name, amen.

IN THE SPIRIT OF WORSHIP

SCRIPTURE: Genesis 14:10-20

VERSE FOR TODAY: Then Abram gave him a tenth of everything (Genesis 14:20, *New International Version*).

HYMN FOR TODAY: "To God Be the Glory"

"To the victor belongs the spoils." This ancient adage still bears much truth in practice, if not in ethics.

The attack on Sodom and Gomorrah by the coalition of Syrian and Babylonian kings left the area in a shambles with many dead. Abraham's nephew, Lot, and his family were captured along with all the women and the plunder from the towns. When Abraham learned of the attack, he mounted an army and pursued the marauders up the Kings' Highway east of Jordan all the way north to Damascus. There he defeated them, rescued Lot and the women from the towns, and reclaimed all the plunder. While the Scripture doesn't say so, Abraham probably also brought back plunder belonging to the defeated kings.

Returning by way of Jerusalem, Abraham met Melchizedek, a priest/king who somehow represented Jehovah God. After receiving Melchizedek's blessing, Abraham gave him a tithe, one tenth, of the spoils ("all that he had"). He returned the captured goods from Sodom and Gomorrah to the rightful owners, keeping nothing for himself.

A principle can be learned here. Christians should give a tithe of their earnings to the church or God representatives—not out of law, but with thanksgiving and out of love and respect for God the Father.

PRAYER THOUGHTS: Father, take my silver and gold. Accept my gifts of tribute to You. In Jesus' name, amen.

My Prayer Notes

_____

_____

_____

_____

_____

_____

_____

_____

_____

_____

_____

_____

_____

_____

_____

_____

_____

_____

_____

DEVOTIONS

· · · · · · · · · · · ·

OCTOBER

October 1

GOD OUR PROTECTOR

SCRIPTURE: Genesis 15:1-6

VERSE FOR TODAY: The Lord is my rock, and my fortress, and my deliverer; my God, my strength, in whom I will trust; my buckler, and the horn of my salvation, and my high tower (Psalm 18:2).

HYMN FOR TODAY: "A Mighty Fortress Is Our God"

Have you ever seen a small child hiding behind his mother's skirt? That little face peeking out occasionally to assess the situation. Are you friend or foe? Just who are you and what is it that you are saying to me? The fear and insecurity that the child is feeling as he faces new people and new situations is minimized as he hides behind his mother's skirt. Suddenly her strength is his strength and he is secure and comforted knowing that she will take care of him. So it is with our God.

We, as Christians, can feel secure for our God is always with us. When life overwhelms us, and we are sad or confused, God is there. When we call upon him He hears and answers us. We can have an incredible security knowing that God's strength is our strength. And oh, what a fortress He is!

Just like that child who clings to his mother in his time of need, let us always remember to cling to our God in our time of need. He will be there to protect us. He is a faithful and loving God. What a wonderful peace is ours when we worship our Creator. How exciting to know that we "can do all things through Christ Jesus who strengthens" us.

PRAYER THOUGHTS: Dear God, praise unto You the Creator. Praise unto You for Your power and strength. Thank You for being our rock and our fortress. Praise unto You, our shield and our comfort. Amen.

October 1-3. **Kelli Wilmoth Bell** is a Christian writer, living in Cincinnati, Ohio. She and her husband, Todd, have a son, Rudyard Griffith, and twin daughters, Chloe Alexandra and Cleo Elizabeth.

THIS WILL I DO

SCRIPTURE: Genesis 15:7-11

VERSE FOR TODAY: All the paths of the Lord are mercy and truth unto such as keep his covenant and his testimonies (Psalm 25:10).

HYMN FOR TODAY: "The God of Abraham Praise"

The bride wore a dress of white satin. The bodice and long train were covered with a hand beaded floral design. Her net veil was crowned with white roses and baby's breath that matched her stunning bouquet of mixed roses, ivy, baby's breath and ribbons. Her entrance into the floral and candle decorated church was dramatic and beautiful. Her handsome groom watched in awe as his bride walked the white linen runner to meet him. Together they exchanged vows and officially became Mr. and Mrs.

In our society we can go to elaborate measures to make a covenant. But it is not the fancy trappings that make the covenant. Rather it is what is in our hearts as we make those promises. The seriousness with which we take the words we are saying can alter the results of our promises. In our culture the promises and vows we make with one another are not always honored.

But the promises of our God are sacred. He always honors the promises He makes. What a joy and peace can be ours because we know our God will do as He says. What a security to know that God's Word is truth and when we honor the covenant we have made with our God, He will be merciful and just. He will be our God; loving and caring for us through eternity.

PRAYER THOUGHTS: Father, thank You for offering us the chance to share a covenant with You. We praise and honor You for You are a God who gives us everlasting life. Help us to honor our commitment to You. In the name of Jesus. Amen.

October 3

THERE ARE ALWAYS RULES

SCRIPTURE: Genesis 15:12-18

VERSE FOR TODAY: "To him that rideth upon the heavens which were of old; lo, he doth send out his voice, and that a mighty voice" (Psalm 68:33).

HYMN FOR TODAY: "Praise Ye the Lord, the Almighty"

As we grow into adulthood we learn to live within life's rules. When we are children, our parents give us guidelines. Keep your room clean. Respect others. Don't fight with your sisters. Don't talk back. Do your homework. Don't talk to strangers. The list goes on and on. Parents set rules and guidelines in order for their children to succeed. As we grow older, society sets boundaries and rules for us. Drive too fast and you get a speeding ticket. Run a red light, receive another ticket. Take what does not belong to you and go to jail. Cheat on a test, receive an 'F'. There are all kinds of rules. In order to live and to prosper in our world we must live and work within the rules and boundaries that society sets. These rules help us to live in harmony with one another.

In order to live and to prosper in God's world we must obey Him and work within the boundaries that He has given us. We must seek His love, forgiveness, and salvation. We must strive toward living a sinless life. God has given us the Bible as a guide. When we live within God's rules and boundaries, He rewards us. He gave His Son for our salvation. When we accept God and the lifestyle He has shown us we are able to have eternal life. We are able to be one with our God.

PRAYER THOUGHTS: God, our Father, Thank You for setting boundaries for us. Thank You for loving us enough to give us guidelines so that we are able to live a better life for You. In the name of Jesus. Amen.

SCORN BRINGS SORROW

SCRIPTURE: Genesis 16:1-5

VERSE FOR TODAY: He who despises his neighbor sins, but blessed is he who is kind to the needy (Proverbs 14:21, *New International Version*).

HYMN FOR TODAY: "Pass Me Not"

Hagar was Sarai's servant, a woman of the desert, probably an Egyptian brought back from Abram's sojourn there. Sarai gave her to Abram to bear a child for her since she was barren. This was a common practice in those days. Despite the fact that God had promised Sarai she would have a son, her impatience and lack of faith caused her to try to "help" God's plan along. After all, she was well past the age of child bearing. But God is a God of miracles, and the consequences of her interference were far-reaching.

As soon as Hagar knew she was with child, her attitude toward Sarai changed. She looked upon her mistress with scorn, loathing, and contempt. Unreasonably, Sarai blamed Abram for Hagar's attitude and she treated Hagar cruelly.

How true-to-life these Old Testament stories are! Their realism clearly portrays the failures and faults of people when their eyes stray from God. This story brings us face-to-face with the One who was working in Abram's life and who is at work in our lives today. If we but "let go and let God" have control, our human relations will take care of themselves.

PRAYER THOUGHTS: Heavenly Father, help us to have the patience to wait upon Your Spirit to lead us, and to not interfere with Your plans for our lives. Help us to be wise and to know what You expect us to do, and what we must leave to Your hand. Keep us from jealousy and give us a humble spirit. In the name of Jesus, amen.

October 4-10. **Garnet Dixon** is a retired school teacher who enjoys her volunteer work as a recorder for the blind, and at Kosair Children's Hospital. She lives in Louisville, Kentucky, with her husband, Arthur.

GOD KEEPS HIS PROMISES

SCRIPTURE: Genesis 16:6-10

VERSE FOR TODAY: "I will so increase your descendants that they will be too numerous to count" (Genesis 16:10, *New International Version*).

HYMN FOR TODAY: "Standing on the Promises"

Driven out by Sarai with Abram's consent, Hagar was followed into the wilderness by God's angel who bade her to return and submit herself to Sarai. How difficult this must have been for Hagar, knowing the resentment that Sarai felt. Yet, she was willing to listen to the angel and risk Sarai's rejection.

God had a plan for Hagar and her son, Ishmael. Although he was not to be Abram's true heir, God promised to make his descendants too numerous to count. Ishmael would found a nation in his own right.

Facing uncertainty and chaos in our lives today, we, like Hagar, may find ourselves in a wilderness of despair. Yet, how often we too find an "angel" from God speaking to us through a loving friend, an encouraging book, an unexpected letter, or a cheerful phone call. God is there to guide us if we but stop and listen. Man in all his weakness can yet have behind him the life-giving consciousness of God. He speaks to us through His Word and encourages us to give our burdens to Him. "Humble yourselves, therefore, under God's mighty hand, that he may lift you up in due time. Cast all your anxiety on him because he cares for you" (1 Peter 5:6, 7, *New International Version*).

PRAYER THOUGHTS: Dear Father, how thankful we are that You walk with us in the dark paths of despair as well as in the bright sunshine on happy and fruitful days. Just to know You are there gives us strength and helps us strive for Your blessing. In Your Son's name, amen.

THE GOD WHO SEES

SCRIPTURE: Genesis 16:11-16

VERSE FOR TODAY: "You are the God who sees me" (Genesis 16:13, *New International Version*).

HYMN FOR TODAY: "Open My Eyes, Lord"

"Thou God Seest Me." In early Puritan homes in America these words were often embroidered, framed, and hung upon the wall. Many times they were taken to mean that the watchful eye of God's unceasing judgment was looking at them. Actually, the words were intended as the glad acknowledgment of the heavenly grace that sees and recognizes our human needs.

Divine mercy can see us through the most tangled human relationships. The same type hostility that developed between Sarai and Hagar can also develop between family members today. The ugly head of hostility, hate and jealousy can also be seen among the church family members.

"He that keepeth Israel shall neither slumber nor sleep" (Psalm 121:4). What a promise this verse contains! To many a person like Hagar, for whom the world seems hopeless and dark, comfort is found in the faith that God sees his need and reaches out to help. God gives directions on how we must live and work together. He encourages us to accept, love, and comfort one another. We need always to remember that without Him, we can do nothing. When no one else knows or seems to care about our problems, "God Sees."

PRAYER THOUGHTS: Blessed Lord, we thank You for the promise that You neither slumber nor sleep, that Your eyes are always on us, caring that our footsteps do not falter and that we do not fall. Give us faith to claim the promises that You have given us. In Christ, amen.

A GOD WHO CARES

SCRIPTURE: Genesis 21:13-17

VERSE FOR TODAY: The angel of the Lord encampeth round about them that fear him, and delivereth them (Psalm 34:7).

HYMN FOR TODAY: "God Will Take Care of You"

Sarah, having borne Isaac, once again decides that Hagar and Ishmael must leave. Whether real or imagined, she thinks Ishmael is mocking Isaac. Abraham is forced to turn out the son whom he has, no doubt, learned to love.

A local museum displays the painting, "The Expulsion of Hagar," by Cavarozzi, that graphically depicts the emotions of Abraham, Hagar, and Ishmael. Abraham is pointing the way for them to go with his right hand and pushing Hagar with the other. Hagar turns imploring eyes to Abraham as a tear runs down her cheek. Ishmael seems removed from the scene, looking into the future as if he already realizes God's plan for him.

Again, a guardian angel watched over Hagar in her distress and helped bring her closer to God, saving her and Ishmael from starvation. Here the meaning of Ishmael's name, "God hears," is clearly portrayed.

God's covenant relationship with mankind, displayed here and throughout the Bible, is initiated by Him, and He sets down its provisions. Isaac is the son of promise, but Ishmael has his place to fill. Likewise, God has covenanted with us and provided a way of salvation. He has given us the choice to accept salvation through His Son, Jesus. It is up to us to accept it.

PRAYER THOUGHTS: Our Father who knows all, sees all, and rules over each of our lives, give us wisdom and understanding. You know our needs and our weaknesses. Give us the strength and knowledge to do Thy will, today and every day. In Christ's name, amen.

GOD HEARS OUR CRIES

SCRIPTURE: Genesis 21:18-21

VERSE FOR TODAY: God was with the boy as he grew up (Genesis 21:20, *New International Version*).

HYMN FOR TODAY: "God Moves in Mysterious Ways"

God's covenant does not fail, and only God sets up its provisions. Ishmael is set aside as the inheritor of the covenant, and Isaac, the son of promise, becomes its recipient. God turns circumstances to His own purposes.

God had a purpose in sending Hagar back to Sarai before Ishmael's birth. It may have been that God wanted Abraham to be a father to Ishmael during his formative years and to have Ishmael circumcised. Certainly, being a part of a strong family with the patriarch Abraham at its head helped to form the man Ishmael became. He fathered twelve sons and founded a nation. Ties of love and affection must have existed between Ishmael and his father, for when Abraham died, Ishmael returned to help Isaac with his burial.

Families remain an important part of God's plan for mankind today. The society is built on the strength of the family. It seems that our society has been weakened by the failure to recognize the value of strong family ties. Just as Ishmael became a wild desert man after being forced from his father's home, so rebellion and disaster result from broken and weakened homes today.

PRAYER THOUGHTS: Loving Father, we thank You for our families and the joys they bring into our lives. May we always cherish them just as we love and care for our Christian brothers and sisters, knowing that as we strive for ways to minister to them, we show our love to You. Use us to build a strong family unit. In Christ's name, amen.

October 9

WHO ARE THESE PEOPLE?

SCRIPTURE: Genesis 37:12-17, 25-28

VERSE FOR TODAY: And as for Ishmael . . . Behold, I have blessed him, and will make him fruitful, and will multiply him exceedingly (Genesis 17:20).

HYMN FOR TODAY: "There's a Wideness in God's Mercy"

The Ishmaelites or Midianites were a group of Bedouin tribes that ranged the desert to the south of Palestine. They were traders in spices, balm, and myrrh, and also engaged in a profitable international slave trade. It was to one of these groups of slave traders that Joseph was sold by his jealous brothers and taken to Egypt.

Most Arabs today claim to be descendants of Ishmael, following the example of Mohammed. As Muslims, they believe that it was Ishmael rather than Isaac whom Abraham was ready to sacrifice at God's command.

God uses the errors of men to further His plans for mankind. This is illustrated graphically in the life of Joseph who was taken down to Egypt by Ishmaelite traders in order that God might save the family of Jacob and prepare a nation to be His chosen people.

Our world today contains many races of people, yet each has the same need—a Savior. God has provided a Savior for all mankind through the death and resurrection of His Son. It is our Christian responsibility to carry this message of salvation to all the world.

PRAYER THOUGHTS: Lord of all, we thank You that You love all mankind regardless of color or race. Keep us free of prejudice and bias and fill us with Your love. Let us become color blind in this world of many races. In Christ's name, amen.

GET UP, LOOK UP, AND LINK UP

SCRIPTURE: 1 Kings 19:9-19

VERSE FOR TODAY: Stir up the gift of God, which is in thee by the putting on of my hands. For God hath not given us the spirit of fear; but of power, and of love, and of a sound mind (2 Timothy 1:6, 7).

HYMN FOR TODAY: "I'll Go where You Want Me To Go"

Through the ages man has tried to hide from God or to run away from Him. Beginning in the Garden of Eden and continuing throughout the Old Testament, we find numerous examples of those who have sinned trying to hide from the Lord. Elijah's case seems different, however, for he was not running away because of his sins but rather because he was depressed from his lack of success. He feared Ahab and Jezebel, but his despondency was greater than his fear.

This is a typical condition of many Christians today. Fear of something that might happen throws them into the slough of despair and they forget all the blessings God has given them. Elijah had been cooped up in the cave of self-pity for too long. God told him to get up, then look up, and finally to link up with others to carry on the work that needed to be done.

The beauty of God's love and His care for us are gifts that should lift us above the mundane problems of life and fill us with joy. The psalmist gives us instructions to "Trust in the Lord and do good; dwell in the land and enjoy safe pasture" (Psalm 37:3, *New International Version*). As we serve God we find true happiness in the knowledge that He will not pass us by.

PRAYER THOUGHTS: Gracious Lord, we know from experience that it is in doing Your will that true happiness is found. We seek Your presence in the everyday happenings of our lives, and may we always listen for the Spirit's guidance in all we do. In His name, amen.

WHAT'S IN A NAME?

SCRIPTURE: Genesis 17:1-5

VERSE FOR TODAY: "You are the Lord God, who chose Abram and brought him out of Ur of the Chaldeans and named him Abraham" (Nehemiah 9:7, *New International Version*).

HYMN FOR TODAY: "I Would Be True"

Have you ever started to introduce someone and realize you can't think of the person's name? We like to hear the sound of our name and are pleased when it is spoken. Names are important to God, too. He often changed the names of those He called to special service, giving them more meaningful ones.

When Abram was 75 years old, God told him to leave his country, his home, and his people. God promised Abram He would make his name great and make him into a great nation.

In our Scripture today, God renewed His covenant with Abram and changed his name Abram ("exalted father") to Abraham ("father of a multitude") to confirm His promise.

The name Abraham brings to mind Christian virtues of love, obedience, faithfulness, trust, patience, compassion, and courage. God said of His faithful servant, "Abraham obeyed me and kept my requirements, my commands, my decrees and my laws" (Genesis 26:5, *New International Version*).

What do our names bring to mind?

What does God say of us?

PRAYER THOUGHTS: Help us, Lord, to live each day in such a manner that what we think, say, and do will witness to others our love for You. In the name of Jesus. Amen.

October 11-17. **Christine Jette** is an active Christian who enjoys music, writing, and reading. She and her husband, Glen, live in Washington Court House, Ohio.

FAITH WORKETH PATIENCE

SCRIPTURE: Genesis 17:6-10

VERSE FOR TODAY: You need to keep on patiently doing God's will if you want him to do for you all that he has promised (Hebrews 10:36, *The Living Bible*).

HYMN FOR TODAY: "Teach Me Thy Will, O Lord"

What joy Abraham must have felt when, after 13 years with no apparent revelation from God, the Lord appeared to him, confirming the covenant He had made earlier with His faithful servant.

During those years as Abraham faithfully served God and patiently waited for divine guidance for his life, he must have pondered over God's covenant promises that he would be the father of many nations, and that with countless descendants he would possess the land of Canaan where he now lived as a stranger. How and when would all this take place?

At times our faith wavers and we feel God is far away. Our lives seemingly have no meaning. We do our best to live as God wants us to and yet feel discouraged and depressed. We learn, as Abraham did, God's plans and purposes cannot be hurried. We must wait upon the Lord, and He will direct us in His time.

We will not hear God audibly as Abraham did. He speaks to us through His Holy Word. If we are to receive His blessings and the promise of eternal life through Jesus Christ, we must faithfully serve Him, keep His commandments, and patiently await His guidance in all we do.

PRAYER THOUGHTS: Increase our faith, O God, that in times of discouragement we will remember You are always near. Help us to be patient, ever seeking Your direction and purpose for our lives. Help us to live our faith in You with patience and assurance that You are indeed directing our lives. In the name of Jesus. Amen.

October 13

ARE WE COMMITTED?

SCRIPTURE: Genesis 17:11-14

VERSE FOR TODAY: Blessed are they who keep his statutes and seek him with all their heart (Psalm 119:2, *New International Version*).

HYMN FOR TODAY: "Come, Ye Christians, Be Committed"

I remember as a child playing with my close friends in an old, crudely built clubhouse. It was "our" place, and only those who knew the chosen password could enter.

Persons who join service and social clubs today are subject to certain requirements to be eligible for the benefits and privileges of those organizations. There is usually a list of what must be done to become and remain an active member.

God commanded obligations to be heeded by Abraham and his descendants if they were to receive His promises. The rite of circumcision was to be observed as an outward sign of their obedience to God, their faith in His promises, and their willingness to fulfill their part of God's covenant with Abraham for generations to come.

Do we witness to others by keeping God's covenants, or have we allowed the preaching of God's Word, the Lord's Supper, and the ordinance of baptism to become merely routine duties to us?

We are members of God's family and joint heirs with Christ in His eternal promises. Let us prayerfully consider our indebtedness to our Heavenly Father for all He has done for us.

PRAYER THOUGHTS: Dear God, we can never repay You for all the rich blessings and promises You have given us. Examine our hearts and help us to be more committed to Your Son, Jesus. We pray in His name. Amen.

NEVER DOUBT GOD

SCRIPTURE: Genesis 17:15-19

VERSE FOR TODAY: "Everything is possible for him who believes" (Mark 9:23, *New International Version*).

HYMN FOR TODAY: "Nothing Is Impossible"

We marvel at the miracles and awesome beauty of God's handiwork which are all around us. They speak of His majesty and power. Not only in nature do we witness God's creativity and planning, but also in the lives of those He chooses to fulfill His purposes.

Abraham was 100 years old and Sarah was 90 years old when God told Abraham that Sarah would give him a son. Abraham laughed at this incredible news. He suggested his son, Ishmael, might be the one through whom all nations of the world would be blessed, but God had chosen Isaac as the inheritor of His covenant with Abraham.

Sarah, whom Paul described as a woman who put her hope in God (1 Peter 3:5), would realize her dream of having a child in the miraculous birth of Isaac. She would be blessed as the mother of nations, and kings of people would come from her. From this aged couple the chosen race would spring.

We dare not substitute our plans for those of God if we want the best for ourselves; nor should we doubt His love, power, and wisdom in directing our lives.

Nothing is impossible with God!

PRAYER THOUGHTS: Almighty Father, Ruler of the universe, take control of our lives. Thank You for Your Word, and for the examples of others who have followed Your teaching. May we, today, trust in You, and let us not lean on our own understanding. When our plans go awry, help us to remember that You know what is best for each of us. Keep us humbly submitted to Your will. Amen.

WHY, GOD?

SCRIPTURE: Genesis 17:21-25

VERSE FOR TODAY: Trust in the Lord with all your heart and lean not on your own understanding (Proverbs 3:5, *New International Version*).

HYMN FOR TODAY: "Trust and Obey"

In a television commercial a mother explains how her dish-washing liquid keeps her hands so soft. Her small daughter keeps asking, "Why? Why? Why?"

Do you ever ask God why? "Why is this happening to me?" "Why am I ill?" "Why can't I have what others have?"

Continually we question why we have to do this or that, or why illnesses, changed plans, and dashed hopes plague our lives. Perhaps it's because we aren't "listening" to God. Perhaps we do things our way instead of patiently waiting for God's direction.

Abraham obeyed God's command that all males in his household and all those bought with his money must be circumcised as a sign of God's covenant with him. He didn't say, "I don't think that's necessary, God."

We don't always know God's plans for us. We do know He teaches, and if we faithfully obey His will, He will direct us. Trusting Him is mandatory if we are to reap the blessings He has for those who keep His commandments.

Instead of "Why, God?" may we learn to say, "If so, God, give me patience to seek Thy will."

PRAYER THOUGHTS: Forgive me, O Lord, when I become impatient with what's happening in my life. Remind me to be still and "listen" for Your direction. Give me wisdom and patience to trust in You. I pray in Jesus' name, amen.

DAILY PRACTICE

SCRIPTURE: Genesis 17:26, 27; Hebrews 6:13-20

VERSE FOR TODAY: Because you know that the testing of your faith develops perseverance (James 1:3, *New International Version*).

HYMN FOR TODAY: "We Have an Anchor"

I recall the patience and perseverance it took for me to learn to ride a bicycle. Trying to steer the bike while balancing it proved to be a trying, wobbling task, accomplished only after persistent practice.

At times our faith wobbles, too. We have to keep practicing it if we hope to perfect it. Regularly attending worship services, partaking of the Lord's Supper, singing His praises, praying, giving, and witnessing keeps our faith alive and growing.

God's covenant with us is not only for Sundays. We must take Him with us on Mondays, sharing with others the knowledge of His promises, and live in accordance with His will through each day of the week.

Sometimes unforeseen situations unbalance our faith, incorrect decisions steer us in the wrong direction, and unexpected upsets bring us sorrow and despair. Our hope is in Christ who is always there to help us regain our balance, turn us around, and heal our grief.

Are we keeping the faith? Will we be ready when Jesus comes again?

PRAYER THOUGHTS: Dear Lord, we thank You for those faithful Christians who have gone before us, setting an example of complete trust in You. Help us to follow their leading. When our faith wavers, may we look to You for guidance and strength. In Christ's name we pray, amen.

PREACH THE WORD

SCRIPTURE: 2 Timothy 2:1-15

VERSE FOR TODAY: Preach the Word; be prepared in season and out of season; correct, rebuke and encourage—with great patience and careful instruction (2 Timothy 4:2, *New International Version*).

HYMN FOR TODAY: "Go Ye Into All the World"

One of my high-school English teachers frequently asked class members to define words. Many often answered, "I know what it means, but I can't explain it." She always replied, "If you can't explain it, you don't know what it means."

Can we explain what we believe and why? Can we knowledgeably answer questions asked by those wanting to learn about our God and His message? As a worker for Christ are we prepared to teach others what we've learned?

A good employee learns his job well. He constantly strives to improve his performance. He meets daily challenges with knowledge and skill. Should we do less for Christ who commanded, "Go ye into all the world and preach the gospel to every creature" (Mark 16:15)?

The task isn't easy, but if we faithfully endure the hardships, God has promised we will inherit everlasting life. There is no greater reward.

Peter said, "Always be prepared to give an answer to everyone who asks you to give the reason for the hope that you have" (1 Peter 3:15, *New International Version*).

Are we eager to share with others what means the most to us?

PRAYER THOUGHTS: I thank You, Lord, for the Bible and its message of salvation. Let my life be a message of love to those around me. Let them see Jesus in me. In His name, I pray. Amen.

QUICK TO SERVE

SCRIPTURE: Genesis 18:1-8

VERSE FOR TODAY: God is not unjust; he will not forget your work and the love you have shown him as you have helped his people and continue to help them (Hebrews 6:10, *New International Version*).

HYMN FOR TODAY: "It Pays to Serve Jesus"

Okay, get ready, get set, SERVE! It just doesn't sound right. When we are young, service has a fun, adult-like quality. The school teacher asks, "Who wants to wipe the chalkboards?" A dozen hands go up. The Sunday-school teacher asks, "Who wants to pass out Bibles?" Little voices cry out, "Pick me! Pick me!"

Somehow *service* loses its attraction as we grow older. Jam-packed schedules, financial stresses, kids, cars, deadlines—they all tend to dampen our enthusiasm to serve. By the time we recognize an opportunity to serve and talk ourselves into it, the opportunity has passed.

Not so with Abraham. He must have had a T-shirt that read "Carpe Diem! Seize the day!" When the three messengers of God appeared outside his tent, he flew into action. He didn't stop to count the costs. He didn't first find out what they could do for him. He didn't question his own worthiness or worry about what he had to offer. He simply served. He recognized the importance of humility and became a servant.

PRAYER THOUGHTS: God, make me ready. Give me a humble spirit, a heart that is willing to give, and a body that is ready to serve. Help me to accept the challenges before me with a willing attitude. In the name of Jesus, amen.

October 18-24. **Kelly Smith** is a Christian writer who lives in Indianapolis, Indiana, where she is employed at the Children's Museum.

DARE TO THINK THE IMPOSSIBLE

SCRIPTURE: Genesis 18:9-15

VERSE FOR TODAY: Trust in the Lord with all your heart and lean not on your own understanding; in all your ways acknowledge him, and he will make your paths straight (Proverbs 3:5, 6, *New International Version*).

HYMN FOR TODAY: "To God Be The Glory"

She stared down at the want ads. "I don't have the right degree. I don't have enough experience. I'm not what anyone is looking for," she muttered.

"Well, you've been praying, right? God will open a door," her friend consoled.

"How's God going to open something when nothing's there?" her voice cracked. "It's hopeless."

How do we react when confronted with the impossible? Sarah laughed. She concentrated on the reality and ignored the imaginable. Everyone knows that she was too old to have a baby, right? Let's be practical. God, however, challenges the practical. He defies the predictable, the realistic. He is not constrained by earthly limitations or human weaknesses.

By folding to something we consider impossible, we are limiting the awesomeness of God's power. We are putting the Creator of all in a box. The same God who designed the world, who parted the Red Sea, who raised the dead, who translated His love for us into the earthly form of His Son, can achieve anything. And the best part is that He still does.

PRAYER THOUGHTS: Dear Heavenly Father, I praise You for Your power and strength. Please grant me the faith to always recognize Your glory. Forgive me when I think Your abilities are limited and I stop believing in miracles. In the name of Jesus. Amen.

THE GREAT ESCAPE

SCRIPTURE: Genesis 19:12-23

VERSE FOR TODAY: For thou, Lord, wilt bless the righteous; with favour wilt thou compass him as with a shield (Psalm 5:12).

HYMN FOR TODAY: "Great Is Thy Faithfulness"

In the lonely darkness of a dormitory room, a young woman weeps. "God, I have made such a mess of things. Please forgive me." No lightning bolts fill the room. Instead a quick peace enters. A heaving chest calms. A racing heart slows. God's mercy is immediate and gentle. William Shakespeare wrote in *The Merchant of Venice*, "The quality of mercy is not strained, but droppeth as the gentle rain from heaven."

Sometimes human predicaments require a more dramatic, more obvious, display of mercy. In our foolishness we entangle ourselves in sticky situations. We need to be rescued. The two men were trying to light a fire under Lot. When their shouts of warning failed to motivate him, they took action. They grabbed Lot and his family and led them out of the city. God, again showing the finite understanding of the human mind He designed, knew there's a time to talk and a time to act.

God's mercy is unlimited, and His means of expressing it are creative and varied. Sometimes it's a subtle feeling that comes from knowing that we are loved. Other times it's a daring rescue or a supernatural feat. However mercy is shown, it has an equally powerful effect on our lives.

PRAYER THOUGHTS: O Father, Your mercy amazes me. Your creative love comforts me when it seems that my world is falling apart. Thank You for saving me from harm, and please forgive my stubbornness when I fail to listen to You and accept Your grace. In the name of Jesus. Amen.

OUR GOD IS A GOD OF LAUGHTER

SCRIPTURE: Genesis 21:1-7

VERSE FOR TODAY: And Sarah said, God hath made me to laugh, so that all that hear will laugh with me (Genesis 21:6).

HYMN FOR TODAY: "He Keeps Me Singing"

Have you ever known someone with a contagious laugh? I have a friend whose laughter is so catching that when she starts giggling, before long, I am laughing, too. Most of the time she seems to be able to see the joy and humor in almost anything. (The Scripture says, "A merry heart maketh a cheerful countenance:" Proverbs 15:13). I'm not even sure why we are laughing. My friend definitely has a gift for brightening up a room.

Often in Scripture God is portrayed as a consuming fire or a strict judge, but God is also a God of joy. God wants our lives to be rich and happy. He wants our cup to overflow so that others can share in our happiness.

God searched Sarah's heart and found the one thing that would make her the most happy. The possibility of having a baby in her old age seemed impossible. But God gave Sarah a son.

The world is full of pain and disappointment, and misery loves company. If we are truly to be the light of the world then we must invite others to experience the blessings Christ bestows on us. Sarah spread the Word of her miracle. She let others hear her laughter so that they might laugh with her.

PRAYER THOUGHTS: Thank You, dear Father, for the gift of laughter. I praise You for the blessings You continually send my way. Help me to spread the good news of Your love to those around me, so that others might experience the pure joy that comes from knowing You. In the name of Jesus. Amen.

TRIANGLES

SCRIPTURE: Genesis 21:8-14

VERSE FOR TODAY: God is our refuge and strength, a very present help in trouble (Psalm 46:1).

HYMN FOR TODAY: "I Surrender All"

I was dismayed to turn on the television recently and find love triangles the subject of a popular talk show. I somehow failed to see the redeeming quality in watching a man, his estranged wife, and a woman with whom he had had an affair, air their petty grievances on national television.

Abraham had a triangle of sorts on his hands. Sarah's jealousy was creating tension in the camp and distress for Abraham. You can almost see him pacing, agonizing, but unable to come up with a viable solution. God saw Abraham's stress and instructed him. God entered a human situation and resolved it.

Sometimes I categorize my struggles into spiritual and carnal. The spiritual ones I eagerly seek God for help. The carnal or human strifes I often label too petty or foolish to bring to God, so I stubbornly try to muddle through them on my own. God wants them all. As creator, God understands our humanness and proved that when He sent His Son to live among us.

Christ will give us strength and wisdom to make the right choices if we simply ask Him. He is our refuge and strength. We can give to Him our every trouble, and He will care for us.

PRAYER THOUGHTS: Thank You, heavenly Father, for caring enough about me to send Your Son to live on earth. Your wisdom surpasses all my understanding, and Your patience with my problems is beyond comprehension. Help me to learn to turn to You in all my times of need. In the name of Jesus, amen.

October 23

THE CONSISTENT CHRISTIAN

SCRIPTURE: Genesis 21:22-27

VERSE FOR TODAY: But thou shalt remember the Lord thy God: for it is he that giveth thee power to get wealth, that he may establish his covenant which he sware unto thy fathers, as it is this day (Deuteronomy 8:18).

HYMN FOR TODAY: "Take My Life, And Let It Be"

While driving through the city recently, a friend commented on the "JESUS SAVES" bumper sticker on the car in front of us. "I would never put that on my car," he said. "That's just asking for trouble. Driving in traffic brings out the worst in people," he explained. "I don't want someone reading that on my bumper just as I cut them off. Sort of blows their whole expectation."

It's true that when people discover that we are Christian it changes what they expect from us. The fact that non-believers automatically expect honesty and integrity from us is a testimony to the Lord we serve. Abimelech and Phichol recognized Abraham's alliance with God. With that recognition came certain expectations. They assumed that Abraham would be a fair businessman. They wanted straightforwardness. They expected him to keep his word and deal justly with them.

Christianity is not something we can take on and off. No area of our life, including our business affairs, is exempt. We must strive to wear the title honorably, and with that responsibility comes the joy of knowing that just as with Abraham, God is with us in everything we do.

PRAYER THOUGHTS: Heavenly Father, forgive me when I fail to reflect You in every facet of my life. I want to be a consistent Christian in my daily walk. Please give me the courage and wisdom to follow Your teaching in whatever I do. In the name of Jesus. Amen.

THE WELL DILEMMA

SCRIPTURE: Genesis 21:28-34

VERSE FOR TODAY: If it be possible, as much as lieth in you, live peaceably with all men (Romans 12:18).

HYMN FOR TODAY: "Let There Be Peace On Earth"

International relations could well be argued the most complex and important issue facing the United States in the 90s. Iraq's invasion of Kuwait, the breakup of the Soviet Union and the death of the Communist Party make diplomacy a crucial commodity.

Abraham had a "desert storm" of his own on his hands. There was a dispute over who had dug the well. Abraham wanted to make sure that Abimelech and Phichol knew that he was a fair man. Rather than quibble over ownership or turn this affair into a violent encounter, Abraham went to great lengths to prove his integrity. The seven ewe lambs, the oath, and the tamarisk tree were symbols of the treaty between the three leaders. Abraham acted as a peacemaker. By making a personal sacrifice, he avoided conflict and trouble. He used his resources wisely, and the name of God was glorified.

Too often we act selfishly when faced with conflict. We get caught up in guaranteeing that we get our "fair share," and we forget the importance of keeping the peace. Diplomacy among His people today brings an atmosphere that allows us to show the love of God to the world. Abraham was diplomatic in his dealing with Abimelech, and the Lord rewarded him.

PRAYER THOUGHTS: Dear God, help me to act sensibly when dealing with others. Help me to put aside my pride and petty desires and work instead at compromising with those with whom I have conflict. Let me be a peacemaker. In the name of my Savior, Jesus Christ. Amen.

GOD WILL PROVIDE

SCRIPTURE: Genesis 22:1-14

VERSE FOR TODAY: So Abraham called the name of that place The Lord will provide; as it is said to this day, "On the mount of the Lord it shall be provided" (Genesis 22:14, *Revised Standard Version*).

HYMN FOR TODAY: "Trust and Obey"

As a child, I never did well when it was time to take a test or exam. I worried before the test, during it, and while I waited for the results. I have difficulty recalling information; therefore, no matter how much I studied, I never did very well on a test. This brought me shame and poor test scores, and it affected my self-confidence.

I would freeze up on exam days. One time I was so nervous that I couldn't even see the paper—it was a blur. I was fortunate to have an understanding teacher who let me go for a walk and take the test outside the classroom.

I believe God allows you and me to be tested today. How do we handle them? He lovingly helps us as we walk through life. He gives us the courage we need to handle the test.

My prayer is that I will have the faith of Abraham—that I will feel a peace on the path to my test. That I will obey God even though I don't understand His reasons. That I will praise God before, during, and after the results of my test—for God always provides.

PRAYER THOUGHTS: Father, I pray that I will prepare for my tests by reading Your Word daily; that I will be able to recall Scripture during times of testing, and that I will trust and obey Your perfect judgment. In the name of my Savior, Jesus Christ. Amen.

October 25-31. **B. J. Bassett** is a writer, teacher, and speaker who lives in Fortuna, California, with her husband. They have four grown children.

GOD'S BLESSINGS

SCRIPTURE: Genesis 22:15-19

VERSE FOR TODAY: I will indeed bless you, and I will multiply your descendants as the stars of heaven and as the sand which is on the seashore. And your descendants shall possess the gate of their enemies (Genesis 22:17, *Revised Standard Version***).**

HYMN FOR TODAY: "Showers of Blessing "

God has blessed me over the years many times, but recently one of the greatest blessings was announced—my first grandchild will arrive in the near future. I am so excited. I have always loved children—my own and other people's children. Now I will be blessed once again—this time with that special relationship of grandparent and grandchild.

After I heard the wonderful news, I went out the next day and purchased yarn to knit a shawl with millions of stitches. With each stitch I say a prayer; I pray that this baby will know Jesus, love Him, and serve Him. Grandmas can do a lot of praying. Something else I did was write a letter to my unborn grandchild. I have a letter that my grandfather wrote to me on the day that I was born. My grandfather died when I was five-years-old, so his letter is one of my dearest treasures. God surely blessed me with loving grandparents. I wrote my letter to my grandchild, telling how much he or she is wanted and loved already. I know I won't be a perfect grandmother, but with God's help I will try my best and praise God for yet another blessing.

PRAYER THOUGHTS: Father, my heart is overflowing with happiness. You have truly blessed me many, many times. Thank You for the blessings of children and grandchildren. Thank You, dear Father, for the greatest gift to mankind, Jesus Christ, and our personal salvation through Him. In His name, I pray. Amen.

HE TALKS WITH ME

SCRIPTURE: Genesis 24:7-18, 25-27

VERSE FOR TODAY: And he said, "O Lord, God of my master Abraham, grant me success today, I pray thee" (Genesis 24:12, *Revised Standard Version*).

HYMN FOR TODAY: "In the Garden"

Prayer has been a part of my life for a long time. Like David, I, too, have cried out to God in despair; like Paul, I have asked forgiveness; and like Gideon, I have put a fleece before the Lord on numerous occasions. I have felt God's power during prayer and have received His blessing with answers to my petitions for myself and others.

One of my ongoing prayers is for my mother who is an alcoholic and suffers from mental illness. Over the years I have pleaded with God for my mother to be healed. I have cried out to God in despair. At times of deepest agony I have felt far from God. I don't understand it, but I do trust God. I know that He is in control of my mother's life, and of my life. It isn't how I would have answered my prayer, but I trust that God will work out all things for good to those who love Him—in His way, and in His time.

Although we may not always like God's answers, He always answers our prayers—with yes, no, or wait.

PRAYER THOUGHTS: Dear Father, I come to You in prayer of thanksgiving today for all the prayers You have answered. You are a great and mighty God, able to do miracles even today. Help me, dear Father, to feel and understand Your answers to my prayers. May I not grow weary in waiting for an answer. Give me wisdom to understand that You, indeed, have the answers to all my prayers. In the name of my Savior, Jesus Christ. Amen.

MIRACLES

SCRIPTURE: Genesis 25:5-11

VERSE FOR TODAY: God blessed Isaac his son (Genesis 25:11, *Revised Standard Version*).

HYMN FOR TODAY: "I Believe in Miracles"

Before I became a published writer, I dreamed about it. I also took writing classes, and did everything in my power to learn the craft of writing. Eventually, I was published more than I had ever dreamed possible. But the biggest miracle for me was something I hadn't dreamed.

The editor of *Focus on the Family* magazine asked if he could include a piece I had written for them in a book with other articles he had chosen. My piece was about our daughter's anorexia, and how prayer and positive peer pressure had saved her life. Our daughter unselfishly gave me permission to write about this difficult time in our lives, and I was delighted to have it included in a book for others to receive help. The book was published in 1990, and for several months it was on *Bookstore Journal's* best-selling list. God had blessed me in a way I never dreamed possible.

Isaac himself was a miracle, having been born to aged parents when it seemed an impossible dream. He was also rescued from being slain as a sacrifice on Mount Moriah (Genesis 22). In retrospect, Isaac surely would agree that God had blessed him in miraculous ways.

PRAYER THOUGHTS: Father, You are truly a God of miracles. May I never forget Your power to do the impossible. Thank You, O Father, that I can see Your hand at work in my life, and the lives of those around me. Give me a faith in You that will remove mountains. I bow to You, my Father, the God of miracles. In Your Son's name, I pray. Amen.

CHOSEN

SCRIPTURE: Genesis 25:19-23

VERSE FOR TODAY: And Isaac prayed to the Lord for his wife, because she was barren; and the Lord granted his prayer (Genesis 25:21, *Revised Standard Version*).

HYMN FOR TODAY: "Give Them All to Jesus"

I have always loved children. I often remember watching young mothers as they enjoyed their children at play. After I was married, I longed for a child of my own. For five years I did not conceive. Many nights I cried myself to sleep. I prayed and asked God for a child, but year after year my prayers were not answered in the way I desired. My husband and I decided to adopt a child. We were so happy when our baby girl was born.

While she was being formed in the womb, God was creating her character. (Thou didst form my inward parts; Thou didst weave me in my mother's womb—Psalm 139:13). He knew all the time what she would be like. Maybe the reason we had to wait so long for a child was because God knew we would need lots of patience raising her. She was beautiful and strong-willed all her life, making parenting difficult at times.

When our daughter was a teenager she had a difficult time, and I was grasping for anything just to have her survive. I thought she would be happier with her natural mother during those most difficult years, but our doctor discouraged it. Today, she is 28 years old and a loving daughter.

God always knows best. He had chosen her to be our child, and he had chosen us to be her parents.

PRAYER THOUGHTS: Father, forgive me when I question Your plan for my life. Thank You for the children You have chosen for me and given me. What a blessing they are. In the name of Jesus. Amen.

GOD LOVES ME

SCRIPTURE: Genesis 25:24-28

VERSE FOR TODAY: When the boys grew up, Esau was a skilful hunter, a man of the field, while Jacob was a quiet man, dwelling in tents (Genesis 25:27, *Revised Standard Version*).

HYMN FOR TODAY: "Jesus Loves Me"

I don't remember a time when I didn't believe in God. And then, as a teenager, I gave Jesus my heart, became a Christian, and have had a personal relationship with Him for over 35 years. During all these many years I have known the fact that Jesus loves me. But it wasn't until recently that I really felt the amazing realization of those words.

I have been in a Twelve-Step program through my church—a program for adult children from addictive and other dysfunctional families. One of the characteristics of adult children from dysfunctional families is that we try to be perfect (which of course is impossible). Through the Twelve-Step program I discovered why I am the way I am. And recently, during my devotional time, I realized that God loves me no matter what I do. If I change, He loves me. If I go backward, He loves me. Even if I stay just as I am today—He still loves me. I realized that it doesn't matter what I do; God will always love me—perfect or imperfect.

Whether I'm a skillful hunter like Esau or quiet like Jacob, God loves me.

PRAYER THOUGHTS: Dear Father, when I think about Your love for me, I am overwhelmed. Teach me to become as You would want me to be. May I be the best that I can be in You, and O Lord, I thank You for Your unconditional love. Thank You for loving me no matter what I do. In the name of my Savior. Amen.

MY BIRTHRIGHT

SCRIPTURE: Genesis 25:29-34

VERSE FOR TODAY: So he swore to him, and sold his birthright to Jacob (Genesis 25:33, *Revised Standard Version*).

HYMN FOR TODAY: "Lord, I Want to Be a Christian"

I can't imagine how anyone could be so careless as to sell his birthright. I don't believe I would do it. I don't care how famished Esau was for food—it was food that would only satisfy his hunger temporarily.

It means a great deal to me to come from a long line of hard-working, loving people. I have always been proud of my heritage—and of my birthright of being the firstborn. I am especially proud of my birthright as a Christian. I feel a responsibility to honor that name—to honor my Lord in my thoughts and actions.

I have often thought about how I would react if I were ever put in an extremely difficult situation where my faith was severely tested by someone who tried to get me to deny my faith in God. Would I stand the test? I feel I would be strong in a time of crisis; but how much could I take? I wonder. My constant prayer is, "Lord, may I always stand for You no matter what happens. May I be grateful that You have grafted me into Your family. Give me courage and wisdom to hold fast to You and Your ways. May I never sell my birthright as Your child—as a Christian."

PRAYER THOUGHTS: Dear Father, You know my concern to always be aware of Your sacrifice for me, to always be strong in my faith, to never dishonor You. Cover me with the blood of Christ that I may be counted worthy to be Your child. Please help me in all these. Amen.

DEVOTIONS

• • • • • • • • • • •

NOVEMBER

November 1

THE POWER OF HIS PEACE

SCRIPTURE: Genesis 26:12-22

VERSE FOR TODAY: He moved on from there and dug another well, and no one quarrelled over it. He named it Rehoboth, saying, "Now the Lord has given us room and we will flourish in the land" (Genesis 26:22, *New International Version*).

HYMN FOR TODAY: "It Is Well With My Soul"

With a smile I recall the first time I stepped into an electronically controlled elevator. (I admit it was a long time ago.) I stepped in, located the control button, started to press hard, but soon realized the slightest flutter of my finger would activate the huge machine.

So often we try *force* as we travel our life's pathway. It is an easy trap to fall into when we live in a world where many people believe might is right.

Isaac sets us an example with his peace-making ways. With ease he could have taken to fighting. Of course he was a forerunner of a far greater Person, the Lord Jesus. He is the One who descended into a world of fighting and fear to spread the message of peace and calm. He came to allay our fears and help us to understand His path of peace is the way to follow.

In the upper room, Jesus spoke peace to His disciples. (Peace I leave with you; my peace I give you—John 14:27). His presence still brings peace, and when we are in touch with Him we take His peace wherever we go.

PRAYER THOUGHTS: Thank You, Jesus, for Your peace. Help us to live and teach Your peace. Please give us wisdom this day to be quiet enough to hear Your voice whispering to us. In the name of Jesus, our Savior. Amen.

November 1-7. **David R. Nicholas**, a minister and writer who lives in the North of England with his wife, Judith, is Communication Officer for Action Partners, a mission agency working in the Sudan.

CHANGING AGREEMENTS

SCRIPTURE: Genesis 26:23-29

VERSE FOR TODAY: And they said, "We see plainly that the Lord has been with you; so we said, 'Let there now be an oath between us, even between you and us, and let us make a covenant with you'" (Genesis 26:28, *New American Standard Bible*).

HYMN FOR TODAY: "To God Be the Glory"

Some years ago we lived near a creek which was called Tommy Trinder's. I'll never forget it, for I had to take the utmost care when driving my automobile around the dog's leg bend in the road at Tommy's. Then the county decided to straighten the road and erase the bend. Such was progress.

Life is full of changes, and not the least of the changes we encounter are changes in people. As someone said, "People are like the weather—so changeable."

Isaac and the Philistines made a covenant, an agreement. The trouble was that the agreement could be broken by both sides. When people are changeable, their agreements are readily broken. On the other hand, God is different. He is constant and the everlasting Father. While we may break our covenants or agreements with God, He never breaks His side of the bargain. This was always the trouble with the Israelites. Again and again they made a promise to God, and repeatedly they broke their side of the agreement.

We, like Isaac, the Philistines, and Israel, are frail—but we have a God who loves us in spite of our frailties. (I have loved you with an everlasting love; I have drawn you with lovingkindness—Jeremiah 31:3). In this we give thanks.

PRAYER THOUGHTS: Heavenly Father, as we live among changing agreements, help us to keep our agreements with You. In Jesus' name, we pray. Amen.

LIVING WATER

SCRIPTURE: Genesis 26:30-33

VERSE FOR TODAY: That day Isaac's servants came and told him about the well they had dug. They said, "We've found water!" (Genesis 26:32, *New International Version*).

HYMN FOR TODAY: "Have Thine Own Way"

Water is so vital to living. "We have found water!" To those who have plenty, that may be an unimpressive statement, but to those without water, it can mean so much.

Most of us take water for granted. We just turn on the faucet and out pours water. We fill a glass and drink the wet liquid. Some time ago, I discovered that water is not as wet as I thought! Curiously enough, water is not really wet enough to wash in. If you try washing your hands without soap, you'll see what happens. When you take your hands out of the water, only small droplets adhere, leaving most of the skin dry. I recall that one soap manufacturer used the phrase, "Makes water better!"

Water is vital to life, but as Jesus put it, there is another kind of water that is required—living water. Water that we drink, take a bath in, or swim in is fine for the physical side of life, but for the spiritual side we need the living water that Jesus offers.

To find water in a parched land can be life-sustaining. But to drink of the living water that Jesus offers gives life eternal.

Isaac's servants found water and were delighted, but how much greater the delight when someone finds the living water of Jesus.

PRAYER THOUGHTS: Loving Lord, while people all around us strive for different things, help us to treasure the living water—our salvation that comes from You. Amen.

LAST WISHES

SCRIPTURE: Genesis 27:1-4

VERSE FOR TODAY: The Lord knoweth the days of the upright: and their inheritance shall be for ever (Psalm 37:18).

HYMN FOR TODAY: "Great Is Thy Faithfulness"

In the southeast corner of our "old farm" was a large elm tree. Mother loved this area of the farm and once expressed a wish to be buried underneath that elm one day. But it was not to be. We moved away, and the land was parceled out to building contractors. Then the wheels of progress bulldozed that southeastern corner to lay what is now Interstate 131.

Today's short Scripture gives us only a wish that the aging Isaac expressed to his favorite son, Esau. In a way it was a dying wish. Perhaps Isaac hoped that God would allow Esau to receive the customary blessing after all; and perhaps Rebekah's plot was a dramatic way of reminding Isaac that the elder son was to serve the younger (Genesis 25:23). In any case, the wish was not fulfilled.

When God's servant dies, he is no longer in control of his earthly wishes. His last will and testament or final wish do not come into play now. His soul is transported to the spiritual realm where the Lord's will is final, but where our deepest longings and desires are fulfilled. It hasn't "entered into the heart of man, the things which God hath prepared for them that love him" (1 Corinthians 2:9).

So much for last wishes.

PRAYER THOUGHTS: We thank You, Eternal Father, that our times are in Your hand, and our inheritance is with You. May our greatest wish be to live each day in accordance with Your will. In the name of our Savior, we pray. Amen.

LEAN, NOT SCHEME

SCRIPTURE: Genesis 27:5-17

VERSE FOR TODAY: "Then take it to your father to eat, so that he may give you his blessing before he dies" (Genesis 27:10, *New International Version*).

HYMN FOR TODAY: "Spirit of the Living God"

Isaac's aim was right. He planned to bless his eldest son. But, like with us today, Isaac planned well but things went wrong.

Though problems may seem to stem from the actions of others, we need to remember that the problem is often in our hands to remedy, with the Lord's help. Like Isaac, I've planned to do certain things and found my plans have been thwarted by others. I've discovered 1 Peter 5:7 gives much comfort at such times: "Cast all your anxiety on him because he cares for you" (*New International Version*).

We must surely learn to lean on the Savior, knowing full well we have a decided advantage over Isaac, for we live in days beyond Calvary rather than days before Calvary. Before Jesus died, He told His disciples He would send another Helper. "These things have I spoken unto you, being yet present with you. But the Comforter, *which is* the Holy Ghost, whom the Father will send in my name, he shall teach you all things, and bring all things to your remembrance, whatsoever I have said unto you" (John 14:25, 26). A Helper who would guide us into all truth. Wisdom is available to us if only we will lean on the Helper who has been provided to guide us.

PRAYER THOUGHTS: Our Loving God, keep us from scheming, and please help us to lean heavily upon You this day. Help us to do this through the love of Jesus, our loving Savior. Amen.

TANGLED WEBS

SCRIPTURE: Genesis 27:18-29

VERSE FOR TODAY: He went to his father and said, "My father." "Yes, my son," he answered. "Who is it?" (Genesis 27:18, *New International Version*).

HYMN FOR TODAY: "Love Divine, All Loves Excelling"

Sir Walter Scott penned these famous words: "O, what a tangled web we weave, When first we practise to deceive."

Blessing was part of ancient Jewish life. Jacob was well aware of the procedure, and he allowed his mother Rebekah to lead him down the pathway of deception. The two plotted to deceive the aged Isaac. How sad. Lies led to hatred and running away, for Esau's anger was fanned into a flame, and he threatened to kill Jacob. Doubtless he was already angry because Jacob had robbed him of his birthright.

We could discuss at length Jacob's deception and the various tricks he used against Laban. The fact remains that God was with him and blessed him because he was the heir of His promise to Abraham.

And yet, deceit is the instrument of Satan, who is the "father of lies" (John 8:44). He has been using it since the temptation of Adam and Eve: "You will not surely die" (Genesis 3:4, 5). Jesus said, "Ye shall know the truth, and the truth shall make you free" (John 8:32). Jesus himself is the truth. As long as we cling to Him, we are holding onto the giver of all truth.

PRAYER THOUGHTS: Father in Heaven, please defend us from the "tricks of Jacob" so that we may live right in Your sight. When we are tempted to be deceptive, let us hold fast to You and to Your truth. Thank You, Father, for giving us power to overcome evil. In the name of Jesus. Amen.

SAFE ON THE HILLSIDE

SCRIPTURE: Genesis 27:30-46

VERSE FOR TODAY: Esau said to his father, "Do you have only one blessing, my father? Bless me too, my father!" Then Esau wept aloud (Genesis 27:38, *New International Version*).

HYMN FOR TODAY: "Blessed Assurance"

Disappointments are a part of life. Hardships can take their toll if we are not careful. Certainly we need to face them rather than try to hide.

William Gladstone, one-time leader of the British Parliament, was in Scotland. As he was climbing a hill, he saw some sheep walking up a hill, away from a valley. Gladstone said to himself, "Those sheep are silly getting out of a sheltered valley and facing the storm on a hill." A little later Gladstone told a shepherd boy about the sheep. The boy said, "Those sheep have more sense than you think. If they stayed in the valley, they would be covered by snow drifts. They are safe on the hillside!"

Like Esau, we lift up our voice and weep at life's disappointments. He cried a great and bitter cry when he heard that his brother had now taken his blessing. Esau was so angry he was dangerous. His rage toward his brother caused him to want to do away with his brother. His disappointment and rage was so great that it was nearly his undoing. A simple lesson for us is that instead of staying in the valley of disappointment, we need to rise up the hill of faith and look to our Lord Jesus. Looking up, we need to ask Him to remind us of His rich promises to us.

PRAYER THOUGHTS: Keep us, Heavenly Father we pray, on the hillside of life. When disappointments in life bring rage and frustration, help us to find safety and protection in Your ways. Let us not be overcome by life's daily disappointment. Let us live looking unto Jesus. In His name. Amen.

SAFE HAVEN

SCRIPTURE: Genesis 28:1-6

VERSE FOR TODAY: "You shall have no other gods before me" (Exodus 20:3, *Revised Standard Version*).

HYMN FOR TODAY: "A Charge to Keep I Have"

In a world full of secular values, it's easy to slip into ways not *quite* contrary to the Christian call. Honesty may be decided by what everybody does as long as it isn't robbing a bank. No one will miss that pen, or a cup of coffee from the office pot.

In ancient Israel, there was a larger danger. A conquering nation imposed its values and religion, as well as its ruler. It was far better to stay within the tribe than merge with those who did not know God. Far better to flee the homeland than to risk heresy.

Many would see a land where "In God We Trust" marks every dollar as a safe haven. To be sure, there are those who would deny the expressions of faith in public, but freedom of religion remains a tenet of our nation. We can study His Word, and obey His commands without fear of danger.

Meanwhile businesses, large and small, and people everywhere are crushed by the small heresies within the tribe of believers. No one notices such very small gods because we are, after all, one nation under God.

Where shall we flee? To whom shall we go? To the rock-solid comfort of the Lord, to the rest in His Word.

PRAYER THOUGHTS: Lord, it may well be that the small sins of this world lead us away faster than a large, untempting sin. Let us rest in Your ways, and not in the cynical view of a world sliding away from You. Let us hold fast to our Safe Haven, Jesus Christ, in whom we pray. Amen.

November 8-14. **Mary Perham** is an award winning writer and the LatchKey Program Coordinator for a pilot program in New York state. She lives in Woodhull, New York.

REWARDS

SCRIPTURE: Genesis 28:6-9

VERSE FOR TODAY: "Now his elder son was in the field; and as he came and drew near to the house, he heard music and dancing" (Luke 15:25, *Revised Standard Version*).

HYMN FOR TODAY: "O Love That Wilt Not Let Me Go"

It's easy to feel compassion for Esau, a man tricked out of his birthright, bereft of affection and finally plotted against by his mother and brother.

It's easy to feel sorry for ourselves when we believe we are living right, and that keeps us from earthly blessings we feel we deserve. We see others with benefits, prizes, and applause while we struggle with (it seems) barely a nod from God. It may seem as if we are robbed of our rightful place.

There is a story in the Bible of another man with an absent, well-loved brother fleeing the pigsties to be embraced by a loving father. The prodigal's brother would have compassion for Esau. There was no fatted calf for Esau.

It is tempting, looking at the "good life" of others, to try to pretend we don't care. It would be much easier to reject God, as Esau tried to reject Isaac. But we must keep in mind that our rewards are not of this world.

Perhaps that's the difference between compassion and self-pity. It was a towering self-pity that drove Esau to leave his tribe. For the elder brother, it was knowledge of his father's compassion that drove him to bitter complaints and toward his father's reassurance of love that never leaves.

PRAYER THOUGHTS: Dear Lord, we become so accustomed to Your loving presence, that it is as automatic as breathing. Keep us mindful of Your compassion in the midst of our self-pity. Amen.

CONDITIONS

SCRIPTURE: Genesis 28:10-22

VERSE FOR TODAY: "You shall worship the Lord your God and him only shall you serve" (Matthew 4:10, *Revised Standard Version*).

HYMN FOR TODAY: "O Worship the King"

Jacob had done nothing great to deserve his vision. He was an ordinary and sinful individual. Yet the Lord stood beside him. This God, who chose to manifest Himself to Jacob, is the God of all the universe.

Although awestruck, Jacob returned to practical matters: *If all the promises are kept, this presence will indeed be the God of Jacob,* he vowed.

His disciples, ordinary men, were awestruck by Jesus. Practical men, they, too, had "if's." Thomas, one of Jesus' disciples, said when he was told by the others that Jesus was alive, "*If* I can see the scars of the nails in His hands, and put my hand in His side, I will believe."

People often say, *"If I pass this test, You are still my God. If my child's fever passes, You are my Lord. If we get there safely, You are God."* It is wise to trust the will of God in our lives with earnest if's that seek the truth of what is beside us.

"All these I will give you, if you will fall down and worship me" (Matthew 4:9, *Revised Standard Version*).

The devil, too, has conditions—arrogant "if's" that seek to replace God.

God, a patient Lord, keeps His promises and leads us to the truth that His promises are already there to be found.

PRAYER THOUGHTS: Teach me, dear Father, to trust you even when things seem bleak. In the name of our Savior, Jesus Christ. Amen.

November 11

IN UNITY

SCRIPTURE: Genesis 29:1-8

VERSE FOR TODAY: But they said, "We cannot until all the flocks are gathered together, and the stone is rolled from the mouth of the well" (Genesis 29:8, *Revised Standard Version*).

HYMN FOR TODAY: "Praise to the Lord"

America prides itself on its independence and on the individuality of each citizen. We may even be drawn to Benjamin Franklin's statement: "The Lord helps those who help themselves."

When a particular time is more troublesome, we reach, for the Lord by instinct, and may seek the comfort of His presence in others. Yet there is this sneaking, subtle sense of wanting to do it all alone. There seems to be more reward, more attention, for *individual* success.

As Jacob arrived at the well, he wondered why the shepherds were waiting to remove the stone to water their flocks. It was time for each individual to get on with his work. Why were they just sitting around?

He asked, "Since it is broad daylight and not yet time to bring the flocks in, why don't you water them and take them back to pasture?" (Genesis 29:7, *Good News Bible*).

They simply told him that they could not water the flock until all flocks were there.

There are times when we must wait on others. Working together in unity gives us a feeling of belonging.

Do I feel a part of the Kingdom of God this day? Do I wait to work in unity?

PRAYER THOUGHTS: Dear Lord, help us to be a community of faithful servants. May we cling to our Savior in unity and love. Amen.

FOREIGN LAND

SCRIPTURE: Genesis 29:9-14

VERSE FOR TODAY: How shall we sing the Lord's song in a foreign land? (Psalm 137:4, *Revised Standard Version*).

HYMN FOR TODAY: "Guide Me, O Thou Great Jehovah"

Travelers far away from their home turf find a wonderful kinship meeting people from their own state, even if those hometowns are miles distant. They are overjoyed if a stranger knows the area from which they come. Suddenly, a connection is made that breaks through boundaries and bonds in warmth. In a strange land, there is a "family."

When visitors attend our worship services, they may fumble through an unfamiliar hymnal, find the posted hymn, and turn to each other with smiles. They know this song; it's theirs, too. Having discovered another common thread of faith, they relax, and believe. Yet, as the Hebrews learned later, there are places so foreign, no song comes. In fact, to sing would be blasphemy. From that struggle comes prayer.

Believing Christians experience both security and struggle, often simultaneously, in an age where the profound jostles the obscene: contrast India's Taj Mahal and Calcutta or the homeless on cathedral steps in our own towns.

How much more important it is, then, to seek out those who know our home, our base, our language, and our Lord. In this we find warmth in a foreign land.

Perhaps then we can understand why Jacob wept.

PRAYER THOUGHTS: Dear heavenly Father, we never need the loneliness of a foreign land when we work with our Savior, Jesus Christ. Help us to find ourselves in You; let our song be that of the redeemed. Amen.

GOALS

SCRIPTURE: Genesis 29:15-30

VERSE FOR TODAY: What is my strength, that I should wait? And what is my end, that I should be patient? (Job 6:11, *Revised Standard Version*).

HYMN FOR TODAY: "For the Beauty of the Earth"

We become aware of our worth in the family of the Lord. Indeed, we are the "King's kids," and what we ask in His name is ours for the asking. What a temptation this presents! All that is good, and bright, and holy is ours. Indeed, it is a banquet of richness.

In His name, people cast their eyes around, asking for an end to poverty, war, and any number of ills. And, as He did Laban, the Lord promises His family the rewards of their labor.

As time goes by, we see our accomplishments are lacking. It isn't as beautiful as we thought it would be. Yes, it's a good work, worthy of attention, but it just isn't quite. It isn't quite as important as we wanted, why this job for me? . . .

How easy it is to tackle the "mega-jobs." There is an innate reward in great deeds, where the love of our kingly Father speeds us on to world-heights. Our own tasks plod and drain us. All this time? For what?

Seven years?

Unlike us, the Lord is past the moment. If Jacob had not married Leah, tribes of Israel would not exist. In fact the royal lineage of Judah would not be.

PRAYER THOUGHTS: Dear Lord, how easy it is to become discouraged when our efforts to bring about the beauty of Your kingdom produce so little. Help us to know that Your way is the beauty we seek. Amen.

WE ARE FAMILY

SCRIPTURE: Genesis 30:25-36

VERSE FOR TODAY: I have learned by divination that the Lord has blessed me because of you (Genesis 30:27, *Revised Standard Version*).

HYMN FOR TODAY: "O Master, Let Me Walk with Thee"

There are moments in the lives of believing Christians when we feel put-upon because of our common faith. Someone calls at the last minute needing items for the church bazaar, knowing they'll be found. The church must have a new roof, so we dig into our pockets, even when we don't have much to pull out. One of the church families is unemployed and needs help for a while. The food pantry needs extra food, and we are asked to provide. Ministers and their families may teeter on the brink of burnout with the never-ending calls on their time.

And we, like Jacob, may be tempted to clear out. We, like Jacob, may resent the impositions. And, in speaking out, we, like Jacob, need someone to say, "You are a blessing to me."

Oh. Somehow, what has become mundane, irritating, and expected is renewed by the Christianity that inspired it. And we, like Jacob, can say to those around us, "My work is my reward."

Every member of the church family needs to be ministered to from time to time. We can recognize again the ties that bind us in service, and go on to the fields refreshed, knowing—like Jacob—we are a blessing.

PRAYER THOUGHTS: Dear Father, let us see our small deeds as steps on our road, measures of our blessing. Let us learn to encourage one another. In the name of Jesus. Amen.

ATTITUDES

SCRIPTURE: Genesis 31:1-8, 15-18

VERSE FOR TODAY: And Jacob noticed that Laban's attitude toward him was not what it had been (Genesis 31:2, *New International Version*).

HYMN FOR TODAY: "In My Life Lord, Be Glorified"

Attitudes! We can't live with them and we can't live without them. None of us likes to be around people with a "bad" attitude. If you've spent much time around teenagers lately, you've probably heard the expression, "He has an attitude." Loosely translated, that means he has a *bad* attitude.

Our attitudes affect the way we view others and how we feel about what goes on around us. Good attitudes enable us to have positive feelings. Bad attitudes usually induce negative thoughts and feelings. Why, then, do we have bad attitudes? Is it because it is easier to find the fault in those around us than to admit we may be wrong? Think about the bad attitudes you've seen demonstrated. Do they come from people seeking to be positive no matter what circumstances they find themselves in? No. Do they come from people striving to live in peace with others? No.

So, in order to have good attitudes, we need to have a positive outlook. We need to pray for changes in our own lives so that whatever is causing the negativism to seep through, will be stopped. And above all it means we have to "love one another" and live in peace. Let's do it!

PRAYER THOUGHTS: Lord, make us mindful of the changes we each need to make in order to serve You more perfectly. Let our attitudes be the same as those of Your Son. Amen.

November 15-21. **Dee Mobley** is a Children's Minister in Marietta, Georgia. She and her husband, Ron, have four children, Nathan, Katie, Drew, and Marcus.

PROMISES, PROMISES

SCRIPTURE: Genesis 31:36-37, 44-54

VERSE FOR TODAY: Laban said, "This heap is a witness between you and me today." That is why it was called Galeed (Genesis 31:48, *New International Version*).

HYMN FOR TODAY: "Seek Ye First"

As my family played *Bible Balderdash* last night, one of the words that came up was "Galeed." I knew the right answer! I knew it because I was in the midst of writing these devotions. Laban and Jacob made a heap of stones to serve as a witness and as a point where each one would stop and not go past the heap onto the other's side to harm them. It was a physical reminder of a promise they had made to each other. It was called Galeed.

We have physical reminders of our promises today. Contracts are signed in which we promise to keep up our end of the bargain on whatever agreement we have made.

Unfortunately today our "promises" are not always taken seriously. A promise today may bring us what we want, but tomorrow we may decide it is too much trouble.

Does the same thing happen with our promises to God? Do we usually, in good faith, make promises to God and tomorrow find it too difficult to live up to our promises? Perhaps we need to be more mindful of our promises. Ask any child about the seriousness of a promise. He gets very upset when someone doesn't keep a promise. It is a serious matter, as it should be. Be sure your promises to God and others are made (and kept!) with the seriousness they deserve.

PRAYER THOUGHTS: Dear God, I thank You for the promises You have made to me that include the most wonderful gift of all, eternal life. Help me to take seriously the promises I make. In Jesus' name, amen.

STRUGGLING THROUGH

SCRIPTURE FOR TODAY: Genesis 32:3-8, 13-18

VERSE FOR TODAY: "Never will I leave you; never will I forsake you" (Hebrews 13:5, *New International Version*).

HYMN FOR TODAY: "No One Understands Like Jesus"

It had been years since Jacob left home, fleeing from Esau's wrath and threat to kill him. Now he was returning home, and a confrontation was inevitable. Had time melted his brother's heart, or hardened it in the old animosity? Jacob struggled with these thoughts as he prepared for the journey, relying on God's promise to be with him (Genesis 32:7, 8).

Everyone has struggles, some minor, others intense and serious. Some we bring upon ourselves, others are thrust upon us. In a newspaper report, an infant girl was born four months premature, on the floor of a "crack" house! Abandoned by her mother, this one-and-a-half-pound baby girl struggles each day to stay alive. Even if she survives, there are constant and difficult struggles ahead of her. Hopefully, God will oversee her future so that she will never feel forsaken.

As a mother, I find it hard to be sympathetic toward a mother like the one in this story. One of my greatest desires is to help my children through their struggles, not cause them. I also want them to look to God for His help and strength, because He will never leave them or forsake them.

We can look to our heavenly Father for comfort and care. He will never abandon us. We are His children.

PRAYER THOUGHTS: I thank You, Lord, for Your steadfastness and constant care. I pray for the babies that are born daily into a struggle just to stay alive because of the sin of this world. Help us to reach out to those who so badly need You to cleanse their lives. In Jesus' name, amen.

HIS STRENGTH

SCRIPTURE: Genesis 32:19-32

VERSE FOR TODAY: Consider him who endured such opposition from sinful men, so that you will not grow weary and lose heart (Hebrews 12:3, *New International Version*).

HYMN FOR TODAY: "Greater Is He That Is In Me"

In the summer, our church family has home Bible studies on Wednesday nights. It is a greatly anticipated time of sharing and growing in the Lord. We often have people visit our studies; people we don't know much about. One such lady came to our home this past summer. She immediately joined in our discussions. She was a very friendly, outgoing person. Her spiritual life had had its ups and downs, and she was trying to get back on track. Almost by accident her story unfolded. Two-and-a-half years before, she and her three children had been in a very tragic car accident. All three of her children were killed. Upon hearing her story, all the things in my life that I had seen as burdens seemed extremely insignificant. The struggle that I was going through could in no way compare to the daily challenge this woman faces.

Somewhat similar to Jacob's experience, we struggle with God and with men. But do we struggle for things that are really important? Sometimes it takes a story like the one I've just told to help us understand what struggles deserve our energies.

Thanks be unto our God, for He cares for us. He wraps us in His arms whether our trials are insignificant or a heavy burden. We can rest in His strength.

PRAYER THOUGHTS: Lord, help us seek Your face and guidance as we struggle through the trials of our lives. In Jesus' name, amen.

November 19

THE FINAL OUTCOME

SCRIPTURE: Genesis 33:1-7

VERSE FOR TODAY: Now there is in store for me the crown of righteousness (2 Timothy 4:8, *New International Version*).

HYMN FOR TODAY: "I Know Whom I Have Believed"

As it happens, I'm writing these devotions at World Series time. It is very exciting because I live just outside of Atlanta, and in this particular World Series the Atlanta Braves are playing. Yes, you're right. For you who are now reading this, that was two years ago. You know whether the Braves ended up winning or losing their first World Series. You know the outcome of this meeting; at this writing, I do not.

Twenty years have passed between the ending of Genesis 32 and the beginning of chapter 33. Jacob did not know what the outcome of his meeting with Esau would be. Jacob was extremely concerned about the reception he would receive from Esau. He did not know the outcome of their meeting; I do.

I also know the outcome of the most important meeting of all time: the meeting of Jesus Christ with my sin (and yours). And isn't it a marvelous outcome? The death on the cross had a wonderful outcome for us. The final outcome; life everlasting.

We may not know the end of most things that happen to us on a day-to-day basis, but we do know that God will see us through as we experience the hard times. We should also remember He is there during the good times and deserves our praise and gratitude.

PRAYER THOUGHTS: Lord, I thank You for conquering my sin and giving me the promise of eternal life. I praise You for the strength and grace You give me on a daily basis, which enable me to meet those challenges that would otherwise defeat me. In Jesus' name, amen.

GIVING AND ACCEPTING FORGIVENESS

SCRIPTURE: Genesis 33:8-14

VERSE FOR TODAY: "Do not judge, and you will not be judged. Do not condemn, and you will not be condemned. Forgive, and you will be forgiven" (Luke 6:37, *New International Version*).

HYMN FOR TODAY: "Dear Lord and Father of Mankind"

Forgiveness is a hard thing to give, especially, sometimes, to ourselves. When other people say they forgive us for something, we often can't believe they really have. Esau forgave Jacob. But Jacob was sure that at some point Esau would realize that Jacob really didn't deserve forgiveness.

You've all heard stories, or know personally, of family disagreements which have led to long-term family feuds. A lack of forgiveness is usually the reason for the continuing problems. One side can't ask for forgiveness while the other can't give it.

Most of us pray often for the forgiveness of our own sins. Do we deserve the forgiveness God says is ours for the asking? No. But because of His grace we will receive it. Can we do less for those we need to forgive? I think not. Can we do less and not forgive ourselves when God has already done so?

Can you imagine how much better our relationships would be if our forgiveness of ourselves and others was as easily attained as God's is? What a peaceful, loving existence we could have.

Our challenge is to become more forgiving persons. Perhaps you can be the example that encourages change in the lives of many because forgiveness is an integral part of your life-style.

PRAYER THOUGHTS: Lord, as I ask for Your forgiveness for the shortcomings in my life, I also pray that I can be a forgiving person, both of myself and of others. Make my life an example for others in that they can see my forgiving nature. Amen.

ACCEPTANCE FOR ALL

SCRIPTURE: Genesis 33:15-20

VERSE FOR TODAY: Each of you should look not only to your own interests, but also to the interests of others (Philippians 2:4, *New International Version*).

HYMN FOR TODAY: "A Charge to Keep I Have"

It is important for us to be accepted. In fact, many experts have agreed that it is one of our most basic needs and, if not met, affects other areas of our lives.

In the elementary school where I teach, there is a special education class for emotionally disturbed children. My heart goes out to those children, their families, and those who work with them on a daily basis. Other children approach them cautiously, if at all. They are different.

When new people come into our church services, are we accepting or do we look at them as intruders into an already established situation? Are we afraid they may have some ideas and opinions different from our own?

It is even more difficult to accept someone who has done wrong and seeks reinstatement. It is hard for both an individual and a congregation to treat the person as though nothing happened. And yet, God forgives and accepts us when we repent. Christians are expected to do the same (2 Corinthians 2:5-7). Esau forgave and embraced his brother. Dare we do less than Esau?

PRAYER THOUGHTS: Lord, make us an accepting people. Help us accept the differences of others and use those differences to Your glory. Forgive us when we fail to be accepting because of our own fears. Help us, dear Father, to see people as You see them. In Your name, amen.

FORGIVENESS OR REVENGE?

SCRIPTURE: Genesis 45:1-8

VERSE FOR TODAY: All things work together for good to them that love God, to them who are the called according to his purpose (Romans 8:28).

HYMN FOR TODAY: "On My Heart Imprint Thine Image"

Joseph was his father's favorite child. He'd been loved and protected all his life. Then, in the violence of his brothers' jealousy, he was sold into slavery. How terrified the young boy must have been. Betrayed by his own brothers, he lived at the mercy of strangers. Betrayed again by his new master's wife, Joseph languished in prison for years. What bitter, self-pitying thoughts must have filled his heart! How often did he ask, "How could they do this to me?" or even, "How could a loving God let this happen to me?"

Yet God prospered Joseph, and each frightening setback became a stepping-stone in His greater plan to save the Hebrews from starvation. Through his pain and struggles, Joseph learned that God controlled every step of his life. When Joseph finally faced the brothers who betrayed him, he had the power to take revenge on all of them, but he forgave them instead because he knew they were used as tools in God's great plan.

When people let us down and life offers painful setbacks, we, too, can forgive others when we realize that God uses these things to accomplish His will in our lives and theirs.

PRAYER THOUGHTS: Lord, thank You for the loving plans You've made for our lives. Help us to trust You at every turn and to offer others the love and forgiveness You've given us. Amen.

November 22-28. **Patricia Dietz** is a free lance writer who enjoys acting, directing, and writing for the Green Bay Community Church drama team. She and her husband, Ed, have two daughters, Rachel and Keren.

GOD'S PROVISION OR MINE?

SCRIPTURE: Genesis 45:9-20

VERSE FOR TODAY: Seek ye first the kingdom of God, and his righteousness; and all these things shall be added unto you (Matthew 6:33).

HYMN FOR TODAY: "Take My Life and Let It Be"

Bill's brow furrowed as he heard the diagnosis. "You have a bleeding ulcer," the doctor told him. "Somehow, you're going to have to unload all that stress."

Bill had been devoted to his work many years, and now had been forced to take a cut in pay. His bills had increased, and his son was in trouble at school. His wife nagged him to spend more time with the family. There seemed to be no time for himself. How could he manage it all?

The famine brought similar trouble for Jacob. Then the message from Joseph came: "God has made me lord of all Egypt" (Genesis 45:9, *New International Version*). Not only alive, but lord of all Egypt? And Pharaoh's words: "Never mind about your belongings, because the best of all Egypt will be yours" (Genesis 45:20, *New International Version*). No wonder Jacob couldn't believe it at first! But he did believe, he trusted, and he came. Jacob and all his family were protected throughout the famine.

God's message to us is the same: Christ is Lord of all. His storehouse is full. If we seek Him first in everything, He promises to supply all our needs.

PRAYER THOUGHTS: Lord, help us to seek Your will in everything as we meet the difficulties in our lives. Teach us to trust in You. Thank You, O Father, for Your provision. In the name of Your Son, and our Savior, Jesus Christ. Amen.

TRAPPED BY LIES

SCRIPTURE: Genesis 45:21-28

VERSE FOR TODAY: Instead, speaking the truth in love, we will in all things grow up into him who is the Head, that is, Christ (Ephesians 4:15, *New International Version*).

HYMN FOR TODAY: "Jesus, My Truth, My Way"

Jerry stared in dismay at the gleaming ice cream machine. He had no idea how it worked. "Why did Erv have to be gone today?" he muttered. Erv, a whiz with machines, had assured Jerry he'd catch on quickly. So Jerry lied, saying he'd managed an ice cream parlor before. The owner believed him and gave him the job, but Erv got sick on Jerry's first day. Now, when the boss came, Jerry would have to admit he didn't even know how to fill and start up the equipment. He'd trapped himself, and the moment of truth was fast approaching.

Joseph's brothers must have felt trapped when, after so long, they had to admit to their father that Joseph wasn't dead—they'd sold him. They had watched their father grieve for his son these many years. Now they would have to tell him that they had caused the grief, and that Joseph was not dead. Their jealous act hadn't gained them Jacob's love, only filled their father with grief. To tell the truth now could alienate him further. But if they didn't tell, how could they return for food?

The passage doesn't say how Jacob felt toward his sons when they confessed, but it does show what a tangled trap we can set for ourselves when we try to hide the truth.

PRAYER THOUGHTS: Lord, help us to live with integrity. Give us the freedom to admit our mistakes and to love and forgive ourselves and others. In the name of Jesus. Amen.

November 25

A GREETING AND A BLESSING

SCRIPTURE: Genesis 47:1-12

VERSE FOR TODAY: Each of you should look not only to your own interests, but also to the interests of others (Philippians 2:4, *New International Version*).

HYMN FOR TODAY: "Blest Be the Tie That Binds"

One Sunday morning, I approached a couple in church who sat off by themselves looking uneasy. When I greeted them they seemed relieved, and after a few moments the woman said, "We're new in town and I miss my old church. We've come here for weeks and I still feel so lonely. We are looking for a church family where we feel we can worship God, and feel that we belong. One or two ladies promised to call, but so far no one has." We sat down to talk, and a valued friendship began.

Many Christians rely on church family for their friendships and can feel lost and isolated in a new congregation. In our fast-paced, activity-focused lives, we don't always stop to look for other people's needs, even though we, too, would be blessed if we did.

The passage says Jacob blessed, or greeted, Pharaoh. These two men must have met with deep gratitude. God had blessed Pharaoh through Jacob's son, protecting the Egyptians from famine, and He had used Pharaoh to bless Jacob with life-giving food and land.

God asks us to put our time and effort into loving and caring for each other. Christ leads us to have kindness and compassion toward one another. Through this He meets our needs.

PRAYER THOUGHTS: Lord, help us to make ourselves available to others, offering each other the same patient, nurturing care that You give us. May we have the attitude of Christ Jesus. In His name. Amen.

SOLD OUT FOR GOD

SCRIPTURE: Genesis 47:13-26

VERSE FOR TODAY: Therefore, I urge you, brothers, in view of God's mercy, to offer your bodies as living sacrifices, holy and pleasing to God—this is your spiritual act of worship (Romans 12:1, *New International Version*).

HYMN FOR TODAY: "Send, O Lord, Thy Holy Spirit"

My six-year-old daughter Keren and I sat watching TV when a segment came on asking for aid for starving children. Keren frowned at the thin, diseased bodies and asked, "Mommy, why don't they go to the store and get some food?"

"Because the stores don't have food, Honey," I replied.

As the Egyptians said to Joseph in today's Scripture passage, "We will not hide the fact from you, Sir, that our money is all gone and our lives belong to you. There is nothing left to give you except our bodies and our lands" (Genesis 47:18, *Good News Bible*). Most of us have never faced hunger without solution—hunger when there is simply no food in the land. Because Jacob loved God, God sent Joseph ahead to provide for the family. But like the Egyptians, Jacob had to entrust himself to Joseph's care to receive that help. In saving Jacob's family, God also saved Egypt.

Just as the people of Egypt put all they owned, even their lives, into Joseph's hands in exchange for life, so God wants us to put every aspect of our lives in His hands and be His servants. In turn, God gives us an *abundant life,* changed to conform to His design.

PRAYER THOUGHTS: Lord, help us to give every aspect of our lives into Your care and to dedicate ourselves to serving You. Amen.

November 27

ADOPTED AS SONS

SCRIPTURE: Genesis 48:1-7

VERSE FOR TODAY: Now if we are children, then we are heirs—heirs of God and co-heirs with Christ (Romans 8:17 *New International Version*).

HYMN FOR TODAY: "Arise, Sons of the Kingdom"

Adoption is a common choice today. People who have no children seek out children who have no parents, and a complete family is born. An adopted family may include brothers and sisters of differing nationalities. But why would a man like Jacob, who had many children, adopt the only two boys of one of his sons?

When a Hebrew man died, his property—the inheritance—was divided equally among the sons, except for the eldest. The firstborn got a double portion—twice as much as his younger brothers. Joseph was Jacob's favorite son, but he was not the firstborn, and Jacob wanted to give a double portion to Joseph. By adopting Joseph's sons, Ephraim and Manasseh, Jacob could give them each an equal share of the inheritance. Thus Joseph got, through his sons, the double portion Jacob wanted him to have.

As members of God's family, our physical traits are not the deciding factor as to whether we belong or not. We were not born with the right to inherit salvation from God. But when we believed in Him, He adopted us as His own children and, as His sons and daughters, we inherit a full portion of His salvation, His blessings, and His promises.

PRAYER THOUGHTS: Thank You, O Father, for adopting us into Your Kingdom. We praise You that we are coheirs with Jesus Christ, Your Son, and our Savior. Help us to realize the great love You have for us and the fullness of our inheritance as Your children. Amen.

MY PLAN OR GOD'S?

SCRIPTURE: Genesis 48:8-14, 17-22

VERSE FOR TODAY: Trust in the Lord with all your heart and lean not on your own understanding; in all your ways acknowledge him, and he will make your paths straight (Proverbs 3:5, 6, *New International Version*).

HYMN FOR TODAY: "Thy Way, Not Mine, O Lord"

The Hebrews believed that the son on whom a dying man placed his right hand would receive the greater blessing. To be at someone's right hand was a position of favor. When Jacob saw Joseph's sons, he asked, "Who are these boys?"

Joseph told his father that he was asking about his own grandsons.

Jacob said, "Bring them to me." And Jacob proceeded to give them his blessing. The Scripture says that Joseph was displeased when his father placed his right hand on Ephraim's head. Though Joseph himself had been a favored younger son, he seems to have felt that it wasn't right for Jacob to place the younger son over the firstborn. Yet Jacob picked Ephraim over Manasseh, prophesying that Ephraim would be the greater of the two.

God doesn't always do the thing that seems most appropriate to us or that fits neatly into our social customs, laws, and moral expectations. We may try, as Joseph did, to push events in the direction we choose, but God's will still prevails. Though, at times, His choices may make us feel uncomfortable and threatened, He asks us to recognize and trust His omnipotence.

PRAYER THOUGHTS: Lord, help us to cling to You instead of to human traditions, to continue to grow in wisdom, faith, and understanding of Your ways. Amen.

POSITIVE PARENTS

SCRIPTURE: Luke 1:5-9

VERSE FOR TODAY: And they were both righteous before God, walking in all commandments and ordinances of the Lord blameless (Luke 1:6, *New King James Version*).

HYMN FOR TODAY: "A Christian Home"

The word "blameless" does not describe parents who never make mistakes, or are never misunderstood. "Blameless" deals with a loving attitude.

Blameless life-styles were the preparation pattern for positive parenthood for Zacharias and Elizabeth. It's the proving ground for parents today as well!

The world is filled with children who need the bright light of parents who are blameless before God and the community.

Practical steps toward positive parenthood include:

*Praying or reading the Bible in front of your children.
*Saying "Sorry, I'm wrong" when you are wrong.
*Talking about spiritual priorities with your children.
*Showing affection to your children and spouse.
*Attending your children's events when possible.
*Giving words of encouragement on a regular basis.
*Honesty in business matters.
*Faithfully worshiping God.

Take a moment to thank God for role models like Zacharias and Elizabeth, as you practice positive parenting traits.

PRAYER THOUGHTS: Dear Father, we have *YOU*! Praise Your name! May we have instilled within us the faith to follow You. Amen.

November 29—December 5. **Derl Keefer** pastors the Three Rivers Church of the Nazarene in Three Rivers, Michigan. He and his wife, Karen, have two children, Jeff and Julie.

WHEN MEN TALK, GOD LISTENS!

SCRIPTURE: Luke 1:10-17

VERSE FOR TODAY: But the angel said to him, Do not be afraid, Zacharias, for your prayer is heard (Luke 1:13, *New King James Version*).

HYMN FOR TODAY: "Sweet Hour of Prayer"

Recently I thought I was having a hearing problem, so I made an appointment for a hearing test. I just knew I would be told that I would have to purchase an expensive hearing aid. The shock came when I was told that my hearing was very good. The assessment was that I just wasn't listening well.

God isn't like that at all. He is in the business of LISTENING. "Your prayer is heard." The angel was saying to Zacharias that God wanted to intervene in a personal way in his life. His prayer for a son was going to be answered, and the boy would be more then he could imagine. "For he will be great in the sight of the Lord . . ." (Luke 1:15, *New King James Version*).

God listens and responds! The God of the universe wants to be involved in a conversation with us. We can pour our hearts out to Him; He won't ignore us. *Warning*: He may not answer just as we want, but rest assured—He will answer after He's heard our sincere prayer. "And I say to you, ask, and it will be given to you; seek, and you will find; knock, and it will be opened to you. For everyone who asks receives, and he who seeks finds, and to him who knocks it will be opened" (Luke 11:9, 10, *New King James*).

PRAYER THOUGHTS: Thank You, God, for hearing the longings of my heart. I am so glad that I can share my hurts, frustrations, and disappointments, as well as the joys, with a God who will listen when others don't have time for me. I know You will never ignore me. Praise Your name. Amen.

My Prayer Notes

_____

_____

_____

_____

_____

_____

_____

_____

_____

_____

_____

_____

_____

_____

_____

_____

_____

_____

_____

_____

_____

DEVOTIONS

DECEMBER

December 1

THE CHALLENGE OF A VISION

SCRIPTURE: Luke 1:18-25

VERSE FOR TODAY: But when he came out, he could not speak to them; and they perceived that he had seen a vision in the temple, for he beckoned to them and remained speechless (Luke 1:22, *New King James Version*).

HYMN FOR TODAY: "In Heavenly Love Abiding"

Sometimes we tire of waiting for God to give us a vision for what we ought to be, do, or think. Receiving a vision is difficult because it takes time and energy to hammer out what needs to happen in us. God chisels away our objections as He did Zachariah's. Three ideas are evident in this passage.

1. A vision comes by faith. This faith believes God has something general and specific for our lives.

2. A vision overcomes restrictions. A 90-year-old man went to his doctor with knee trouble. The physician asked, "At your age, what do you expect?" His quick response was, "I expect you to fix this knee because my other knee's the same age, and it works fine."

3. A vision stretches us. It helps us see beyond our limits. Phillips Brooks said we never become truly spiritual by sitting down and wishing. We must undertake something so great that we cannot accomplish it unsighted.

Today's assignment: Ask God to give you a vision big enough to overcome obstacles that hinder your faith.

PRAYER THOUGHTS: Dear Father, Your Word tells us that where there is no vision, the people perish. We do not want to be a perishing people; but, rather, people of faith who accomplish much in our world. May we accept Your vision for us today, tomorrow, and the rest of our lives. Give us wisdom to accept the challenge. In the name of Jesus, our Savior, we pray. Amen.

JOHN, THE PROPHET OF REPENTANCE

SCRIPTURE: Luke 3:1-6

VERSE FOR TODAY: He went into all the region around the Jordan, preaching a baptism of repentance for the remission of sins (Luke 3:3, *New King James Version*).

HYMN FOR TODAY: "Christ Receiveth Sinful Men"

John was a voice of one calling in the desert, as it is written by the prophet, Isaiah. When it came to the matter of salvation, he didn't waste any breath. The job description of a prophet was to be a "forth-teller" of God's truth. He was to proclaim God's Word in the present tense to a spiritually needy people. John fit that Biblical role. As a practicing Nazarite, John looked the part of an ancient prophet of God with his long hair and beard. He probably had fire in his eyes and a commanding, bold voice that caught the eyes and ears of the people. His message, repentance for sin, was an old message needed since Adam's day. This message of repentance set the stage for the teaching and ministry of Jesus.

Today's world needs to hear that same message . . . repent! Oh, how the world laughs and scoffs at the idea, but the need is so great. Without repentance, life has no real meaning . . . empty love . . . hollow joy . . . situational ethics . . . immoral morality . . . Hell eternally. Repentance brings real life, full love, joy, ethical honesty, right morals, and an eternity in Heaven. Why would anyone not repent?

Take time to write your "John" today and thank him for the message of hope through repentance that he preaches.

PRAYER THOUGHTS: Dear God, repentance brings me to the point of saying, "Woe is me, for I am an unclean sinner." Forgive, cleanse, purify, and make me Yours for all eternity. In the name Christ, my Savior. Amen.

THE ACTION OF REPENTANCE

SCRIPTURE: Luke 3:7-14

VERSE FOR TODAY: And the people asked him, saying, What shall we do then? (Luke 3:10).

HYMN FOR TODAY: "And Can I Yet Delay?"

"Conviction is that operation of the spirit which produces with man, a sense of guilt and condemnation because of sin" (H. Orton Wiley, *Christian Theology*). God's responsibility is conviction, and our accountability is action.

God desires that we change our sinful actions to righteous accomplishments and attitudes. That occurs when Jesus enters our lives, but we must invite Him to be our Savior and Lord.

A change of heart and action occurs when we are willing to accept the Word of God, and obey it. James Stewart once said, "It is very much easier to spend a dozen hours discussing religion than one half hour obeying God."

Bruce Larson wrote about two men who went fishing on a Wednesday night. One fisherman said, "You know, I feel guilty being here on prayer meeting night because I know our minister is trying so hard to get people to attend, and as board members, we probably ought to be there tonight." His fishing buddy board member replied, "I couldn't be there, even if I was at home. My wife is sick." He was guilty, but not guilty enough to change.

When God talks with us, our response must be, "What shall I do?"

PRAYER THOUGHTS: Dear Father, I realize how important it is to hear Your convicting voice. Help me not to avoid it, but may I move quickly to respond. If there is something You want of me, teach me to say, "I am willing to act upon it—NOW!" In the name of my Savior. Amen.

JESUS IDENTIFIES WITH US

SCRIPTURE: Luke 3:15-22

VERSE FOR TODAY: When all the people were being baptized, Jesus was baptized too (Luke 3:21, *New International Version***).**

HYMN FOR TODAY: "When We See Christ"

On the east side of the Jordan River at Bethany (John 1:28), people from all over the countryside streamed to hear the soul-stirring messages of John the Baptist. What he said was used by the Holy Spirit to convict people of their sin. His preaching and magnetic personality led people to wonder if he was the long-awaited Messiah for Israel. John answered their questioning minds with a firm "No" and a prophecy that soon the Messiah would come to them to separate the wheat from the chaff. Jesus would do that very thing, but not arbitrarily and not without love. I think John imagined that the Messiah would preach hard truth both poignantly and with vigor—without compassion.

When Jesus came to John at the Jordan and asked to be baptized, it stunned John, for, after all, he thought the Messiah should have "first billing" (Matthew 3:15). And of the Messiah, John says, "I am not good enough even to carry his sandals (Matthew 3:11, *Good News Bible*).

Jesus, the Son of God, came to identify with guilty, sinful humanity. Jesus had no personal need for baptism, but, in this act, He offered himself as the substitute and representative for sinful mankind. His action showed that reconciliation and redemption would be possible because of Him. Praise God!

PRAYER THOUGHTS: Thank You, God, for bringing the sinless Jesus into the world so that we might be reconciled to You. Because Jesus identified with us, we can follow His example to a holy lifestyle. May our lives be raised from death to life through Him. Amen.

A LOVING JESUS

SCRIPTURE: Luke 7:18-28

VERSE FOR TODAY: When the men came to Jesus, they said, "John the Baptist sent us to you to ask, 'Are you the one who was to come, or should we expect someone else?'" (Luke 7:20, *New International Version*).

HYMN FOR TODAY: "He the Pearly Gates Will Open"

John, languishing in prison, could not talk personally to Jesus. Men shared bits and pieces of information with him, but that was certainly different from direct conversation. Additionally John the Baptist had a preconceived idea of how the Messiah would accomplish His goal of salvation. John was convinced the Messiah would come wielding a spiritual sword and cut down anyone who would dare disagree with the truth (Matthew 3:12), and envisioned Him as an axe ready to cut at the roots of wrongdoings (Luke 3:9).

Jesus came with His own plan of how to accomplish the bringing of salvation to people. Christ came with an attitude of care, love, mercy, and compassion. John was expecting something totally different and could not understand Christ's action. Is it any wonder he asked a couple of his disciples to check on Jesus? John needed to understand Jesus.

You, also, must understand the Master. You must see Him for who He is in the whole spectrum of life. Your faith must reach out to a loving Jesus. Christ is much more than a good man who did wonderful things, or a prophet, or a great preacher; He is the Savior of souls, showing justice with compassion.

PRAYER THOUGHTS: Dear Lord, please help me to see Your loving compassion as something I am to show to others. Help me to reach out to those hurting, failing, depressed, and lost, that they can see my Jesus! Let my life be filled with love for mankind. In the name of my Savior, Jesus Christ. Amen.

WHAT A GREETING!

SCRIPTURE: Luke 1:26-31

VERSE FOR TODAY: Therefore the Lord Himself will give you a sign: Behold, the virgin shall conceive and bear a Son, and shall call His name Immanuel (Isaiah 7:14, *New King James Version*).

HYMN FOR TODAY: "Angels, from the Realms of Glory"

Imagine having an angel come to call! The young girl, Mary, must have looked around to see if he was really speaking to her. And then she realized that he was. "Be happy," he said, "God has chosen you because He thinks highly of you. The Lord is with you; you are blessed among all women."

I suspect Mary's eyes grew large as she looked up at the heavenly visitor. Her hands probably clasped themselves across her breast and felt her heart beating wildly. *Who, me?* she thought. *Why?* She was troubled and wondered about the strange greeting.

The angel, Gabriel, hastened to reassure her. "Don't be afraid, Mary. You have found favor with God . . . He wants you to bear His Son, Jesus."

Why does God choose certain people for unusual assignments? It seems that sometimes His chosen people pay a tremendous price of pain and suffering. They endure hardships as much as those who don't know the Lord. The difference is that the Lord walks beside them and gives them peace and joy. That relationship is worth it all. God never forces His love or His will on anyone. Mary had a choice! Aren't we glad she was willing?

PRAYER THOUGHTS: How wonderful it is, Our Father, to read again the story of the angel coming to Mary. Fill our hearts with holy expectation of the wonders of this advent season. Amen.

December 6—12. **Dorothy Snyder** is a retired businesswoman who enjoys free lance writing. She lives with her husband, Wilbert, in Boulder, Colorado.

December 7

THE "IMPOSSIBLE" DREAM

SCRIPTURE: Luke 1:32-38

VERSE FOR TODAY: Then the angel said to them, "Do not be afraid, for behold, I bring you good tidings of great joy which shall be to all people (Luke 2:10, *New King James Version*).

HYMN FOR TODAY: "O Come, O Come, Emmanuel"

One time when attending a camp in the mountains, a bird flew into the chapel during a service. The big door was open as were some of the windows. We people were just as surprised as the bird. Some of us tried to direct it to the open door or windows, but it flew instead against the closed windows, recovered, and finally with much flapping found its way through the open door again. A youngster piped up, "If I were a little bird I could have showed it the way out." I thought, *Why, that's what Jesus came to do. That's the Incarnation!*

Mary didn't understand. She had questions. And the angel patiently explained how God himself had planned this unusual birth. He promised that He would empower, "overshadow" her, and that her baby would be called the Son of God. He stated that "with God nothing will be impossible."

Mary realized then that her lot was ordained by God, and she humbly accepted with model words of patient trust.

God often asks us to do certain things for Him. Sometimes they seem hard. Paul Tournier once said, "Saying 'yes' to God is saying 'yes' to life." We need not fear the direction God will lead us, because He will lead us to life!

PRAYER THOUGHTS: Father, we thank You for sending Your Son, Jesus, into our world. At this Christmas season, please open many hearts to hear Your message of peace and joy. Let us be used to proclaim Your message. In the name of Jesus. Amen.

SHARED JOYS

SCRIPTURE: Luke 1:39-45

VERSE FOR TODAY: And she will bring forth a Son, and you shall call His name JESUS, for He will save His people from their sins (Matthew 1:21, *New King James Version*).

HYMN FOR TODAY: "What Child Is This?"

The angel, Gabriel, had told Mary that her cousin Elizabeth was also going to have a baby. This, too, was unusual because Elizabeth was quite old. But Mary was so excited that she walked "with haste" four or five days south into the hill country where her cousin lived. What a meeting of special joy and significance that must have been. In fact, when Elizabeth greeted her cousin, she felt life in the baby she carried. God also revealed to her that Mary was to bear the long-awaited Savior.

Mary stayed with Elizabeth for about three months. What do you suppose they talked about? If we could eavesdrop, we might have heard those two sharing their confidences: "What happened exactly?" "Tell me all about it." "Really?" "Then what did the angel say?" "And what did you say?" Elizabeth wasn't jealous. She rejoiced and affirmed Mary's experience. She was content that her son would be the forerunner of the Messiah.

Belonging to the extended family of Christians provides for our sharing—not only our belief in the God of the impossible but the wholesome exchange of perplexities, sorrows, and joys. We find comfort in knowing we have many brothers and sisters in Christ.

PRAYER THOUGHTS: Our Father in Heaven, we are grateful that Your Son, Jesus, entered our world through a human family. We thank You for relationships. We thank You for our extended families. Lead us to reach out and help those who do not have families at this holiday season. In the name of our Savior, amen.

MARY'S SONG

SCRIPTURE: Luke 1:46-56

VERSE FOR TODAY: . . . And His name will be called Wonderful, Counselor, Mighty God, Everlasting Father, Prince of Peace (Isaiah 9:6, *New King James Version*).

HYMN FOR TODAY: "There's a Song in the Air"

In her humility Mary's heart exploded in praise. Her words echoed language from the Old Testament prayers of praise with which she was familiar.

Mary's song, the Magnificat, proclaimed words of hope for the hopeless. God in His mercy "scattered the proud," "put down the mighty," "exalted the lowly," "filled the hungry," and "sent the rich away empty."

Her exaltation defined her worship: "Holy is His name," "His mercy is on those who fear Him," "He has shown strength," "He has helped Israel," and "in mercy He spoke to our fathers."

And Mary's heart spilled over in personal gratitude: "My soul magnifies the Lord," "My spirit rejoices in Him," "He has regarded my lowly state," "All generations will call me blessed," and "He has done great things for me." What a wonderful feeling it must have been for a young woman to be used by her Creator!

George Frederick Handel composed the oratorio, "Messiah," in 24 days. A servant came in while he was writing the Hallelujah Chorus and found the composer weeping. When he could speak, he told the servant, "I think I did see all Heaven before me and the great God himself."

PRAYER THOUGHTS: Our Father, we praise You and worship You. Thank You for sending us Your Son, Jesus. Fill our hearts with awe and gratitude for Your great work of creation and redemption. In Jesus' name, amen.

THE FORERUNNER

SCRIPTURE: Luke 1:57-66

VERSE FOR TODAY: And all those who heard them kept them in their hearts, saying, "What kind of child will this be?" And the hand of the Lord was with him (Luke 1:66, *New King James Version*).

HYMN FOR TODAY: "Go, Tell It on the Mountain"

Elizabeth's neighbors and relatives came to rejoice with her when her baby was born. At the baby's circumcision, those same friends thought the child should be named Zacharias. But Elizabeth said, "No, he shall be called John." They couldn't believe it and plainly disapproved, so they called upon his father. Because Zacharias hadn't spoken for nine months, he motioned for a writing tablet and wrote, "His name *is* John." He didn't write *will be*, for after all, hadn't the angel commanded it? Suddenly his speech returned and his first words were praise.

Fear is a natural reaction when we witness the supernatural. And this happening became the talk of the countryside. Everyone wondered about this baby, John. They said, "What kind of child will this be?" The name John means "God is gracious," and, as preordained, John was an unusual person.

His parents knew he was to be a man with a mission, the forerunner of the Messiah. Playing second fiddle to someone else is not an easy assignment, but John's parents wisely prepared and trained him for his part in the plan of redemption. When the time came for John to "go public," his forerunner message was a call for repentance.

PRAYER THOUGHTS: O God, our Heavenly Father, how grateful we are for Your love and care. Show us how to share Your caring love to those who don't know "how great Thou art." Help us to "go public" with the message of redemption for mankind through Your son, Jesus. In His name, amen.

PROPHECY FULFILLED

SCRIPTURE: Luke 1:67-80

VERSE FOR TODAY: The voice of one crying in the wilderness: "Prepare the way of the Lord; Make straight in the desert A highway for our God" (Isaiah 40:3, *New King James Version*).

HYMN FOR TODAY: "Come, Thou Long Expected Jesus"

The sign read, "Pilot Car. Follow Me." Then I saw a carrier truck with an oversized load. The pilot car was a forerunner like John the Baptist, going ahead and preparing the way.

Zacharias and Elizabeth had given up hopes of ever having a child. John's birth had followed unusual happenings in their family: the angel's announcement to Zacharias and his inability to speak for nine months. Now at John's birth, the child was given a strange name and his father suddenly recovered his speech.

Zacharias' pent-up emotions broke out into spontaneous praise, similar to Mary's song. The outburst of prophecy recalled the promises of God made 400 years before, that God would visit His people. But the prophets had also spoken of one who would come before to prepare the way. And Zacharias knew that his son was that person.

We don't know much about John's childhood, but Luke reports that "the child grew and became strong in spirit" (Luke 1:80, *New International Version*). I'm sure John's parents were fully aware of their great responsibility.

What a privilege to be the parents and to train the herald of the Messiah! The prophecy of the forerunner was fulfilled in their son, John.

PRAYER THOUGHTS: O God, we are humbled as we read of Your great preparations for the coming of our Savior. We are overwhelmed that You love us so much. Help us to welcome Him with purified hearts. Amen.

POLLUTION

SCRIPTURE: Malachi 3:1-5; 4:5, 6

VERSE FOR TODAY: Sow for yourselves righteousness; Reap in mercy, Break up your fallow ground, For it is time to seek the LORD, Till He comes and rains righteousness on you (Hosea 10:12, *New King James Version*).

HYMN FOR TODAY: "Watchmen Tell Us of the Night"

When the oil spilled into the waters of the Gulf of Alaska, no one could bring in fresh water to overcome the pollution. Purity isn't catching, but pollution is. I remember the parable of the rotten apple—one bad apple will spoil the whole barrel.

The standards Moses received from God had been neglected. The Israelites had allowed the pagan religions to dilute even their offerings. The prophets spoke without fear. Malachi was God's voice thundering about pollution.

But judgment was not the only word from the Lord. Forgiveness through the cross of Jesus was also in the heart of God. John would come ahead of Jesus, preaching repentance. Confession and a change of heart still bring God's forgiveness. God confronts us with our own set of substitute gods, our pride and ambitions, our inconsistencies. Nevertheless, His forgiving heart still yearns to hear a response to His love. John preached repentance. And after John came Jesus. Hopefully we can respond,

"O holy Child of Bethlehem!
Descend to us, we pray;
Cast out our sin and enter in,
Be born in us today."
(*Fourth verse of song*, "O Little Town of Bethlehem).

PRAYER THOUGHTS: Holy Father, purify our hearts, our words, and our actions. "O come to us, abide with us, our Lord Emmanuel." Amen.

December 13

A KING AND THE KING

SCRIPTURE: Luke 2:1-7

VERSE FOR TODAY: And she gave birth to her firstborn, a son. She wrapped him in cloths and placed him in a manger, because there was no room for them in the inn (Luke 2:7, *New International Version*).

HYMN FOR TODAY: "Away in a Manger"

Augustus, the Caesar, was ruler of the Roman empire at the time of birth of Jesus Christ. Augustus was a king who cared nothing about his subjects other than what he could exploit from them through taxes and other means. He was not willing to make sacrifices of any sort for them. As we turn to Jesus, we see a King who is the King of kings. However, if we contrast His life to that of Caesar Augustus there are glaring differences. Conditions around the birth of Augustus were lavish in every respect. Augustus was the heir to the throne of Julius, the Caesar.

According to Scripture, Jesus was the heir to the throne of David, but the circumstances surrounding His birth were very mean and depressing. There was no room in the inn for Mary and Joseph. Mary was ready to give birth to Jesus. How devastating this must have been for the poor family. The stable was the maternity ward and the manger was the bassinet. The King of kings became the great sacrifice needed to redeem mankind. Unlike Augustus, He cared for His subjects enough to die for them. It is ironic to see that "no room" was found in the inn, but there was room on the cross at Golgotha.

PRAYER THOUGHTS: O God, we magnify Your name today because of Your great power. We thank You for Jesus Christ who voluntarily bore the cross for the world. We can never repay You for what You have done for us. So, in our humble way, we thank You. Amen.

December 13-19. **Ulysses Rhea** is Christian Education Administrator for the Lincoln Heights Missionary Baptist Church in Cincinnati, Ohio. He and his wife, Bennie, have one daughter, Stephanie.

A VISIT FROM HEAVEN

SCRIPTURE: Luke 2:8-14

VERSE FOR TODAY: "This will be a sign to you: You will find a baby wrapped in cloths and lying in a manger" (Luke 2:12, *New International Version*).

HYMN FOR TODAY: "Angels, from the Realms of Glory"

Signs have been used by man to indicate many things through the centuries. The sign that the angels gave to the shepherds was an unmistakable sign. God was arranging the circumstances in such a way that the shepherds would not make a mistake.

From the language of the angels, it is obvious that the shepherds were looking for a Messiah. The long-awaited Messiah has finally arrived! News traveled slowly in those days, so God dispatched a choir of angels to make this all-important announcement.

There are many signs today that indicate the second advent of the King. We must be ready when He comes. When we read the Word of God, we will be aware of the signs concerning the second coming. We are warned in Scripture to "watch," for we know not when the Son of man will return.

We must be thankful to God for the first coming of the Savior-King. Above all, let us thank Him for preparing a way for our redemption through the Savior.

Jesus was sent on earth to give life and give it more abundantly. The news and sign given to the shepherds on that dark night was the greatest turning point in the history of man's spiritual existence.

PRAYER THOUGHTS: Father, keep us ever mindful of the great blessing in the gift of Jesus Christ. We realize that without that gift our lives would be still in darkness. In Your Word we find that Jesus is the way, the truth, and the light. Amen.

December 15

THEY FOUND HIM

SCRIPTURE: Luke 2:15-20

VERSE FOR TODAY: So they hurried off and found Mary and Joseph, and the baby, who was lying in the manger (Luke 2:16, *New International Version*).

HYMN FOR TODAY: "O Little Town of Bethlehem"

It is remarkable to see the obedience of the shepherds after they were given the instructions concerning the Messiah. There was no hesitation or questioning of the validity of this command. The shepherds had a great opportunity to witness to the other people in the area. So they took advantage of the situation.

How many times in our lives have we allowed great opportunities to witness pass us by? Too many times in our work, school, and home environment we neglect to speak out for Christ. God is not willing for anyone to be lost (2 Peter 3:9).

The Great Commission (Matthew 28:16-20) insists that we who are saved witness to the rest of the world. Samuel told Saul, the king, that obedience is better than sacrifice (1 Samuel 15:22). When we are obedient to parents, and other authorities, God is pleased. Obedience always brings blessings.

The Scripture is filled with recorded events where obedience resulted in blessings. Abraham was obedient and he was blessed. Moses, Samuel, David, Paul, and many others are good examples of obedient servants who were blessed because of obedience.

PRAYER THOUGHTS: O God, we pray today for an obedient spirit. We need Your guidance in the everyday events of our lives. We look to You for instructions because we are Your servants. Our goal is to please You with our work and obedience. In Jesus' name, amen.

TO BE NAMED, SAVIOR

SCRIPTURE: Luke 2:21-24

VERSE FOR TODAY: On the eighth day, when it was time to circumcise him, he was named Jesus, the name the angel had given him before he had been conceived (Luke 2:21, *New International Version*).

HYMN FOR TODAY: "I Love the Name Jesus"

A wise young couple will be concerned as to the meaning of the name they choose for their unborn child. Some may already know what name they will give their child because it is a family name. Others may say that they want to see the child before the name is given. Christian parents often choose a name that will encourage godly character.

Mary and Joseph did not choose Jesus' name. His name meant *Savior*, and the angel told Mary before He was born what to name Him (Luke 1:31). Are we prayerful in naming our children?

It is refreshing to see obedience on the part of Mary in this story. If she had been selfish or catered to her own whims, she might have named Jesus something else. But we see that her obedience paid off. She was blessed and is still honored as a great woman to this present day.

The name *Jesus* was very appropriate for the Son of God, because He became the Savior of mankind. He knew His assignment well and proceeded to accomplish the goal even at the cost of His life (Philippians 2:8). His example of obedience lies before each Christian today. We need to strive to emulate Christ in our lives, because what we do for Christ will last!

PRAYER THOUGHTS: God, we thank You for the example of Jesus Christ. May He continue to inspire us to a life of selflessness. May we remember in Your Word that he who seeks to save his life will lose it, but he who loses his life for Christ's sake will gain it. Amen.

SIMEON MEETS THE MESSIAH

SCRIPTURE: Luke 2:25-35

VERSE FOR TODAY: "For my eyes have seen your salvation, which you have prepared in the sight of all people, a light for revelation to the Gentiles and for glory to your people Israel" (Luke 2:30-32, *New International Version*).

HYMN FOR TODAY: "Fairest Lord Jesus"

God is faithful in keeping His promises. The Holy Spirit had told Simeon that he would not die before seeing the Anointed One. Simeon was concerned about Israel's future, but when he saw God's promise wrapped in a human manifestation, he praised the God who loves His people!

Promises raise hope and build expectations. However, when promises are not kept, hope dwindles and expectations disappear. How many promises have you kept lately? Or, better still, how many promises have you broken lately? We have made promises to many people in our lives, such as parents, teachers, bosses, our children, and ourselves. We must admit that we have failed to keep some promises.

To fail in keeping a promise is not an unpardonable sin, but God is not pleased. He is interested in seeing us keep our promises especially when the building of His kingdom is advanced. God is very patient with us and expects us to conform to His will in every facet of our lives, but we find ourselves constantly asking for forgiveness for our failures. Even in the midst of our failures, God is good, and He will never fail us!

PRAYER THOUGHTS: O God, we thank You for the promise of a Savior-King. He has been all that we need. He protects, guides, and helps in many ways. We are striving everyday to follow His example. Amen.

LOOK AND LIVE

SCRIPTURE: Luke 2:41-45

VERSE FOR TODAY: When they did not find him, they went back to Jerusalem to look for him (Luke 2:45, *New International Version*).

HYMN FOR TODAY: "Look and Live"

In every area of life, we find that people are looking and searching for something. In many cases they are searching for who they are. "I want to find myself," they may say.

Every year, Jesus' parents went to Jerusalem for the feast of the Passover. When Jesus was twelve years old, they went to Jerusalem with their friends and family as usual. When the festival was over, they started home, but Jesus remained behind talking with the Jewish teachers. Along the way, His parents realized that He was not among the group and they quickly returned to Jerusalem to find Him.

Jesus is very concerned that we find Him today. He is available, and He can be found if we just look for Him. Paul declared to the Corinthians that "if anyone is in Christ, he is a new creation; the old has gone, the new has come!" (2 Corinthians 5:17, *New International Version*). Finding Christ is a life-changing experience. A new kind of love infuses our heart. A new way of walking graces our steps. A new way of talking emanates from our mouth. We become new creatures. Things that impressed us in the past stay in the past. Values that were high on our list become secondary to us after finding Christ. How sweet it is to find and know Him. He lifts our burdens, gives us joy, and gives us a new lease on life. In Him, we can live!

PRAYER THOUGHTS: Heavenly Father, it is so sweet to know Jesus. He is all we need. Please keep us mindful of the great sacrifice He made for the whole world. In His precious name we pray, amen.

A TALK WITH JESUS

SCRIPTURE: Luke 2:46-52

VERSE FOR TODAY: Everyone who heard him was amazed at his understanding and his answers (Luke 2:47, *New International Version*).

HYMN FOR TODAY: "Just a Little Talk with Jesus"

In this world of varied means of communication, we find that many Christians forget about the *ultimate* means of communication: prayer. Communicating or talking with Jesus is a must for Christians throughout life. He is able to guide in all aspects of our lives. We seem to make great efforts to communicate with world resources, but neglect the One who is the origin of the resources. Meditation, prayer, and worship are very important ways to communicate with Jesus. As a result of serious communication with Him, we will be amazed at what He says and does, just as those teachers in the temple were amazed by Him nearly 2000 years ago.

I find it very refreshing to talk with Jesus at the beginning of each day. Once that is done, the day seems to move along smoothly. The Scripture says, "pray without ceasing" (1 Thessalonians 5:17). It is wonderful to spend time in communication with our good friend, Jesus. Talking with Him puts me in the proper frame of mind to deal with whatever the day has in store for me. Praying at the beginning of the day is fine, but praying through the day makes it easier to cope no matter what the circumstances.

Talking to Jesus will eventually mature the Christian. Praying at all times makes my day go better. "How about you?"

PRAYER THOUGHTS: Lord, we need to know Your will for our lives each day. Keep us aware that communication with You is very important. We love You because of what You mean to us. Amen.

REPENTANCE IS ESSENTIAL

SCRIPTURE: Matthew 3:1-12
VERSE FOR TODAY: Repent ye, and believe the gospel (Mark 1:15).
HYMN FOR TODAY: "Whiter Than Snow"

The Jewish people expected Elijah to return again, but John the Baptist came dressed as Elijah had dressed (2 Kings 1:8), preaching repentance for remission of sins. Christ, after His resurrection, told His disciples to preach this message. Peter did so on the Day of Pentecost.

John came as a forerunner to prepare the way for the coming of Christ, the Messiah. John preached fearlessly. Wherever he saw sin, he denounced it. People came out to the desert from Jerusalem, the province of Judea and the country near the Jordan River to hear John preach. Many people confessed their sins. John preached a turning *from* sin and a turning *to* God.

A young man was caught stealing sheep, and in punishment his forehead was branded with the letters S T, which stood for sheep thief. He knew he could not run away from the fact he stole sheep, so he decided to stay home and win back the respect of his neighbors and himself. He repented of his behavior. When he became an old man, a stranger came to the village and asked one of the natives what the letters stood for. The villager replied, "It all happened a great while ago, and I have forgotten the particulars, but I think the letters stand for SAINT."

PRAYER THOUGHTS: Dear Lord, wash me and I shall be whiter than snow. Create in me a clean heart that I may better serve You. Amen.

December 20-26. **Arlena Hasel and** her husband, John, continue to serve Christ and His church in Clermont, Florida, where they reside after 35 years of ministry with the Oakley Baptist Church in Cincinnati, Ohio.

MY BELOVED SON

SCRIPTURE: Matthew 3:13-17

VERSE FOR TODAY: This is my beloved Son, in whom I am well pleased (Matthew 3:17).

HYMN FOR TODAY: "Glory to His Name"

A father once said, "Our kid has his faults, but we love him and he looks good to us." Actually, love sees more in the beloved than others can ever see. We look good to those who love us. Love sees more, for it sees the beloved when surrounded by love.

None of us know what Christ looked like. There were no photographs—only the artists' paintings. Isaiah 53:2 says, "There is no beauty that we should desire him." Another father might say, "What's so special about the young man Jesus?"

God the Father looked at His Son and said, "This is my beloved Son, in whom I am well pleased." In that short statement God verified Scriptures found in Psalm 2:7 and Isaiah 42. Jesus knew God was His Father and that His life would lead to the cross for our sins. His short life would be one of a suffering servant.

Often a child will never hear the words from a parent, "I'm proud of you" or "I love you." Thus a deep longing to be loved is never fulfilled. In the Gospel of John, Jesus said: "And he that sent me is with me: the Father hath not left me alone; for I do always those things that please him" (John 8:29). Let us seek to live lives pleasing to our Father!

PRAYER THOUGHTS: Dear Heavenly Father, we are Your children. Sometimes our lives please You and sometimes they don't. Thank You for your unconditional love. Thank You for sending Your beloved son, Jesus, to be our Savior and King. Help us to live by His example. In His name, we pray. Amen.

THE SATANIC "IFS"

SCRIPTURE: Luke 4:1-8

VERSE FOR TODAY: Get thee behind me, Satan (Luke 4:8).

HYMN FOR TODAY: "Yield Not to Temptation"

Have you ever thought, If I were rich, I'd do so and so; If I get well, I'll never miss church again; If I get home from the war, I'll really live for the Lord!

Satan played some "if" games with Jesus. He said, "If thou be the Son of God, command this stone that it be made bread" (Luke 4:3). "If thou . . . wilt worship me, all shall be thine" (Luke 4:7). "If thou be the Son of God, cast thyself down from hence" (Luke 4:9). The promised bread, power, and glory all looked good.

Jesus quoted Scripture to Satan. Jesus chose His Father's plan for His life—not Satan's. It would take Him through service and suffering—to the cross and to the crown.

Martin Luther once said, "The devil came to me and said, 'You are a great sinner and you will be damned.' Luther answered, 'I am a great sinner, that is true. I confess it. You say I will be damned. That is not good reasoning. It is true I am a great sinner; but it is written, "Jesus Christ came to save sinners;" therefore, I shall be saved.' So I cut the devil off with his own sword; and he went away mourning, because he could not cast me down by calling me a sinner."

There are no "ifs" that we can not overcome "if" we allow Christ to be the center of our lives. He, alone, can give us the power to overcome sin.

PRAYER THOUGHTS: Our Father, help us to know Your Word so we can withstand the wiles of Satan when He tempts us. Let us ever stand on Christ, the solid rock. Amen.

SENSATIONALISM OR THE CROWN?

SCRIPTURE: Luke 4:9-15

VERSE FOR TODAY: Be strong in the Lord, and in the power of his might (Ephesians 6:10).

HYMN FOR TODAY: "Stand Up, Stand Up for Jesus"

Jesus was sent to lead people to God. In doing so, He could not escape the cross—whether He was the powerful conqueror or the gentle, kind, loving Jesus. He went aside for forty days to contemplate the task before Him and to decide His course of action. Then Satan appeared with offers to make Jesus an instant sensation *if* He would only follow the tempter's advice. Jesus showed His power over each temptation and ordered Satan to leave Him. Jesus' life would be that of a suffering servant, experiencing death on the cross for our sins. But, for Him, there would be a crown of righteousness.

How do we measure up when tempted? Do we cave in or do we stand firm? Can we call on the power of God by quoting Scripture to the tempter (or to ourselves)?

Young Joe was poor in spelling, but Mabel, an excellent speller, sat opposite him. On an examination Joe forgot many of the words, and the tempter encouraged, *Look on Mabel's paper; she has them right.* Joe copied several words and the teacher saw him. Just as a pupil came to collect the papers, Joe tore his up. The teacher knew he decided to take a zero rather than hand in a dishonest paper. Later she said to Joe, "I saw your struggle, and I'm proud of a boy who conquered temptation."

PRAYER THOUGHTS: Our Father, how good it is to know we have a Lord and Savior who was "in all points tempted like as we are, yet without sin" (Hebrews 4:15). Help us to live by His words, we pray, amen.

THE WISE SEEK JESUS

SCRIPTURE: Matthew 2:1-6

VERSE FOR TODAY: Where is he that is born King of the Jews? for we have seen his star in the east, and are come to worship him (Matthew 2:2).

HYMN FOR TODAY: "We Three Kings of Orient Are"

The wise seek Jesus. Noel Paton has a picture entitled, "De Profundis," with the words of the psalmist inscribed upon it: "Out of the depths have I cried unto thee." Christ is pictured kneeling upon a rock and stretching over a dark abyss to help a woman who is painfully climbing up to Him. The woman, with wings of faith, shows that only when there is faith in Christ can there be rescue by Him. It is necessary, therefore, not to cry, but to arise; not only to arise, but to climb; not only to climb, but to believe. God, in saving us, demands something of us.

The Wise-men went to a great deal of time and expense to take the arduous journey to find the child Jesus. When they found Him, they then worshipped Him and presented gifts worthy of a King. Years later, as recorded in the Gospel of John, certain Greeks came to Philip saying, "Sir, we would see Jesus."

A young minister asked an older minister for some advice. He was told that in every village, town, and hamlet of England could be found a road which, if followed, would lead to London. "Just so, every text which you choose to preach from in the Bible will have a road that leads to Jesus. Be sure you find that road and follow it. This is my advice to you."

PRAYER THOUGHTS: Our Father, thank You for our spiritual heritage which has led us to Jesus, Your Son. Help us to seek His ways. May we show wisdom in our daily way. In the name of our Savior, Jesus. Amen.

O WORSHIP THE KING

SCRIPTURE: Matthew 2:7-12

VERSE FOR TODAY: They saw the young child with Mary his mother, and fell down, and worshipped him (Matthew 2:11).

HYMN FOR TODAY: "O Come, All Ye Faithful"

A few literary men were assembled in a club room in London one day a number of years ago. One of the men asked, "Gentlemen, what would we do if Milton were to enter this room?"

"Ah," replied one in the circle, "we would give him such an ovation as might compensate for the tardy recognition accorded him by the men of his own day."

"And if Shakespeare entered?" asked another.

"We would arise and crown him master of sonnet," one said.

"And if Jesus Christ were to enter?" asked another.

"I think," said Charles Lamb amid an intense silence, "we would all fall on our faces."

When the Wise-men found the young child with Mary his mother, they fell down and worshipped Him.

Some travelers in Texas saw a large sign that read: "Go and worship God in the church of your choice." Another car pulled up beside them and waited for the red light to change. A child was heard to ask, "Daddy, what does worship mean?" The father replied, "It means to go to church and listen to the preacher preach." In Revelation 7:12, worship in Heaven is described as God's angels falling down before Him, saying, "Amen: Blessing, and glory, and wisdom, and thanksgiving, and honor, and power, and might, be unto our God for ever and ever. Amen."

PRAYER THOUGHTS: Holy, Holy, Holy! Merciful and mighty! We worship You, this day, O God. We praise You for Your Son. Amen.

ETERNAL SAVIOR

SCRIPTURE: Isaiah 42:1-9

VERSE FOR TODAY: I the Lord have called thee in righteousness, and will hold thine hand (Isaiah 42:6).

HYMN FOR TODAY: "Son of God, Eternal Savior"

The hymn writer speaks of Jesus as King of love and Prince of peace. He is the beloved Son who is well-pleasing to God. He became the sacrificial lamb for our sins. In John 12:32, Jesus said: "And I, if I be lifted up from the earth, will draw all men unto me." He finished His God-given task by being lifted up on the cross where He continues to draw men and women to Him.

Several verses of Isaiah 42 are quoted in Matthew 12:18-20. God's Son would be a servant to the people as He ministered to their needs. He brought hope to the Gentiles. With Jesus' coming, all people were invited to share in and accept the love of God. Through Jesus, God was reaching out to all people to offer this love. This great love is portrayed in the hymn, "The Ninety and Nine." In this hymn, we sing of Jesus' love as He reaches out to the lost. He is not willing that any should perish.

God speaks of His beloved Son in many places in the Bible. A good father will train, lead, and educate his child. He is not just the father *of* the child, but the father *to* the child. This is the picture that our God wants us to have of Him.

Jesus said, "when you have seen me, you have seen the Father." No wonder He was well-pleasing to God!

PRAYER THOUGHTS: Our Father, may others see Jesus in us. We know that when we follow You, it is easier for others to believe in You. May we bear Your name well. Amen.

CARING FOR THOSE IN NEED

SCRIPTURE: Luke 4:16-19

VERSE FOR TODAY: Blessed is he that considereth the poor: the Lord will deliver him in time of trouble (Psalm 41:1).

HYMN FOR TODAY: "God Will Take Care of You"

A young woman age twenty-two is pregnant. The father of the baby wants nothing to do with the woman or the baby. What's more, her adopted parents have disowned her. She wants to keep her baby. Where will she turn for help? A young family is on the verge of homelessness. They have small children and the father is jobless. Where will they turn for help? A father is dying. The mother is working and caring for the father. The children are left alone to cook, clean and go to school. They are scared and lonely. Where will they turn for help? An elderly woman finds herself house bound for the first time in her life. She doesn't know how she will order food, pay bills, or care for herself. Where will she turn for help?

As Christians, we are God's helping hands. He uses us as instruments to carry out His will and to share His love and His care. May we, as members of God's family, care for others in a practical as well as spiritual way. God loves us and uses us to share His love with others.

PRAYER THOUGHTS: Dear God, Thank You for the love You give. Thank You for the care You have for all people. You know us all. Use us to help others who are in need. Let us never forget or turn a blind eye on anyone when we may be able to offer practical and spiritual help. Thank You, O Father, that we can be a part of Your Kingdom, the Kingdom of love, mercy, and plenty. In the name of Jesus. Amen.

December 27-31. **Kelli Wilmoth Bell** is a Christian writer, living in Cincinnati, Ohio. She and her husband, Todd, have a son, Rudyard Griffith and twin daughters, Cleo Elizabeth and Chloe Alexandra.

GOD'S SERVANT

SCRIPTURE: Luke 4:20-24

VERSE FOR TODAY: And he said, Verily I say unto you, No prophet is accepted in his own country (Luke 4:24).

HYMN FOR TODAY: "I'll Go Where You Want Me to Go"

A famous talk show host was invited to turn on the Christmas tree lights of a small New England town. When he arrived he was shown the way to a local restaurant where he was to wait until he would be needed to perform his duties at the Christmas ceremony. The host and his wife arrived and seated themselves at the designated restaurant. When the waiter arrived they ordered two cups of coffee. Upon hearing this the waiter angrily told them, "customers who are only ordering coffee are not allowed in the restaurant." The host and his wife embarrassedly went to a coffee shop. You see, the waiter had not recognized the famous host.

Isn't it wonderful to have the assurance that our God will always recognize us? In fact, the Bible states that He knows us so well that even the very hairs on our head are numbered (Matthew 10:30). He knows and cares for each of us. We need never be afraid. He is concerned about us. He loved us enough to give us His only Son to die in our place so that our sins can be forgiven. How blessed we are that our Creator loves us and wants the best for us. May we who have sought Christ and want to serve Him, feel His power and His love in our lives.

PRAYER THOUGHTS: It is difficult for us, O Father, to understand Your love and acceptance of us, but we praise You for caring for us. Show us, dear Father, where You want Your servants to be. Praise to You our Great Creator. In the name of our Savior, Jesus Christ. Amen.

HUMBLE BEFORE OUR GOD

SCRIPTURE: Luke 4:25-32

VERSE FOR TODAY: Great is the Lord, and greatly to be praised in the city of our God, in the mountain of his holiness (Psalm 48:1).

HYMN FOR TODAY: "How Great Thou Art"

The awesome power of our God surrounds us. It can be seen everywhere. His power is seen in a baby's gentle laugh and the rain's soft patter. It is in the tears of joy and in the tears of sadness. God's greatness is in the air we breathe and in the breeze beneath a robin's wings. It is in the beauty of the mountains and the strength of the sea. God's power is in every part of His world and in every being He created to live in His world.

Our God is indeed a God to be revered and worshipped. Wherever we are, we can be assured that our God is there. The psalmist says, "Great is our Lord and mighty in power; his understanding has no limit. The Lord sustains the humble . . ." (Psalm 147:5-6).

How wonderful that we may humbly approach the throne of God and sing praises to our creator. How touching to know that the God of such power and such greatness knows each of us as individuals and is concerned about our smallest frustrations. How special a confidence is ours because we who seek Him know that He hears us and watches over us.

PRAYER THOUGHTS: Blessed is our God, our Creator. Praise to His power and His greatness. Help us, O Father, to humble ourselves before You. We know that You speak with authority. Thank You that Your Word shows us how Jesus, our Savior, spoke with authority. Let us accept Him in our town, our church, and our lives. In His name, amen.

GOD CARES FOR HIS PEOPLE

SCRIPTURE: Isaiah 40:1-11

VERSE FOR TODAY: He shall feed his flock like a shepherd: he shall father the lambs with his arm, and carry them in his bosom, and shall gently lead those that are with young (Isaiah 40:11).

HYMN FOR TODAY: "Under His Wings"

For me, being pregnant is a wonderful, yet frightening experience. This was especially true when my twins entered the world six weeks early following a routine doctor's visit. I watched while doctors, nurses and advanced technology helped my girls battle for their lives. They were tiny, their spirits were strong and I knew the hand of God was upon them. I knew that God's love and care was with all of us and I had to trust in Him. To my joy, the twins were able to come home happy and healthy after two and one-half weeks in the hospital. Through all the ups and downs, the fears and the joys of those few weeks, I always felt a certain calm and peace because I knew God was in control. I could feel His love upon my heart.

In our Scripture lesson today, we are told that "the word of our God stands forever." We can rest assured that He will comfort us in our need.

As Christians, we must trust in, and cling to, our God. His glory has been revealed to man through His Son, Jesus. He has shown us His love and His promise to care for us. In life's trials it is easy to lose sight of the fact that our loving God is in control of our world. Let us never lose sight of Him and His love for us.

PRAYER THOUGHTS: Our God, we trust in You. We praise You for the love and care You give us constantly. Help us even through life's pains to seek Your comfort. Thank You for Your everlasting love and care. May we live with the confidence that You, indeed, care for us. Praise You, our constant Friend. In the name of Jesus. Amen.

WRITTEN ON MY HEART

SCRIPTURE: Jeremiah 31:29-34

VERSE FOR TODAY: And they shall teach no more every man his neighbour, and every man his brother, saying, know the Lord from the least of them to the greatest," (Jeremiah 31:34).

HYMN FOR TODAY: "Tell Me the Story of Jesus"

As a grade school student I enjoyed many successes but year after year I had one glaring fault—I simply talked too much. Each year every report card ended with a comment "Kelli is a wonderful student but she talks too much" One year my frustrated teacher instructed me to write, "I will not talk in class" five hundred times. Needless to say, I was furious. But the lesson was learned. Those words were "written on my brain." I would not soon forget to be quiet during class.

God asked His people to teach His word to their children that they might not forget His word. "Thou shalt teach them diligently unto thy children, and shalt talk of them when thou sittest in thine house, and when thou liest down, and when thou risest up" (Deuteronomy 6:6-7).

God wants His words and His laws to be written on our hearts. He wants us to carry His words with us wherever we go, and in whatever we are doing. When we learn His words and know them so well that they are a part of our being, it is easy to feel God's love and presence. Just as I remembered to be quiet in class, let us remember to do God's will. Let us seek His way. Let us know His love.

PRAYER THOUGHTS: O God, thank You for giving us Your word—the Bible. Let us always remember to seek You and to know Your ways. Praise You, our Father. In the name of Jesus, our Savior, amen.